Briefcase on Commercial Law

Second Edition

Michael Connolly, LLB, Barrister
Senior Lecturer in Law
University of Westminster, London

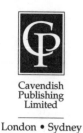

Cavendish
Publishing
Limited

London • Sydney

First published in 1995 by Cavendish Publishing Limited, The Glass House, Wharton Street, London, WC1X 9PX, United Kingdom

Telephone: +44 (0) 171 278 8000   Facsimile: +44 (0) 171 278 8080

E-mail: info@cavendishpublishing.com

Visit our Home Page on http://www.cavendishpublishing.com

Connolly, Michael

Briefcase on Commercial law – 2nd ed

1. Commercial law – England   2. Commercial law – Wales

I. Title   II. Commercial law

346.4′2′07

ISBN 1 85941 255 6

Printed and bound in Great Britain by Biddles Ltd, Guildford and King's Lynn

Contents

Table of cases

Part 1 Agency

1   The agent's authority

In the following chapters the principal has been identified as (P), the agent as (A), the third party as (T) and the undisclosed principal as (UP).

1.1   Actual authority

Freeman & Lockyer v Buckhurst and Kapoor (1964) CA
For the facts, see below, 1.3.1.
   Diplock LJ stated:

> An 'actual' authority is a legal relationship between the principal and the agent created by a consensual agreement to which they alone are parties. Its scope is to be ascertained by applying ordinary principles of construction of contracts, including any proper implications from the express words used, the usages of the trade, or the course of business between the parties.

1.1.1   Express actual authority

Ireland v Livingston (1872), see below, 6.1.1.

1.2   Implied actual authority

Hely-Hutchinson v Brayhead (1968) CA
Hely-Hutchinson (T) was the managing director of a struggling company, Perdio. Brayhead (P) were considering a takeover of Perdio in the medium term future. Richards (A) was the chairman of Brayhead. He also acted as *de facto* managing director with the acquiescence of Brayhead's board, concluding contracts without the board's express consent. Hely-Hutchinson proposed to Richards that he (Hely-Hutchinson) would inject money into Perdio (to keep it alive until Brayhead was ready for the take-over) if Brayhead would indemnify him. Richards agreed to this and, in his capacity as chairman of Brayhead, sent letters of indemnity to Hely-Hutchinson. Accordingly, Hely-Hutchinson advanced money to Perdio. Nonetheless,

Perdio became bankrupt, so Hely-Hutchinson sought the indemnity from Brayhead. Brayhead resisted the claim stating that Richards had no actual authority as chairman to give such an indemnity.

Held although Richards had no *express* actual authority to give the indemnity, authority could be *implied* from the circumstance that the board acquiesced when Richards acted as managing director. The Court of Appeal also found that the board's acquiescence amounted to a representation which clothed Richards with apparent authority (see below, 1.3).

Hamer v Sharp (1874)

An estate agent was instructed to 'find a purchaser' for some property and advertise it at a certain price. The agent signed an agreement of sale which made no references to any stipulations in the title.

Held the court would not exercise its equitable discretion to grant specific performance because of the inadequacies in the agreement. *Obiter* in any case the agent was given no authority to sign an agreement of sale, he was only authorised to find a purchaser for the vendor to deal with.

Rosenbaun v Belson (1900)

An estate agent was instructed to sell property and it was agreed that he would be paid commission on the purchase price accepted.

Held the agent had implied authority to sign the memorandum of contract.

1.2.1 Estate agents and earnest money

Sorrell v Finch (1977) HL

Levy set up an estate agents business under the name of 'Emberden Estates' (A). He fraudulently collected deposits from six separate prospective purchasers, including the plaintiff's (T), on a single property, owned by the defendant (P), who had instructed Emberden Estates. Levy signed the plaintiff's receipt without stating in what capacity. The plaintiff's cheque was made out to 'Emberden Estates'. Subsequently, Levy absconded with the money. The plaintiff sued the defendant as principal, asserting that his agent, Emberden Estates, had (implied actual) authority to collect a deposit and therefore the principal should be liable for it.

Held estate agents in general have neither implied nor apparent authority to accept a deposit. Hence the principal vendors could not be held liable should the agent default.

1.2.2 Customary authority

Dingle v Hare (1859)

The agent was authorised to sell manure. There existed a commercial custom that a warranty was supplied with manure. The agent sold some manure with a warranty. In an action for breach of the warranty, it was argued that the agent had no authority to give warranties.

Held as the custom was notorious and reasonable, the agent had implied authority to issue a warranty with the manure.

Robinson v Mollett (1875) HL

A broker (A) was instructed to buy 50 tons of tallow. There existed a custom in the tallow trade that brokers would buy in bulk in their own name in order to supply several principals. The principal did not know of this custom.

Held the custom was unreasonable because the effect of it was that the agent acted as principal in his own right, with the potential conflict of interest which went with it. If the principal had known of the (unreasonable) custom when authorising the particular transaction then the agent would have had authority to act in accordance with that custom. But as the principal in this case did not know of the custom, the agent had no implied authority so to act.

1.3   Apparent (or ostensible) authority

Rama Corporation v Proved Tin (1952)

Slade J stated:

> Ostensible or apparent authority ... is merely a form of estoppel ... and you cannot call in aid of an estoppel unless you have three ingredients: (i) a representation; (ii) a reliance on the representation; and (iii) an alteration of position resulting from such reliance.

Freeman and Lockyer v Buckhurst and Kapoor (1964) CA

Kapoor (A) was appointed by the board (P) of Buckhurst to handle a land sale. Kapoor assumed the duties of managing director and the board acquiesced in this. Subsequently, Kapoor hired architects (T) to obtain planning permission on the land. This action was beyond his actual authority (given with land sale duty), but within the normal authority of a managing director. The architects claimed their fee from Buckhurst.

Held Buckhurst had represented to the architects that Kapoor was a managing director with the authority to hire architects. Thus Buckhurst were bound to pay the architects because of Kapoor's apparent authority. Diplock LJ explained apparent authority thus:

> An 'apparent' or 'ostensible' authority ... is a legal relationship between the principal and the contractor [third party] created by a representation, made by the principal to the contractor, intended to be and in fact acted upon by the contractor, that the agent has authority on behalf of the principal to enter into a contract of a kind within the scope of the 'apparent' authority, so as to render the principal liable to perform any obligations imposed upon him by such contract. To the relationship so created the agent is a stranger. He need not be (although he generally is) aware of the existence of the representation but he must not purport to make the agreement as principal himself. The representation, when

acted upon by the contractor by entering to a contract by the agent, operates as an estoppel, preventing the principal from asserting that he is not bound by the contract. It is irrelevant whether the agent had actual authority to enter into the contract.

In ordinary business dealings the contractor at the time of entering into the contract can in the nature of things hardly ever rely on the 'actual' authority of the agent. His information as to the authority must derive from either the principal or from the agent or from both, for they alone know what the agent's actual authority is. All the contractor can know is what they tell him, which may or may not be true. In the ultimate analysis he relies either upon the representation of the principal, that is apparent authority, or upon the representation of the agent, that is, warranty of authority.

The representation which creates 'apparent' authority may take a variety of forms, of which the commonest is representation by conduct, that is, by permitting the agent to act in some way in the conduct of the principal's business with other persons. By so doing the principal represents to anyone who becomes aware that the agent is so acting that the agent has authority to enter on behalf of the principal into contracts with other persons of the kind which an agent so acting in the conduct of his principal's business has usually 'actual' authority to enter into.

Hely-Hutchinson v Brayhead (1968) CA
For the facts, see 1.2.

During his judgment, Lord Denning MR contrasted apparent (or ostensible) authority with actual authority:

Ostensible or apparent authority is the authority of agent as it *appears* to others. It often coincides with actual authority. Thus when the board appoint one of their number to be managing director, they invest him not only with implied authority, but also with ostensible authority to do all such things as fall within the usual scope of that office. Other people who see him acting as managing director are entitled to assume that he has the usual authority of a managing director. But sometimes ostensible authority exceeds actual authority. For instance, when the board appoint a managing director, they may expressly limit his authority by saying he is not to order goods worth more than £500 without the sanction of the board. In that case his *actual* authority is subject to the £500 limitation, but his *ostensible* authority includes all the usual authority of a managing director. The company is bound by his ostensible authority in his dealings with those who do not know of the limitation. He may himself do the 'holding out'. Thus if he orders goods worth £1,000 and signs himself 'Managing Director for and on behalf of the company', the company is bound to the other party who does not know of the £500 limitation, see *British Thompson-Houston v Federated European Bank* (1932) ...

1.3.1 Representation

Summers v Solomon (1857)

The defendant (P) employed his nephew (A) to run his jewellery shop. In practice the nephew would order jewellery from, *inter alia*, the plaintiff jewellery supplier (T) and the defendant would pay for it. The nephew left the job, but the supplier was not told that the nephew's agency had been terminated. Later, the nephew obtained some jewellery from the supplier – purportedly under the old arrangement – and absconded with it. The supplier, still under the impression that the agency existed, approached the defendant for payment.

Held the defendant had represented to the supplier that the nephew had authority to order jewellery by omitting to inform him of the termination of the agency. Thus, the nephew had apparent authority to order the jewellery and the defendant was liable.

Chapleo v Brunswick Permanent Building Society (1881) CA

The directors of an unincorporated building society (P), could, by its rules, borrow money up to a certain limit. The building society employed a secretary (A) to receive loans from investors. At a time when the prescribed limit had been exceeded, the secretary received a loan from the plaintiff (T). The secretary then absconded with the money and the plaintiff asserted that the building society had represented the secretary as having (apparent) authority to receive loans despite the limit.

Held the building society rules, deriving from an Act of Parliament, are a matter of law. The representation must be one of *fact*, not law.

Farquharson Bros v King (1902) HL

The clerk (A) of the plaintiff timber company (P) was given limited power to sell to certain customers and general written authority to sign delivery orders on the plaintiff's behalf (which enabled the warehouse to release timber to the delivery note holders). By abusing his authority, the clerk had timber delivered to himself in the false name of 'Brown'. In that name he sold the timber to defendants – who knew nothing of the fraud. When the fraud was discovered the plaintiff timber company sued for the recovery of the timber or its value. The defendants argued that the plaintiffs had represented that the clerk had (apparent) authority to sell the timber to them.

Held there was no representation that the clerk had authority so to act. The defendants knew nothing of the plaintiff timber company; the clerk sold in his own false name.

Attorney General for Ceylon v Silva (1953) PC

A Crown customs officer (A) found some goods and mistakenly thought that they were unclaimed goods. Consequently, he put them up for auction and the goods were sold to Silva (T). In fact, the goods belonged to the Crown (P), who would not hand them over to Silva.

Held the Crown were not bound by the act of their agent because: (i) there was no actual authority for the agent to sell Crown property; and (ii) there was no representation by the Crown that the agent had authority to sell the goods; the only representation by the Crown as to the agent's duties was by statute, which gave no authority to act so. The representation here that the agent had authority to sell the goods was made by the agent himself. Accordingly, the Crown were not liable.

Note ──

This case was approved by the House of Lords in *Armagas v Mundogas* (1986) (see below).

Egyptian Int Foreign Trade Co v Soplex, *The Raffaella* (1985) CA

The credit manager, Mr Booth (A), of the defendant bank (P), put his single signature to a letter of guarantee. He had no actual authority to do this. However, Mr Booth assured the plaintiffs (T) 'in London one signature is sufficient'.

Held although the bank had not made a representation that Mr Booth had authority to issue the letter with only a single signature, they had conferred authority on Mr Booth to make representations as to his authority. Therefore although the representation here came from the agent, the bank were bound by the apparent authority of their agent, Mr Booth.

Armagas v Mundogas, *The Ocean Frost* (1986) HL

The plaintiffs (T), through their broker, J, were negotiating to purchase a ship, *The Ocean Frost*, from the defendants (P). The plaintiffs planned to let the ship back to the defendants on a three year charterparty – this would finance the sale. The broker, J, stood to gain if the deal went through. The defendants' vice president (transportation) and chartering manager, M (A) was negotiating with J. He told J that the defendants were unwilling to enter into a three year charterparty, but would enter into a one year charterparty. J then offered M a bribe and M signed a three year charterparty to the satisfaction of the plaintiffs. However, he also signed a one year charterparty, leading his principal (the defendants) to believe they were bound only by a one year charterparty. The ship was duly let to the defendants, who after one year, returned it. The plaintiffs, understanding the charterparty to be for three years, sought damages for breach of contract. They argued that M had actual (implied), or apparent, authority to sign the three year charterparty.

Held although M had been appointed as vice-president (transportation) and chartering manager, there was no usual or customary authority (to sign a three year charterparty) incidental to that position. Neither was there a representation by the defendants that he had such authority. The only representation was by M, the agent.

First Energy v Hungarian International Bank (1993)

Jamison (A) was the senior manager of the Manchester office of the Hungarian International Bank (P). First Energy approached Jamison at the bank for finance for a project. Jamison initially told First Energy that he had no authority to sanction a loan to them, but later said (falsely) that he had been given such authority. A loan was arranged but the bank refused to advance any money.

Held on the facts, there was a contract. The bank had put Jamison in a position where he had apparent authority to make a representation that he had been given authority to sanction the loan. In these circumstances, the representation may come from the agent.

Note ───

Compare this case with *Armagas v Mundogas, The Ocean Frost* (above). See, also, Reynolds (1994) 110 LQR 21.

Re Selectmove Ltd (1995) CA

Selectmove (T) owed the Inland Revenue (P) some £24,000. They met a tax collector, Mr Pollard (A) and offered to pay off the debt at £1,000 per month. Pollard stated that he had no authority to accept an offer that low, but he would consult a superior and if Selectmove did not hear from him, they could presume that the offer had been accepted. Selectmove did not hear from Pollard and started making the monthly payments. Presently, though, the Inland Revenue sought the entire debt. Selectmove argued that they had an agreement with the Inland Revenue to pay off the debt in instalments; and that that agreement was made by their agent, Pollard, who had apparent authority to accept the offer.

Held (i) silence *can* amount to acceptance of an offer, where this is not *imposed* on the offeree (so cases such as *Felthouse v Bindley* were distinguished); (ii) there was nothing to suggest that the Inland Revenue made a representation to Selectmove that Pollard had authority to convey the Inland Revenue's acceptance by silence.

Q What if Pollard had agreed to convey the acceptance actively, for instance by a letter, and had falsely done so; would that have made this case indistinguishable from *First Energy v HIB* (above)? If silence *can* amount to acceptance, why should an active acceptance make the case different?

1.3.2   Reliance

Overbrooke v Glencombe (1974)

A catalogue for a property auction stated in the conditions of sale that the auctioneer (A) had no authority to give representations or warranties. The catalogue was distributed before the auction. At the auction the third party (who was in possession of a catalogue) asked the auctioneer if a particular property was subject to local authority interest. The auctioneer incorrectly stated that it was not. The third party purchased the property on the strength of the auctioneer's reply but refused to complete the sale when he discovered that a local authority slum clearance scheme may affect the property.

Held the reliance must be reasonable. The third party was bound by the contract as it was unreasonable for him to rely on the auctioneer's representation in light of the catalogue statement.

1.3.3 Alteration of position

Norfolk County Council v Secretary of State for the Environment (1973)
A company (T) applied to their local council (P) for planning permission to build an extension to their factory. The council's planning committee resolved to refuse permission but, by mistake, the planning officers (A) sent a note to the company which stated that permission had been granted. In reliance on that notice the company ordered machinery for the factory. Two days later the mistake was discovered and the company was informed that permission has been refused. The company cancelled the order for machinery and incurred no expense in doing so. The company claimed that the council were estopped from denying planning permission.

Held although the company acted in reliance on the notice they had not done so to their detriment: they were no worse off than if the mistake had not been made. Unless the third party alters his position to his detriment, he cannot claim under apparent authority, which operates as an estoppel. The council were entitled to refuse planning permission.

1.3.4 Conduct subsequent to the contract

Spiro v Lintern (1973)
Mr Lintern (P), as sole owner, wished to sell his house so he asked his wife (A) to instruct an estate agent to find a purchaser. Unknown to Mr Lintern, his wife entered into an agreement (as apparent vendor) with Spiro to sell. Mrs Lintern represented herself as principal so there was no question at this stage of apparent authority. When Mr Lintern discovered the truth he did nothing to disabuse Spiro; in fact he allowed Spiro to incur expenses with architects and builders on the property. Before this sale was completed Mr Lintern attempted to sell to another for a higher price and Spiro brought an action of specific performance. Mr Lintern claimed that: (i) his wife had no authority to sell on his behalf; and (ii) his wife made the contract as principal and as she did not own the house an action for specific performance against her must fail.

Held Mr Lintern, by his (subsequent) conduct of allowing Spiro to incur expense on the property without disclosing the truth, was estopped from denying the contract with Spiro. Specific performance was ordered. The court also held that the alteration of position in such a case must be to the detriment of the claimant. This requirement was satisfied by the expenses incurred by Spiro.

Worboys v Carter (1987) CA

Carter (P) owned the lease on Lower Ledge Farm. His business was in trouble and the farm became run down. Then Clark (A) offered help, and advised selling the farm lease; but Carter objected to this idea. In the event Clark persuaded him to sign a document which did no more than appoint Clark as his agent. Clark mistakenly thought that this gave him authority to sell the farm and he went ahead with a sale to Worboys. Worboys then requested of Carter on several occasions a date by which Carter might vacate the farm; but Carter would not give it. Worboys measured up Lower Ledge Farm in Carter's presence and to the knowledge of Carter Worboys sold his own farm, on the expectation of moving in to Lower Ledge Farm. Carter confined his objections to the sale to his agent Clark; he was unhelpful to Worboys but said nothing to indicate that the sale was off. Eventually, Worboys sued for specific performance.

Held Clark had no actual or apparent authority to sell the farm. However, Carter's conduct (acquiescence) in the presence of Worboys amounted to a representation that he approved of the sale. Worboys relied upon that representation by, amongst other things, selling his own farm; Carter was estopped from denying the contract and specific performance was granted.

1.4 Usual authority (the doctrine of *Watteau v Fenwick*)

Edmunds v Bushell and Jones (1865)

Jones (UP) employed Bushell (A) to manage his business under the name 'Bushell & Co'; the drawing and accepting of bills of exchange was incidental to such a business. However, Jones stipulated that Bushell should not accept bills of exchange. Bushell accepted a bill of exchange. An action was brought to hold Jones liable on the bill.

Held that Jones was liable notwithstanding that this was a case of an undisclosed principal where the agent had acted outside of his actual authority.

Miles v McIlwraith (1883) PC

The defendant (P), who sat in the Queensland Legislative Assembly, was a part-owner of a ship. It was unlawful for a person to sit in the Assembly and at the same time make contracts with the government. So no authority was given to the agents to let the ship on behalf of the owners (including the defendant) to the government. However, it was agreed between the owners and the agents that the owners would let the ship to the agents so that agents might then let the ship to the government. In this way no contractual relationship would be established between the defendant and the government. It was found that the government either did not know or did not care that the ship was owned, not by the agents, but by the defendant; this was a case of undisclosed principal where the agents had acted within their usual authority. The issue was whether there was a contractual relationship between the defendant (part-owner) and the government.

Held the defendant had not contracted with the government; the agents had no actual or apparent authority to bind the principal defendant.

Q Compare this decision with *Watteau v Fenwick* (below); did the court in *Watteau v Fenwick* establish a contract between the principal and third party, or merely an obligation on the principal to pay a debt to the third party?

Watteau v Fenwick (1893)

The defendant (P), purchased a beerhouse from Humble (A). Humble remained as manager with his name above the door as licensee. Humble's authority was restricted to the purchase of beer. However, the plaintiff (T) regularly supplied cigars and bovril to Humble on credit, in the belief that Humble was the owner of the beerhouse. The suppliers knew nothing of the real principal. The plaintiff remained unpaid and after discovering the truth sued the real principal for the money owed. This was a case of undisclosed principal where the agent has acted outside of his actual authority. There was no actual authority – the principal had expressly limited Humble's authority to the purchase of beer. There was no apparent authority either because there had been no representation that Humble was an agent; only that he was the owner.

Held the defendant principal was liable. Wills J held (Lord Coleridge CJ concurring) that once it is established that the defendant was the real principal, the ordinary doctrine as to principal and agent applies – that the principal is liable for all the acts of the agent which are within the authority usually confided to an agent of that character, notwithstanding limitations, as between principal and agent, put upon that authority.

Notes

1 Wills J based his decision upon two grounds: by analogy with the law of partnership and the case of *Edmunds v Bushell* (above). However, Powell, *The Law of Agency*, 2nd edn, 1964, pp 73–78, noted that the analogy with partnership law was mistaken, s 5 of the Partnership Act 1890 stating no more than the doctrines of implied and apparent authority. Montrose, (1939) 17 Can Bar Rev 693, has pointed out that the reported facts of *Edmunds v Bushell* are not clear and there may have been apparent authority.

2 *Watteau v Fenwick* has been doubted but never overruled, so it is still, theoretically at least, good law. See *The Rhodian River* [1984] 1 Lloyd's Rep 373, p 378 (per Bingham J); *McLaughlin v Gentles* (1919) (SC of Ontario); *Sign-O-Lite v Metropolitan Life* (1990) (below). It was followed once in the English courts in *Kinahan v Parry* (1910) (below), a decision which, on appeal, was reversed on different grounds.

3 *Watteau v Fenwick* cannot be explained on conventional agency theory: in a case of undisclosed principal there cannot be apparent authority because no representation could come from principal (see above, 1.3, especially *Freeman and Lockyer v Buckhurst*); and where the agent acts outside of his actual authority, the doctrine of undisclosed principal cannot apply (see *Keighley, Maxted v Durrant* (below, 3.2.4)).

4 Several commentators have offered alternative theories. See Treitel, *The Law of Contract*, 9th edn, 1995, pp 633–35 (by analogy to vicarious liability in tort); Hornby [1961] CLJ 239 ('apparent ownership'); Fridman, *Law of Agency*, 7th edn, 1996, pp 69–76 (a form of actual implied authority); Goodhart and Hanson (1931) 4 CLJ 320, p 326 ('pure estoppel by conduct') and Fishman (1987) 19 Rutgers LJ 1 (inherent agency power).

5 For other commentary on *Watteau v Fenwick* see, as well as the above, Collier [1985] CLJ 363; Goode, *Commercial Law*, 2nd edn, 1995, pp 173–74; Fridman, 'The demise of *Watteau v Fenwick*' (1991) 70 Can Bar Rev 329 and *Bowstead and Reynolds on Agency*, 16th edn, 1996, pp 416–19.

Kinahan v Parry (1910)

The defendants (UP), owners of Carne Park Hotel, appointed Mortimer (A) as its manager. Mortimer's name appeared above the door as licensee. A licensee would usually be free to purchase what he likes from whom he likes. However, a *manager's* authority would usually be limited by the principal. Kinahan (T), believing Mortimer to be the licensee, sold Mortimer some whisky, and gave him credit. Kinahan knew nothing of the existence of the owners. When they discovered that Mortimer was merely a manager and that the defendants were the true owners, they sued the defendants for the price of the whisky.

Held following *Watteau v Fenwick* (above), the defendants were bound by the act of their agent (Mortimer) so long as he had acted within the usual authority of a licensee, which is what he appeared to be (NB the name above the door.) That was the case here and so the defendant was bound to pay.

Note ───
This decision was reversed by the Court of Appeal on the different
ground that Kinahan had sold the whisky to Mortimer personally and so
no issue of agency arose.

Sign-O-Lite v Metropolitan Life (1990) Can

Baxter owned a shopping mall. Sign-O-Lite (T) contracted with one of
Baxter's companies in 1978 for the installation and rental of an electronic
sign. Metropolitan Life (UP) then acquired ownership of the mall from
Baxter and employed another of Baxter's companies, the Baxter Group, as
agents, to manage the mall. In 1985 the Baxter Group concluded a new
contract with Sign-O-Lite for the rental of the electronic sign. In doing this,
the Baxter Group exceeded their authority. Sign-O-Lite were unaware of
the change of ownership of the mall and believed, reasonably, that it was
dealing with the same principal as it had in 1978, albeit with a different
company name. So this was a case of undisclosed principal where the
agent had acted outside of his authority (in other words a *Watteau v
Fenwick* situation). A dispute arose over the 1985 contract and the plaintiff,
Sign-O-Lite, tried to enforce it against the now disclosed principal. One
issue for the court was whether *Watteau v Fenwick* was applicable.

Held the doctrine of *Watteau v Fenwick* was not good law in British
Columbia and so had no application. An undisclosed principal was not
liable for unauthorised acts of the agent, even if within the scope of such
an agent's usual authority.

Note ───
See Fridman (1991) 70 Can Bar Rev 329.

2 Agency by operation of law

2.1 Agency of necessity

The Choko Star (1990) CA

A ship leaving Argentina became stranded on a river bed. The ship's master (A) made a contract with salvers (T) to refloat the ship. The master purported to act on behalf of the shipowners (P1) and the cargo owners (P2), although neither party had expressly authorised him to act so. After they had refloated the ship, the salvers looked for payment from the shipowners and the cargo owners. The shipowners settled, but the cargo owners contended that they should not bear any of the cost of refloating the ship because the master had no authority to make the contract on their behalf. In particular, there was no agency of necessity because it was possible for the master to obtain instructions (see *Springer v GWR*, below, 2.1.2) from the cargo owners – something which he had not done. The salvers contended that, in the absence of agency of necessity, the master had actual implied authority to act. They relied on *The Unique Mariner* (1978), where the master of a ship that had run aground was held to have had implied actual authority to make a contract with salvers. As with the instant case, there was no necessity in *The Unique Mariner* because the master could get instructions from the owners.

Held where agency by necessity could not operate because an element was not present (impracticable to obtain instructions) there was no basis for implying authority for the master to act on behalf of cargo owners. No such term could be implied to give the contract (between the cargo owners and the shipowners) business efficacy: the shipowners could claim expenses for the preservation of the cargo in appropriate circumstances. If the 'innocent bystander' test were applied, the cargo owners would not have said, 'Of course the master need not inquire of us; we will be bound by any salvage contract he makes, provided that it is itself on reasonable terms'. *The Unique Mariner* could be distinguished on the basis that, in that case, the master acted on behalf of *ship*owners, not, as in the instant case, *cargo* owners.

Notes————————————————————————

1 See Brown (1992) 55 MLR 414; Munday [1992] LMCLQ 1; Reynolds [1990] JBL 505.

2 That position has now been reversed for shipping cases. Section 224 of the Merchant Shipping Act 1995 has incorporated the International Salvage Convention 1989. Article 6 of that Convention provides that a ship's master, and her owner, have authority to make contracts with salvers on the behalf of cargo owners. It also restates the position in *The Unique Mariner* in that the master has authority to make salvage contracts on behalf of the shipowner. These provisions came into force on 1 January 1996 (s 316(2)).

2.1.1 There must be a genuine necessity and the agent must act *bona fide*

Prager v Blatspiel (1921)

Not long after the outbreak of the First World War the plaintiff, from Romania, contracted to buy a number of furs from the defendants, in London. The furs were largely paid for and delivery was to be at the behest of the plaintiff; he intended to wait until the war was over. Then Romania was occupied by the Germans and communication between the parties became impossible. The furs were stored and were increasing in value. The German occupation continued and towards the end of the war the defendants began to sell off the furs locally. When the war ended the plaintiff demanded delivery, only to be told that the furs had been sold off under an agency of necessity. The plaintiffs sued in conversion.

Held there was no agency of necessity. For an agency of necessity to exist there must be a 'definite commercial necessity' against which the agent acts *bona fide*. Here, on the facts, there was no necessity – the buyer was willing to wait for delivery and the goods were appreciating in value. Further, it was clear from the facts that the defendants had not acted *bona fide*.

2.1.2 Impracticable to obtain instructions

Springer v GWR (1919) CA

The defendant railway company was engaged by the plaintiffs to transport tomatoes from the Channel Islands to London, by ship to Weymouth and by train to London. The ship was detained at the Channel Islands for three days by bad weather. When the ship eventually arrived at Weymouth, unloading was delayed for two days by a strike of the railway company's employees. For fear of the tomatoes going bad, the railway company sold them locally, without communicating, as they could have done, with the plaintiffs. The plaintiffs brought an action for breach of contract of carriage. The railway company justified their action under an agency by necessity.

Held for an agency of necessity to exist it must be 'practically impossible to get the owner's instruction in time as to what should be done'. In the circumstances, the railway company ought to have communicated with the plaintiffs when the ship arrived at Weymouth, so as to get instructions. There was no agency of necessity and the railway company was liable to the plaintiffs.

2.1.3 Where no contract is made between principal and third party

China-Pacific v Food Corp of India, *The Winson* (1982) HL

The defendant cargo owner (P) chartered a ship to carry wheat from the USA to Bombay. The ship became stranded on a reef and her master entered into a standard (Lloyd's) contract with the plaintiff salvers (A). To assist the salvage operation the salvers unloaded much of the wheat and stored it in warehouses in Manila. This protected the wheat from deterioration. The salvers incurred expense in doing this and had acted without the express authority of the cargo owners. They then claimed from the cargo owner reimbursement for the storage charges incurred.

Held there existed no agency by necessity because: (i) on the facts there was no emergency; (ii) the doctrine (of agency by necessity) should only apply where a contract has been made between the principal and the third party, and not where the agent is simply reclaiming expenses incurred, which was the case here. The appropriate remedy in this case was under the law of bailment; the salvage company were bailees of the cargo owners and were entitled to reimbursement on that ground; and (iii) per Lord Simon, *obiter*, in this case there was evidence that the salvor's purpose in storing the wheat was to ensure a lien (see below, 6.2.7) for themselves against the cargo owners. The doctrine (of agency by necessity) only applies where the agent acts *bona fide* in the interest of the principal and not himself (See *Prager v Blats*piel above, 2.1.1.) However, it was unnecessary to decide the point.

On the second point of the decision, Lord Diplock said:

Whether one person is entitled to act as agent of necessity for another person is relevant to the question whether circumstances exist which in law have the effect of conferring on him authority to create contractual rights and obligations between that other person and a third party that are directly enforceable by each against the other. It would, I think, be an aid to clarity of legal thinking if the use of the expression 'agency of necessity' were confined to contexts in which this was the question to be determined and not extended, as it often is, to cases where the only relevant question is whether a person who, without obtaining instructions from the owner of goods, incurs expense in taking steps that are reasonably necessary for their preservation is in law entitled to recover from the owner of the goods reasonable expenses incurred by him in taking those steps.

2.2 Agency by cohabitation

Phillipson v Hayter (1870)

A wife purchased a gold pen and pencil case, a seal skin cigar case, a seal skin tobacco pouch, a guitar and a Russia purse (leather prepared with birch bark oil).

Held the presumption of authority arising from cohabitation is confined to necessaries suitable for the style in which the husband chooses to live. This was not the case here and there was no presumed authority.

Debenham v Mellon (1880) HL

A wife and her husband were, respectively, the manageress and manager of a hotel, where they cohabited. The husband expressly forbade his wife from purchasing goods as agent on his behalf; instead he gave her an allowance for clothes. Normally, she purchased clothes from the plaintiff in her own name. On one occasion, however, she bought clothes and pledged her husband's credit.

Held there was no express agency – this was forbidden by the husband. There was no agency implied from cohabitation because the couple were not cohabiting in a domestic situation. They lived together in a hotel (the address being known to the plaintiff) as manageress and manager, not as a family. The husband, then, was not liable to the plaintiff on the debt.

3   Ratification

3.1   Ratification may be implied from conduct

Waithman v Wakefield (1807)

Mrs Wakefield ordered some dress material from the plaintiffs (T) on her husband's (P) account. In doing this, she had acted outside of any actual or apparent authority. The plaintiffs, being unpaid, then visited Mrs and Mr Wakefield and demanded the return of the goods. Mr Wakefield disowned the transaction and agreed to return the goods. But Mrs Wakefield refused and her husband backed down in favour of his wife. So the plaintiffs sued Mr Wakefield for the price of the goods. Mr Wakefield argued that he was not bound by the unauthorised act of his wife.

Held the act of ratification need not be express, it may be implied; the act by Mr Wakefield of keeping the goods amounted to an act ratifying the transaction. He was then liable to the plaintiffs.

3.2   Rules for ratification

3.2.1   Principal must exist at time of contract

Kelner v Baxter (1866)

The promoters (A) of a company entered into a contract to buy some wine. After the company was formed the promoters – now its directors (P) – purported to ratify the contract.

Held as the company did not exist at the time of the purported contract, it could not now ratify the act. An agent cannot act for a non-existent principal. The promoters were held personally liable on the contract.

Note ———————————————————————

Section 36C(1) of the Companies Act 1985 provides that unless otherwise agreed, the agent shall be personally liable on any contract purportedly made on behalf of a non-existent company.

Newborne v Sensolid (GB) Ltd (1953) CA

Leopold Newborne (A) was forming a company to be called 'Leopold Newborne (London) Ltd' (P). He agreed to sell some tinned ham to

Sensolid (T), and signed the contract 'Leopold Newborne (London) Ltd' with his name underneath. Later (in a falling market), Sensolid refused to take delivery of the ham. Newborne sought damages for non-acceptance and the writ was issued in the name of the company, 'Leopold Newborne (London) Ltd'.

Held: (i) as the company did not exist at the time that the contract was made, any contract with that company was a nullity. Accordingly, Sensolid could not be sued upon the contract with 'Leopold Newborne (London) Ltd'; (ii) Newborne could not sue personally on the contract because, on the facts, he had purported to act on behalf of the company and not for himself. *Kelner v Baxter* (above) was distinguished.

Coral (UK) v Rechtman (1996)

Altro were a well known, large trading group, based in Vienna. They traded through a number of subsidiaries. Rechtman was a director of one of them, 'Altro Mozart Food Handels' ('Handels'). Rechtman negotiated a contract to sell 12,000 tonnes of sugar to Coral and he signed the contract, 'For and on behalf of Altro Mozart Food GmbH'. In fact, at the time, this company did not exist. The sugar was not delivered and so Coral tried to sue for non-delivery. Altro put forward Handels as the defendants, arguing that Rechtman was acting for that company when signing the contract. However, Coral were concerned about the solvency of Handels and, relying on *Kelner v Baxter* (above), tried sue Rechtman personally on the contract.

Held the identity of the parties to a contract should be decided in each case as a question of fact; the deciding factor being the intention of the parties (at the time that the contract was made). In this case, it was clear that Rechtman had acted in good faith and that Coral were not worried which particular subsidiary of the Altro group they dealt with. There was no intention at the time of the contract that Rechtman should, personally, be a party to it. Hence Rechtman could not be held personally liable for the non-delivery of the sugar.

3.2.2 Principal must be ascertainable at the time of the 'agent's' act

Hagedorn v Oliverson (1814)

An insurance broker (A) effected a policy on goods on behalf of persons (P) as yet unknown who may have an interest in the goods on board a ship.

Held any interested person may ratify the insurance so far as it covers his interest and the underwriters will be bound.

Watson v Swann (1862)

The plaintiff (P) asked an insurance broker (A) to effect a general policy on goods. However, the underwriters were not prepared to issue such a policy. So the broker declared the goods on the back of a policy effected at an earlier date; the underwriters then initialled it. The goods were subsequently lost and the plaintiff sued on that policy.

Held as the policy was effected before the broker was approached by the plaintiff it could not be said to have been effected on the plaintiff's behalf. Consequently, as the 'principal' was not ascertainable at the time that the agent effected the policy, ratification was not possible. Willes J stated:

> The law obviously requires that the person for whom the agent professes to act must be a person capable of being ascertained at the time. It is not necessary that he should be named; but there must be such a description of him as shall amount to a reasonable designation of the person intended to bound by the contract.

Note ———

Bowstead and Reynolds on Agency, 16th edn, 1997, para 2-063, comments that this proposition might be too restrictive.

Southern Water Authority v Carey (1985)

A building contract between the employer (T) and the main contractors (A) provided that the main contractors entered into the contract (including an exemption clause) for the benefit of themselves and any sub-contractors used. Later a sub-contractor (P), who was engaged after the main contract was made, was sued for negligence by the employer. The sub-contractor tried to ratify the contract so as to rely on the exemption clause therein.

Held at the time the contract was made, the sub-contractor was not ascertainable to the employer (although the main contractor had them in mind). So the sub-contractor could not be allowed to ratify the contract. *Watson v Swann* (above) applied.

3.2.3 Principal must be competent at the time of the agent's act

Williams v Moor (1843)

Contracts for work and materials and goods supplied and delivered were entered into allegedly by the defendant (P), who was at the time an infant, and therefore incompetent to enter into a legal relationship. When he reached full age the defendant confirmed the contracts. The plaintiff then brought an action for debt incurred upon those contracts. The defendant argued that as the contracts were made by an infant they were void and thus incapable of ratification.

Held on general principle, an infant, upon reaching full age, may ratify, and so make himself liable on, contracts made during his infancy. See, also, *Dibbins v Dibbins* (1896) below, 3.2.5.

3.2.4   Undisclosed principal cannot ratify

Keighley, Maxted v Durant (1901) HL

The defendant (P) authorised his agent to purchase wheat at a certain price in the joint name of the defendant and his agent. The agent purchased wheat from Durant at a higher price than authorised and in his own name. So this became a case of undisclosed principal where the agent acted outside of his authority. Nonetheless, the defendant, being satisfied with this act, ratified the deal. Subsequently, the defendant changed his mind and refused to take delivery of the wheat. Durant (T) sued for damages, arguing that the contract had been ratified.

Held an undisclosed principal cannot ratify. Lord Macnaghten stated:

> As a general rule, only persons who are a party to a contract, acting either by themselves or by an authorised agent, can sue or be sued on the contract. A stranger cannot enforce the contract, nor cannot it be enforced against a stranger. That is the rule; but there are exceptions. The most remarkable exception, I think, results from the doctrine of ratification in English law. That doctrine is thus stated by Tindal CJ in *Wilson v Tumman* (1843): 'That an act done, *for another*, by a person, not assuming to act for himself, but for such other person, though without any precedent authority whatever, becomes the act of the principal, if subsequently ratified by him, is the known and well established rule of law. In that case the principal is bound by the act, whether it be for his detriment or his advantage, or whether it be founded on a tort or on a contract, to the same effect as by, and with all the consequences which follow from, the same act done by his *previous* authority.' And so, by a wholesome and convenient fiction, a person ratifying the act of another, who, without authority, has made a contract openly and avowedly on his behalf, is deemed to be, though in fact he was not, a party to the contract. Does the fiction cover the case of a person who makes no avowal at all, but assumes to act for himself and no one else? If Tindal CJ's statement of the law is accurate, it would seem to exclude the case of a person who may intend to act for another, but at the same time keeps his intention locked up in his own breast; for it cannot be said that a person who so conducts himself does assume to act for anybody but himself. But should the doctrine of ratification be extended to such a case? On principle, I should say certainly not. It is, I think, a well established principle in English law that civil obligations are not to be created by, or founded upon, undisclosed intentions.

Therefore, the contract was unenforceable against the defendant.

Spiro v Lintern (1973)

For the facts, see above, 1.3.3.

Held although Mr Lintern could not be said to have ratified the contract by his (subsequent) conduct of allowing Spiro to incur expense on the property without disclosing the truth, he was estopped from denying the contract with Spiro.

3.2.5 Time for ratification

Bird v Brown (1850)

Carne and Telo (Liverpool) ordered goods from Illins (P) in New York. The goods were duly sent, but were not paid for. On behalf of Illins, but without any authority, Brown (A) stopped the goods in transit (see below, 14.4). Brown told the ship's master to hand over the goods to him (Brown). Carne and Telo then demanded the goods from the ship's master and tendered the freight charge. The ship's master refused to hand over the goods and delivered them to Brown instead. So Carne and Telo sued Brown for conversion. Later Illins tried to ratify Brown's act of stoppage. The issue was whether Carne and Telo's title to the goods had been divested by the stoppage.

Held: (i) when Carne and Telo demanded the goods the transit ended and with it the unpaid seller's right to stoppage; (ii) as the ratification came after the right to stoppage had lapsed, it was ineffective. Therefore Brown's act and the subsequent ratification of it did not divest Carne and Telo of title to the goods and the action for conversion succeeded. Rolfe B stated:

> ... the authorities ... shew that in some cases where an act which, if unauthorised, would amount to a trespass, has been done in the name and on behalf of another, but without previous authority, the subsequent ratification may enable the party on whose behalf the act was done, to take advantage of it and to treat it as having been done by his direction. But this doctrine must be taken with the qualification that the act of ratifying must take place at a time, and under circumstances, when the ratifying party might himself have lawfully done the act which he ratifies.

Bolton v Lambert (1889) CA

A third party made an offer to an agent who, without authority, accepted it on behalf of his principal. Then the third party revoked the offer. The principal then ratified his agent's acceptance and sued the third party for specific performance.

Hence, the ratification related back to the acceptance (the agent's acceptance was not a nullity) and so the revocation of the offer had no effect. There was a binding contract.

Metropolitan Asylums v Kingham (1890)

On 18 September, the defendant (T) tendered to supply eggs regularly to the asylum over a six month period beginning on 30 September. On 22 September, the asylum's board (A) resolved to accept that offer but omitted to affix a seal to the resolution, so the acceptance was not valid. All the same the board's manager (A) sent a letter of acceptance. On 24 September, the defendant withdrew his offer because it contained a mistake as to the price. On 6 October, the board ratified their resolution and the seal was affixed.

Held a ratification must take place within a reasonable time; a reasonable time cannot extend beyond a time when the contract is to commence. Ratification was, therefore not possible in this case.

Dibbins v Dibbins (1896)

The survivor (P) of a partnership had an option to buy the deceased partner's share within three months of the death. His solicitor (A) took up the option on the survivor's behalf. However, as the survivor was insane, that is, not competent, the solicitor had no authority to do so. Subsequently, an order was made under the Lunacy Act 1890 authorising notice to be given on the survivor's behalf, but this was after the three month period.

Held the second notice was outside the time limit and so was too late to ratify the first notice.

Watson v Davies (1931)

A third party offered to sell property to a deputation (A) of a charity (P). The deputation accepted the offer subject to approval by the full board of the charity. Some time later the third party revoked the offer. Later, the full board ratified the acceptance of the deputation and sued for specific performance

Held an acceptance by an agent, made *expressly* subject to ratification, is a nullity until ratified. Therefore this offer stood as no different to an unaccepted offer which, of course, could be revoked at any time. There was no binding contract.

Note

Compare *Watson v Davies* with *Bolton v Lambert* (above).

Presentaciones Musicales v Secunda (1993) CA

In April 1988, solicitors issued a writ without authority on behalf of the plaintiff company. In May 1991, the company ratified the solicitors' act. However, by statute, a writ *issued* in May 1991 would be to late and the claims would be struck out. So, for the ratification to have been effective, it must have been retroactive.

Held the ratification was retroactive and so the writs were good. *Per* Dillon LJ (Nolan LJ concurring) the rule was that ratification is retroactive with the exception (from *Bird v Brown* (above)) that if a time is fixed for doing an act, whether by statute or by agreement, ratification will not operate to extend that time. A writ issued without authority is not a nullity and so a ratification made after the expiry of the time limit did not extend that time: the writ was valid from its inception.

Per Roch LJ, the exceptions to the general rule were: (i) where the act had been avoided or undone; (ii) where the ratification would divest a third party of property rights (as in *Bird v Brown*). Hence, the ratification of the writ was unaffected by these exceptions.

1 The Court of Appeal was divided in its opinion of *Bird v Brown* (above), Dillon LJ giving it a wider interpretation than Roch LJ. See Brown (1994) LQR 531.

2 Leave to appeal was refused by the House of Lords [1994] 1 WLR 937.

3.2.6 Adoption of the transaction operates as a ratification of the whole transaction

Re Mawcon (1969)

A liquidator (P) was appointed to Mawcon Ltd. However, a court order allowed the directors (A) of Mawcon to continue the business so long as they did not incur any debts. In breach of their authority, the directors hired lorries from Vallance Ltd (T) and incurred a debt of £512. The lorries were used in Mawcon's business and the liquidator collected the proceeds of that business from the creditors. However, Vallance remained unpaid and sued the liquidator for the £512.

Held by collecting the proceeds generated by the use of the hired lorries the liquidator ratified the acts of the directors. But it was not open to the liquidator to retain the proceeds of the transactions in which the lorries were employed and at the same time repudiate the authority of the directors to hire the lorries. Adoption of part of the transaction operated as a ratification of the whole transaction, or transactions as a whole. A principal could not pick out of a transaction those acts which were to his advantage.

Keay v Fenwick (1876) CA

Dale, the managing owner (A) of a ship, sold it without authority, through shipping agents (T). Later, the other part-owners (P) of the ship ratified the sale and collected the proceeds. The shipping agents claimed their commission from the part-owners.

Held by adopting the transaction the part-owners were liable for the shipping agents' commission. The commission was part of the transaction.

3.3 Void acts

Danish Mercantile v Beaumont (1951)

A solicitor (A) commenced proceedings without the authority of the client (P). This would normally mean that proceedings would be stayed.

Held the client's ratification would cure the defect in the proceedings.

Note

This case was approved by the House of Lords in *Ward v Samyang Navigation* (1975).

Bedford Insurance Co v Instituto D Resseguros Do Brasil (1985)

Bedford Insurance (P) authorised brokers (A) to issue marine insurance subject to a limit as to the size of the financial risk. By the Insurance Companies Act 1974, a person must be authorised to carry on a marine insurance business and by the Insurance Companies Act of 1984 it is an offence to carry on an unauthorised marine insurance business. In 1981 and 1982, the brokers issued policies beyond the limit imposed by their principal. However, after discovering this in 1983, Bedford purported to ratify the brokers' acts so that they could recover from their indemnifiers.

Held the effect of the statute was that the insurance policies were void *ab initio*; even if they were made with the principal's authority they would be void. However, if the acts had not been illegal, ratification would have been effective.

Whitehead v Taylor (1839)

The agent of the landlord distrained goods without the landlord's consent. At a later time the landlord ratified this act.

Held the unlawful distraint was retrospectively made lawful by the act of ratification.

3.3.1 Companies

Ashbury Railway Carriage & Iron Co v Riche (1875) HL

The directors (A) of a company (P) concluded a contract outside the scope of the memorandum of association. The contract was therefore *ultra vires* and void.

Held as the company had no power to make the contract, it had no power to ratify, even with the assent of every shareholder.

3.3.2 Forgeries

Brook v Hook (1871)

An agent forged the signature of his brother in law (P) on a promissory note made out in favour of the plaintiff (T). Before the note matured the plaintiff met the principal and, after discovering the truth, threatened legal proceedings. In an effort to protect his agent the principal purported to ratify the act.

Held the act of forgery was illegal and therefore void. It was not possible to ratify a void act. The court relied upon the distinction between void and voidable acts. A voidable act could be ratified.

Note ———————

It could be said, however, that the true principle of this case is that as the agent forged the principal's signature there was no agency situation; instead the 'agent' was actually purporting to be the principal. See *Bowstead and Reynolds on Agency*, 16th edn, 1996, p 68.

4 Relationship between the principal and the third party

4.1 Principal's liabilities to the third party

4.1.1 Agent acts without authority

Commerford v Britanic Assurance (1908)

The agent of the defendant insurance company (P) represented to the plaintiff (T) that a certain policy would pay out £75 in the case of her husband's death. This was true. He further represented that if the husband died from an accident – as opposed to disease – the policy would pay out £150. This was untrue and the agent had no authority (actual or apparent) to make this statement. That representation was not ratified. After her husband died in a drowning accident the plaintiff sued the principal insurance company for £150.

Held as the agent had no authority to make the statement and it had not been ratified the principal insurance company were not liable to the plaintiff.

4.1.2 Principal settles with agent

Wyatt v Marquis of Hertford (1802)

A third party, who was owed money by the principal, took a security offered by the agent. He gave the agent a receipt as if for the payment, although none had been made. When the principal saw the receipt he paid the agent, mistakenly thinking that the agent had paid the third party. Presently the third party sued the principal for the (still unpaid) debt.

Held the action failed because the third party was estopped by his conduct of issuing a receipt. This led the principal, believing that the debt had been discharged, to settle with his agent.

Irvine v Watson (1880)

The agent ordered some oil from the third party. It was delivered and the third party did not require prepayment. This was unusual in the trade, but there was no trade custom that there should be prepayment. The principal settled with the agent, who later became insolvent. The third party remained unpaid and sued the principal.

Held the rule that a principal may be exonerated is based upon estoppel and not simply that it is unjust for the principal to pay twice. Here the principal was liable as the third party had made no representation that the debt had been settled by the agent. In particular, although delivering the oil before payment was unusual, there was no trade custom as such, consequently delivery did not amount to a representation that payment had been made.

4.2 Principal's rights towards the third party

4.2.1 Third party settles with agent

Linck v Jameson (1885)

A broker (A) sold goods to a third party, who paid the broker. The broker absconded without paying over the money to his principal. The principal brought an action for price against the third party.

Held the agent had no authority (actual or apparent) to receive payment. Further, the mere fact that the principal had authorised the agent to receive payments on previous occasions did not amount to apparent authority. The third party was still liable to the principal.

Butwick v Grant (1924)

Butwick (P) employed Chait (A) to sell sports coats to Grant (T). Grant ordered 63 and they were later delivered with an invoice in the name of Butwick. Chait collected payment from Grant and gave him a receipt. However, Chait got into financial difficulty and could not hand the money on to his principal, Butwick, though he had intended to do so. Butwick sued Grant for the price of the goods, the issue being whether the agent had authority to collect the money.

Held authority to sell does not necessarily imply authority to receive payment for the goods: Grant would have to pay Butwick.

Hine Bros v SS Insurance Syndicate (1895) CA

An insurance broker (A) was authorised to receive payments only in cash. This was in accordance with trade custom. The broker took a payment from a third party by bill of exchange and then become insolvent. The principal sued the third party for the payment.

Held the third party was still liable to the principal because: (i) the agent had no authority to take a bill of exchange; and (ii) there was no trade custom that payment may be made by bill of exchange.

5 Doctrine of undisclosed principal

5.1 General rule

Curtis v Williamson (1874)

Boulton, appearing to act on his own behalf, purchased some gunpowder from the plaintiffs. Later, the plaintiffs discovered that Boulton was acting on behalf of an undisclosed principal – the defendant mine owners. Then Boulton filed a petition of liquidation and the plaintiffs filed an affidavit in those proceedings in an attempt to recover the debt owed for the gunpowder. However, the plaintiffs then changed their mind and sued the defendant principal.

Held once an undisclosed principal is discovered the third party may elect to sue that principal. Secondly, the filing of the affidavit against the agent did not prevent the action against the principal.

Sui Yin Kwan v Eastern Insurance (1994) PC

A company called Axelson (UP) owned the ship *Osprey*. They asked their shipping agents, Richstone (A), to insure the ship, including personal injury to the crew. Richstone did this in their own name – which is normal. The *Osprey*, while moored in Repulse Bay, Hong Kong, was hit by typhoon *Ellen*. Many of the crew were lost and relatives of two of them sued Axelson for negligence and got judgment. They were awarded $HK1 million. However, Axelson had already gone into liquidation, so the relatives stepped into the shoes of Axelson and sued the insurance company (T). The insurance company argued that they had only dealt with Richstone, and knew nothing of Axelson, the undisclosed principal.

Held the doctrine of undisclosed principal applied: where an agent acts within his actual authority the undisclosed principal may intervene and acquire the rights/liabilities of the agent. Here, the agents acted within their actual authority and so the relatives could recover from the insurance company.

Note
See Hallady [1994] LMCLQ 174.

Boyter v Thomson (1995) HL (SC)

Thomson (P), a private seller, sold a cabin cruiser through a commercial agent to Boyter (T). Boyter knew nothing of the agency and thought that the agent was the owner. The cruiser proved not to be of merchantable quality and, upon discovering the agency, Boyter sued Thomson under s 14 of the Sale of Goods Act (see below, 9.4). Section 14(5) provides that where an agent sells goods the principal shall be liable under s 14(2) and (3) in the normal way, provided that the principal sells in the course of a business, *or if he does not, the buyer knows this or reasonable steps have been taken to bring this to his attention.* As this was a case of undisclosed principal Boyter had no way of knowing that Thompson was a private seller. In reply Thomson argued that s 14(5) did not apply to cases of undisclosed principal.

Held s 14(5) applied to cases of undisclosed principal and Thomson was liable to Boyter for breach of contract.

5.2 Exceptions to the general rule

5.2.1 Express terms of the contract

UK Insurance Association v Nevill (1887)

Nevill (P) and Tully (A) were part-owners of a ship. Tully was a member of the UK Insurance Association (T) and he insured the ship with them; Nevill was unknown to the Association. The Association's rules stated that only members were liable for premiums. Presently, Tully went bankrupt and the Association sought the premium from Nevill.

Held the terms of UK Insurance Association expressly excluded an undisclosed principal. Therefore Nevill was not liable for the premium.

5.2.2 Implied terms of the contract

(Grace) Humble v Hunter (1848)

Grace Hunter was the owner of the ship *Ann*. She tried to sue upon a contract (charterparty) signed by her son (A): 'CJ Humble Esq owner of the good ship or vessel called the *Ann*'.

Held an undisclosed principal could not come forward to assume rights or liabilities on the contract when (impliedly) excluded by the terms of that contract. Here, the agent (the principal's son) had described himself as the owner of the ship.

5.2.3 Personality of the principal

Archer v Stone (1898)

Before signing a contract to sell a house, the seller (T) asked the agent if he was acting for a particular principal. The agent replied that he was not.

This was untrue and a misrepresentation. When the truth was discovered the seller refused to go ahead with the sale. The purchaser (undisclosed principal) brought an action for specific performance.

Held the action failed because of the misrepresentation.

Nash v Dix (1898)

Trustees were selling a former chapel building. They refused an offer on behalf of a Roman Catholic committee because the committee intended to use the building as a Roman Catholic place of worship. The committee then asked the manager of a mineral water company to buy the building and offered to buy it from him at a £100 profit. The trustees, who believed that the manager wanted the building for his company, agreed to sell the building to the manager. The manager had been aware of their mistake, but he said nothing. Upon discovering the truth, the trustees refused to complete the sale and the manager brought an action for specific performance.

Held granting specific performance, the manager was buying for himself, with a view to reselling. There was no agency arrangement and so the identity of the probable sub-buyers (the committee) was irrelevant to that sale.

Said v Butt (1920)

Said (P) wished to attend the opening night of the play *Whirligig* at the Palace Theatre, London. However, at the time he was in dispute with the theatre owners and he knew that the theatre would not knowingly admit him on such an important evening. So Said employed Pollock (A) to purchase a ticket on his behalf without revealing the agency. In due course, Said went along to the opening night but was refused entry to the theatre by Butt (the theatre's managing director) who spotted him in the foyer. Said sued Butt; the issue for the court was whether a binding contract existed between the theatre and Said.

Held there was no contract. McCardie J emphasised the specific importance of a first night; accordingly, the management would be particular as to who attended.

Dyster v Randall (1926)

Dyster (P) wished to purchase some land owned by Randall, who distrusted Dyster. That land was for sale but Randall would not sell it to Dyster and Dyster knew this. So Dyster employed Crossley (A) to buy the land without revealing the agency. When Randall discovered the truth, he sought to renege on the contract. Dyster brought an action for specific performance.

Held the agent's silence did not amount to a misrepresentation. This was not a personal contract and so the identity of the purchaser was irrelevant. Specific performance granted.

5.3   Set-off and the undisclosed principal

Rabone v Williams (1785)

An agent, acting for an undisclosed principal sold the defendant some goods. The defendant was owed money by the agent. Subsequently, the principal intervened on the contract to sue the defendant for the price of the goods. The defendant argued that he should be able to set off the debt owed by the agent against his liability to the principal.

Held where the agent delivers goods in his own name, thus concealing the agency, the purchaser contracts with the agent and enjoys the right of set-off against the agent. If the real principal intervenes on the contract, the purchaser's right of set-off on the contract remains. The defendant may have his set-off against the real principal.

Cooke v Eskelby (1887)

A firm of brokers (A) owed money to Cooke (T). Sometimes the brokers sold goods on behalf of a principal and sometimes on their own behalf; this was known to Cooke. On one occasion the brokers sold some cotton to Cooke; in this instance the brokers were acting for an undisclosed principal. When the real principal intervened on the contract to sue the defendant for the price of the goods, Cooke argued that he should be able to set off the debt owed by the brokers against his liability to the real principal.

Held the set-off was not effective against the real principal. The doctrine which allows a set-off against an agent to be effective against his (undisclosed) principal is based upon estoppel. Consequently, it only operates where the principal has represented to the third party that the agent is the principal. That was not the case here because Cooke was not bothered if the brokers were acting as agent or principal.

6 Relationship between the principal and the agent

6.1 Agent's duties

Commercial Agents (Council Directive) Regulations 1993 SI 1993/3053

3 Duties of a commercial agent to his principal

(1) In performing his activities a commercial agent must look after the interests of his principal and act dutifully and in good faith.

(2) In particular, a commercial agent must:

(a) make proper efforts to negotiate and, where appropriate, conclude the transactions he is instructed to take care of;

(b) communicate to his principal all the necessary information available to him;

(c) comply with reasonable instructions given by his principal.

Notes————————————————————————————

1 These Regulations now govern the principal-agent relationship; if the common law is inconsistent with them, the Regulations will prevail.

2 The Regulations only apply to 'Commercial Agents' who are defined in s 2 as self-employed intermediaries who have authority to negotiate the sale or purchase of goods on behalf of the principal, be it in the agent's or the principal's name.

3 See, generally, Reynolds [1994] JBL 265; Schmidt [1996] SLT (News) 13 and 'Commercial Agents Regulations – Update' (1997) 19(4) Buyer 3–5

6.1.1 To act

Turpin v Bilton (1843)
An agent was instructed to insure his principal's ship. The agent failed to do so. Consequently, when the ship was lost, the owner was uninsured.

Held the agent was liable to his principal for the loss caused by his failure to act.

Ireland v Livingston (1872)
Livingston (P) wrote to Ireland (A) in Mauritius authorising them to buy and ship 500 tons of sugar adding: '50 tons more or less of no moment, if it

enables you to get a suitable vessel.' These instructions were ambiguous and capable of two meanings: either one bulk was required to be sent in one ship or two or more bulks could be sent in two or more ships. The agents took the latter meaning and shipped 400 tons with an intention to ship a further 60 tons when available at a later date. Livingston refused delivery and wrote to cancel any further order. The agents sued for breach of contract.

Held as the instructions were capable of two meanings it was reasonable for the agents to take one of those meanings. In the circumstances, they acted reasonably and Livingston was bound to accept the cargo.

Cohen v Kittel (1889)

The principal instructed his agent to place bets on horses at Sandown Park and Newmarket. The agent failed to do so and the principal sued him for loss of winnings.

Held that as a wagering agreement is not enforceable, the agent cannot be held liable for failing to carry out an unenforceable act.

6.1.2 Principal's best interests

Fray v Voules (1859) CA

An attorney (A) employed to conduct a case reached a compromise on the advice of counsel. This compromise was against the express instructions of his client (P).

Held an attorney has no authority to enter into a compromise against the directions of his client even if he is acting *bona fide* in the best interest of his client and on counsel's advice.

The Hermione (1922)

The crew (P) of *The Hermione* spotted another ship, *The Daffodil*, in trouble. They towed it into bay and salvaged its cargo of rubber before it sank. (*The Daffodil* then became the property of the insurance company (T).) The crew were entitled to the salvage value of the rubber. So they employed a solicitor (A) to negotiate with the insurance company, stipulating not to settle below £10,000. The solicitor settled for just £100 and was sued by the crew.

Held the solicitor was liable because he went outside his instructions and failed to act in his client's best interests. (The judge valued the cargo at £500 and awarded £400 damages.)

Waugh v Clifford (1982)

Clifford, a firm of builders, employed solicitors (A) to negotiate a settlement with Waugh, a dissatisfied house purchaser. The solicitors arranged a compromise with Waugh whereby Clifford would repurchase the property. Clifford then wrote to the solicitors instructing them not to agree this compromise, but by an error the solicitor dealing with the matter was not informed and the compromise was agreed. Following that, Waugh brought an action for a specific performance. Clifford argued that the solicitor had no authority to agree that compromise.

Held specific performance was granted. Although there was no actual authority (authority expressly withdrawn), the solicitor had apparent authority to agree the compromise.

Re Debtors (No 78 of 1980) (1985)

Harrison and Holmes had a bankruptcy order set aside. The trustees in bankruptcy appealed against this decision. Harrison and Holmes instructed their counsel to negotiate a compromise. Counsel agreed a compromise with the trustees whereby the appeal would be conceded but Harrison and Holmes would be given time to raise money in order to prevent their house being sold. Later, Harrison and Holmes argued that they were not bound by the compromise because, if they had known its details, they would have never agreed to it.

Held Harrison and Holmes were bound by the compromise. Counsel conducting a case on behalf of a client had unlimited apparent authority in relation to settlement, compromise and any matter that seemed fit to him. There are two limitations to this authority: (i) he may not introduce wholly extraneous matters; and (ii) he is bound by any express limitations put on his authority by his client, even if the other side did not know of such limitations. None of these limitations applied in this case.

6.1.3 Personal performance

De Bussche v Alt (1878) CA

The owner of a ship, De Bussche (P), engaged an agent to sell it at a minimum price of $90,000, at any port where it happened to be on its travels. The agent, with the consent of De Bussche, engaged the defendant, Alt (sub-agent), in Japan to sell the ship. After languid efforts to sell the ship Alt purchased it for himself for $90,000 and then re-sold it in Japan for $160,000. De Bussche then sued Alt alleging that Alt was his agent and so must account for the profit made.

Held the general rule is that an agent cannot delegate obligations which he has personally undertaken to fulfil. However, a right to delegate may be implied from the conduct of the parties, usages of the trade, the nature of the particular business or where there is an unforeseen emergency. In this case, where the ship was to travel from port to port it must have been contemplated by the parties that a sub-agent may be appointed in any of those ports. At the time of the 'resale' of the ship there existed between De Bussche and Alt a relationship of principal and agent. Consequently, Alt should account for the profit made.

Calico Printers v Barclays Bank (1931)

The plaintiffs (P) engaged Barclays Bank (A) to insure their goods in Beirut. As Barclays had no office in Beirut they instructed a sub-agent – the

Anglo-Palestine Bank – to insure the goods. This was done with the consent of the plaintiffs. The sub-agent failed to insure the goods and they were destroyed by fire. The plaintiffs sued, among others, the sub-agent for breach of the agency contract.

Held an agent undertakes responsibility for the whole transaction; where a sub-agent is in breach of duty the principal must look to the agent and not the sub-agent. In turn the agent may look to the sub-agent. This is because, generally, there is no privity of (agency) contract between the principal and the sub-agent. Privity between principal and sub-agent can only exist when the principal has authorised the agent to create such privity between the principal and a sub-agent; this would require 'precise proof'.

Q This case was decided before *Donoghue v Stevenson* (1932) and *Hedley Byrne v Heller* (1964). Do you think that nowadays the sub-agent would be liable to the principal in negligence?

Allam v Europa Poster Services (1968)
The defendant company (A) was authorised by site-owners (P) to issue notices to several parties (T) terminating licences to use the site. The defendant company employed a firm of solicitors (sub-A) to send out the notices, one of which went to the plaintiffs. They claimed that the notice was invalid because, *inter alia,* the defendant company could not delegate that task.

Held the role delegated to the solicitors was purely ministerial, involving no discretion or confidence; it must have been contemplated by the parties (principal and agent) that solicitors would be engaged to issue the notices. Thus, the maxim *delegatus no potest delegare* (delegates cannot delegate) had not been breached.

6.1.4   Care and skill

Chaudhry v Prabhakar (1989) CA
Chaudhry (P) asked Prabhakar (A), a friend who knew more about cars than she did, although he was not a qualified mechanic, to help her buy a second-hand car. She stipulated that it should not have been involved in a traffic accident. Prabhakar recommended a car being sold by a car sprayer and panel beater. Prabhakar had noticed that the bonnet had been repaired but made no inquiries. In reply to a specific question, Prabhakar stated that the car had not been involved in a traffic accident. Chaudhry purchased the car for £4,500 and later discovered that it had been involved in a traffic accident and was not roadworthy. Although Prabhakar had acted without payment, Chaudhry sued him for breach of the duty of care arising from the (gratuitous) agency.

Held Chaudhry could recover from the gratuitous agent. He owed a duty of care and his skill was to be measured objectively. He fell below the standard expected.

6.1.5 Conflict of interest

Oliver v Court (1820)

Court (A) was employed to sell by auction an interest in an estate. However, at the auction nobody made an offer. The next day Court himself purchased the interest. This was not discovered until 12 years later.

Held an agent is not entitled to purchase for himself things which he was entrusted to sell. The court exercised its discretion to set the transaction aside after 12 years.

Bentley v Craven (1853)

Craven (A), one of several partners in a firm (P) of sugar refiners, also carried on business as a sugar dealer, and accordingly could buy at below market price. He was engaged by the firm to buy sugar on their behalf. Unknown to the firm he purchased sugar belonging to himself at market price and made a profit.

Held an agent employed to buy cannot buy his own goods for his principal. The principals may either rescind the contract or adopt it and claim the profit made by the agent. In this case, the principals chose to adopt the contract and were entitled to the agent's profit.

Aberdeen Railway Co v Blaikie bros (1852) HL(Sc)

Thomas Blaikie (A) was a partner in Blaikie Bros, a firm of iron-founders. He was also a director, and for a time, the chairman, of the Aberdeen Railway Co (P). During this time the company agreed to purchase railway ironware from Blaikie Bros. However, the company refused to complete the contract because it considered the price to be exorbitant. Blaikie Bros sued for damages.

Held the action would fail because the contract was void. This was because Thomas Blaikie had put himself in a position of conflict of interest. Lord Cranworth LC stated:

> A corporate body can only act by agents; and it is, of course, the duty of those agents so to act as best to promote the interests of the corporation whose affairs they are conducting. Such an agent has duties to discharge of a fiduciary character towards his principal; and it is a rule of universal application that no one having such duties to discharge shall be allowed to enter into engagements in which he has or can have a personal interest conflicting, or which could possibly conflict, with the interests of those he is bound to protect. So strictly is this principle adhered to that no question is allowed as to the fairness of unfairness of a contract so entered into.

McPherson v Watt (1877) HL

A solicitor (A) was appointed by two ladies (P) to sell their houses. The solicitor wanted the properties for himself but did not disclose this. Instead, he arranged the purchases nominally in the name of his brother. The solicitor and his brother brought an action seeking specific performance to enforce the sales.

Held specific performance was refused. The solicitor placed himself in a position of conflict of interest. His obligation to arrange a purchase on the best possible terms conflicted with his desire to own the property.

Allison v Clayhills (1907)

Allison was a businessman who employed Clayhills, a solicitor, from time to time. Clayhills took a 15 year lease on the Grey Horse inn from Allison with an option to purchase. After Allison died, the trustees of the will tried to have the transaction set aside on the ground that Clayhills acted as solicitor for both parties and Allison had no independent advice.

Held the transaction would not be set aside. A solicitor owes a duty to his client not to put himself in a position of conflict of interest.

He may deal with his client where the matter is entirely outside of the confidential relationship of the parties. Conversely, the duty may continue after the employment of the solicitor has ceased: it depends on the circumstances of the case. For example, by his employment, the solicitor may gain special knowledge or a personal ascendancy over his client which continues after the employment has ceased.

In such cases where a conflict of interest does arise, the onus is on the solicitor to prove the validity of the transaction by showing that the client was fully informed of all the facts, understood the transaction and that the transaction itself was a fair one. In the circumstances, the transaction was an entirely separate matter from the solicitor-client relationship of the parties and it would not be set aside.

Armstrong v Jackson (1917)

Jackson (A), a stockbroker, was instructed by Armstrong (P) to buy some shares in a certain company for him. In fact Jackson sold shares belonging to himself to Armstrong, although he led Armstrong to believe that they had been purchased on the open market. Five years later, Armstrong discovered the truth and sued Jackson. Meanwhile, the shares had fallen in value.

Held the agent was in breach of his duty by placing himself in a position where his duty and interest would conflict. The transaction was set aside even though the shares had fallen in value. Jackson had to repay the money paid for the shares and Armstrong had to give up the shares to Jackson.

Demarara Bauxite v Hubbard (1923) PC

Mr Hubbard died in 1915 and Mrs Hubbard (P) was introduced to Humphries (A), a solicitor, to deal with the probate. From then on Mrs Hubbard sent all her legal work to Humphries. In 1919, Hubbard agreed to sell some land to Humphries; Humphries knew that others would pay a higher price for it, but he did not disclose this. Then, however, Mrs Hubbard was offered a higher price and she refused to complete the sale to Humphries. He brought an action to enforce the sale. There were two issues to decide: (i) did a relationship of solicitor and client exist between

Humphries and Mrs Hubbard? And (ii) if it did, had Humphries' conduct rendered the sale unenforceable?

Held on the first issue, although Humphries was not technically acting for Mrs Hubbard at the time the sale was agreed, a relationship of confidentiality naturally arising from previous dealings still existed between the parties. On the second issue, the solicitor must prove two things. First, that he fully disclosed all of the facts to her. This was not done. And secondly, that Mrs Hubbard received competent independent advice. There was no evidence of this either and so the sale would not be enforced.

Harrods v Lemon (1931)

The estate agency department of a company (A) arranged a sale of property on behalf of the vendor (P). However, in ignorance of this the surveying department of the same company produced a report on behalf of the purchaser which effectively reduced the price of the property. When the truth was discovered, the vendor was informed that the agents were in a position of conflict of interest. However, he was content to complete the sale at the lower price.

Held as long as the principal had full knowledge of the facts and consented there was no breach of duty by the agent.

Kelly v Cooper (1993) PC

Cooper, a firm of estate agents, were instructed separately by two neighbours, Kelly (1st P) and Brant (2nd P), to sell their respective properties. Cooper found a single buyer for both properties and the transactions were completed. When Kelly discovered that Cooper had also acted for his neighbour, he brought an action against Cooper claiming that they had put themselves in a position of conflict of interest by taking on a neighbour's property.

Held the contract of agency between Cooper and Kelly did not include a term (express or implied) preventing the estate agents from seeking to earn a commission from rival vendors.

6.1.6   Gifts

Wright v Carter (1903) CA

Wright (P) executed a deed giving property in trust to his solicitor (A). This was a gift.

Held the deed was void. While the relationship of solicitor and client exists there is a presumption of undue influence against the receiver of a gift, who has the burden of rebutting that presumption. The presumption is one which is extremely difficult to rebut.

6.1.7 Bribes – definition

Industries & General Mortgage Co v Lewis (1949)

Lewis (P) employed an agent to deal with a third party (IGM) who arranged a loan to Lewis. Without informing Lewis, IGM agreed to pay the agent half of the fee that they received from Lewis for arranging the loan. IGM had no dishonest intention of influencing the agent to act to his principal's disadvantage.

Held this was a bribe and the third party was ordered to pay Lewis the amount of the bribe in damages or for money had and received. A bribe at civil law involves three elements:

(i) the third party makes a payment to the agent of the principal with whom he is dealing;

(ii) the third party knows that the agent is acting for that principal; and

(iii) the third party does not disclose to the principal that he has made the payment to the agent.

If these circumstances are proved, there is an irrebuttable presumption that the agent was influenced by the bribe and that he breached his duty to his principal.

Anangel Atlas v IHI (1990)

Campbell (A) was a navel architect who designed a ship for IHI. He also helped to promote the ship. Campbell then acted for Anangel (P) to negotiate the purchase of a ship from IHI (T). During this period, Campbell received payments from IHI in respect of design royalties and promotion costs. Anangel alleged that as these payments were secret they could recover them as money had and received.

Held Anangel's claim would fail. They knew of Campbell's connections with IHI and the payments were reasonable and did not affect the price of the ship.

6.1.8 Bribes – remedies

Boston Deep Sea Fishing & Ice Co v Ansell (1888)

Ansell, the director (A) of the plaintiff company (P), placed orders with certain other companies (T) on behalf of the plaintiffs. For doing so, those certain other companies paid him bonuses and a commission.

Held Ansell must account to his own plaintiff company for the bribes plus interest. Further, the plaintiffs were entitled to dismiss Ansell immediately without compensation upon discovering the truth.

Lister v Stubbs (1890) CA

Lister (P), a firm of silk-spinners, regularly employed their foreman, Stubbs (A), to purchase materials for dyeing. Stubbs often purchased goods from Varley, who secretly paid him commission, some of which

Stubbs invested. Upon discovering the payments, Lister sought to recover the money paid and to trace the investments.

Held the relationship between Stubbs and Lister was that of debtor and creditor, and not of trustee and beneficiary. Thus Lister could recover any money held by Stubbs in respect of the secret commission, but they could not trace the investments.

Note ───────

This case was disapproved by the Privy Council in *Attorney General for Hong Kong v Reid* (1993) (below). See *Birks* [1993] LMCLQ 30.

Andrews v Ramsay & Co (1903)

Andrews (P) instructed Ramsay (A), a firm of estate agents, to sell his property for a commission of £50. Ramsay sold the property to Clutterbuck (T), who secretly paid a fee of £20 to Ramsay. When Andrews found out, he demanded the return of the £20 payment *and* the £50 commission.

Held Andrews was entitled to both the £20 payment and the return of the commission.

Hippisley v Knee Bros (1905) CA

Hippisley (P) employed Knee Brothers (A) to sell goods. It was agreed that Hippisley would pay for Knee Brothers' expenses. Knee Brothers sold goods and earned commission. In the event Knee Brothers incurred printing expenses, and they claimed the full price of this despite receiving themselves a discount. This was a custom of the trade (not known to Hippisley) and Knee Brothers were acting honestly.

Held Knee Brothers were in breach of their duty and should account for the discount as a secret profit. However, as Knee Brothers acted honestly they were entitled to keep their commission.

Mahesan v Malaysia Government Officers' Co-operative Housing Society (1979) PC

A third party sold land to a housing society (P) at an inflated price and made a net profit of $443,000. He managed this by bribing the director (A) of the society with $122,000 taken from the profit. By the time the truth was discovered the third party had fled the country. The society sued their director for both the bribe and damages representing the true value of the land and the price that they had paid for it (in other words, the net profit made from the fraud – $443,000).

Held these claims are alternative; the principal cannot recover both the bribe and damages – that would amount to double recovery.

Logicrose v Southend United Football Club (1988)

McCutcheon (A), the chairman of Southend United (P), negotiated with Logicrose (T) an agreement whereby Logicrose would use Southend United's football ground on certain days as a market place. During the negotiations the issue of a market licence arose. McCutcheon falsely stated to Logicrose that a certain offshore company held the licence and would require £70,000 in compensation to relinquish the licence. In fact McCutcheon controlled this offshore company. Logicrose paid the 'compensation' and a contract for the use of the football ground for a market was concluded between Logicrose and Southend United. So here, the agent took a bribe from the third party (who was innocent and thought that he was making a goodwill payment to another company which in fact was owned by the agent). When the truth was discovered the Football Club dismissed McCutcheon.

Held Southend United were entitled to dismiss their agent for taking a bribe. They could also recover the bribe and rescind the contract with the third party. Recovering the bribe does not amount to an adoption of the transaction. Further, the bribe does not have to be returned to the third party on the basis of *restitutio in integrum* when the principal rescinds the contract.

Attorney General for Hong Kong v Reid (1993)

The defendant (A) was once the assistant Director of Public Prosecutions for Hong Kong. He took bribes and favoured certain criminals. With that money, he purchased properties in New Zealand.

Held he held these properties (as far as they represented the bribes) on constructive trust for the Crown as beneficiary. Should the value of that property increase, the Crown, and not the defendant, could claim the profit. This was because the defendant could not be allowed to profit from an investment with a bribe. Should the value of the property fall below the amount due, the defendant would be liable for the difference.

Note ─────

Lister v Stubbs (above) was disapproved. See Birks [1993] LMCLQ 30; Crilley [1994] Restitution L Rev 57; Pearce [1994] 2 LMCLQ 189.

6.1.9 The agent must not take advantage of his position to acquire a benefit

Keech v Sandford (1726)

A lease of a market had been devised to the trustee (A) for the benefit of an infant. However, when the lease expired the landlord was not willing to renew it for the trust, but he was willing to renew it for the trustee personally. The trustee then renewed the lease for himself.

Held the rule that no advantage must be taken from the position of trustee is strict – it was ordered that the trustee hold the lease on trust for the infant beneficiary.

Boardman v Phipps (1965) HL

The Phipps Trust (P) owned a small holding of shares in a company. Boardman and one other, as agents for the trust, were entitled to attend a shareholders' meeting of the company and make inquiries into the company's affairs. They learned that the value of the company's assets was high yet the profits were low; and they realised that the company would benefit from selling its non-profit making assets. The Phipps Trust could not have raised the money to buy a controlling interest in the company; neither did the trustees desire to do so. However, Boardman and the other agent, acting in good faith and openly, purchased a controlling interest in the company and carried out the desired reorganisation. This proved to be highly profitable to the shareholders; and so both the Phipps Trust and the agents benefited greatly from the initiative taken by the agents on their own behalf. Yet the knowledge which led to the initiative was derived from their position as agents. One of the beneficiaries under the Phipps Trust brought an action calling for the agents to account to the Trust for the profits made.

Held (3:2) that the agents, having used information from their position as agents, would have to account for any profits made using that information. However, as they acted in good faith they were entitled to generous payment for their work and skill.

6.2 Principal's duties

Commercial Agents (Council Directive) Regulations 1993 SI 1993/3053

4   Duties of a principal to his commercial agent

(1) In his relations with his commercial agent a principal must act dutifully and in good faith.

(2) In particular, a principal must:

(a) provide his commercial agent with the necessary documentation relating to the goods concerned;

(b) obtain for his commercial agent the information necessary for the performance of the agency contract, and in particular notify his commercial agent within a reasonable period once he anticipates that the volume of commercial transactions will be significantly lower than that which the commercial agent could normally have expected.

(3) A principal shall, in addition, inform his commercial agent within a reasonable period of his acceptance or refusal of, and of any non-execution by him of, a commercial transaction which the commercial agent has procured for him.

6.2.1 Remuneration and implied terms

Commercial Agents (Council Directive) Regulations 1993 SI 1993/3053

6 Form and amount of remuneration in absence of agreement

(1) In the absence of any agreement as to remuneration between the parties, a commercial agent shall be entitled to the remuneration that commercial agents appointed for the goods forming the subject of his agency contract are customarily allowed in the place where he carries on his activities and, if there is no such customary practice, a commercial agent shall be entitled to reasonable remuneration taking into account all the aspects of the transaction.

7 Entitlement to commission on transactions concluded during agency contract

(1) A commercial agent shall be entitled to commission on commercial transactions concluded during the period covered by the agency contract:

(a) where the transaction has been concluded as a result of his action; or

(b) where the transaction is concluded with a third party whom he has previously acquired as a customer for transactions of the same kind.

(2) A commercial agent shall also be entitled to commission on transactions concluded during the period covered by the agency contract where he has an exclusive right to a specific geographical area or to a specific group of customers and where the transaction has been entered into with a customer belonging to that area or group.

8 Entitlement to commission on transactions concluded after agency contract has terminated

Subject to reg 9 below, a commercial agent shall be entitled to commission on commercial transactions concluded after the agency contract has terminated if:

(a) the transaction is mainly attributable to his efforts during the period covered by the agency contract and if the transaction was entered into within a reasonable period after that contract terminated; or

(b) in accordance with the conditions mentioned in reg 7 above, the order of the third party reached the principal or the commercial agent before the agency contract terminated.

9 Apportionment of commission between new and previous commercial agents

(1) A commercial agent shall not be entitled to the commission referred to in reg 7 above if that commission is payable, by virtue of reg 8 above, to the previous commercial agent, unless it is equitable because of the circumstances for the commission to be shared between the commercial agents.

(2) The principal shall be liable for any sum due under para (1) above to the person entitled to it in accordance with that paragraph, and any sum which the other commercial agent receives to which he is not entitled shall be refunded to the principal.

11 Extinction of right to commission

(1) The right to commission can be extinguished only if and to the extent that:

(a) it is established that the contract between the third party and the principal will not be executed; and

(b) that fact is due to a reason for which the principal is not to blame.

(2) Any commission which the commercial agent has already received shall be refunded if the right to it is extinguished.

(3) Any agreement to derogate from para (1) above to the detriment of the commercial agent shall be void.

Way v Latilla (1937) HL

It was agreed between principal and agent that the agent would send the principal information concerning gold mines in West Africa. No express terms were agreed as to remuneration, but the principal led the agent to believe that a commission would be paid.

Held there was an implied term in the contract of agency that the agent was entitled to a reasonable remuneration on a *quantum meruit*, that is payment for what the service was worth.

Kofi Sunkersette Obu v Struass (1951) PC

There was an express term in an agent's contract that he would be paid £50 expenses per month. Commission would be paid at the principal's discretion. The agent claimed that he was entitled to a reasonable commission on a *quantum meruit*.

Held the court would not interfere with the express terms of the contract which provided that the commission was payable only at the principal's discretion. Thus, *Way v Latilla* (above) was distinguished because in that case the matter was left open.

6.2.2 Remuneration according to custom

Miller v Beale (1879)

The principal employed an auctioneer to sell property.

Held there is an implied term that the auctioneer is entitled to the usual and reasonable commission.

Wilkie v Scottish Aviation (1956)

Wilkie was employed by the defendants as a surveyor. There was no express term as to his fees. After the work was completed Wilkie sent the defendants a bill for over £3,000. This was based upon the Scale of Professional Charges of the Royal Institute of Chartered Surveyors. The principal paid just £1,000 and Wilkie sued for the difference.

Held the fees would only be payable according to the Scale if it was customary, reasonable and notorious.

6.2.3   Loss of the right to remuneration

Marsh v Jelf (1862)

An auctioneer (A) was employed to sell property by auction. In fact he sold it privately.

Held the auctioneer was not entitled to commission because he had breached his duty to the principal. See, also, *Andrews v Ramsay* (1903) above, 6.1.8.

Mason v Clifton (1863)

Clifton (P) employed Kingdon (A) to raise loans for him on usual mortgage terms. Kingdon engaged the assistance of Mason, who went to much trouble to obtain the loans. However, they were not on terms required by Clifton. Nevertheless, Mason sued Clifton for his commission or for remuneration for his trouble and labour.

Held the claim would fail because Kingdon, and not Mason was employed as agent by Clifton. In any case the loans obtained were on different terms to those required, and so Mason (and Kingdon) would not be entitled to commission. Nor would they be entitled to remuneration because they had not done what they were required to do, that is, obtain loans on usual mortgage terms.

6.2.4   Effective cause

Toulmin v Millar (1887) HL

An agent was instructed to find a tenant and the person he introduced to his principal actually purchased the property.

Held for the agent to be entitled to commission there had to be a contractual relationship with the transaction concerned. Consequently, no commission need be paid to the agent for doing something (introducing a purchaser) not within the agency agreement.

Millar v Radford (1903) CA

An agent was instructed to find a tenant or purchaser for a property. The agent found a tenant and was paid his commission. Some 15 months later the tenant purchased the property. The agent claimed a further commission on the basis that he had found a purchaser.

Held that it was not enough for the agent to be a cause in the sequence of events leading up to the sale (the *causa sine qua non*). The agent had to show that he was the effective cause of the sale (the *causa causans*). Here the agent's involvement ceased when the tenant entered the property. He did not bring about the sale and so was not entitled to commission on that sale.

6.2.5 Agent's right to earn commission

French v Leeston (1922) HL

A shipbroker (A) negotiated a charterparty (an agreement to let a ship) lasting 18 months between a shipowner (P) and a third party. The shipbroker's commission depended upon the continuation of the charterparty. However, after four months the shipowner agreed to sell the ship to the third party, thus terminating the charterparty.

Held there was no implied term preventing the principal terminating the charterparty. To imply such a term would interfere with the right of the principal to deal with his property as he wished. Therefore the principal was not in breach of the agency agreement.

Luxor v Cooper (1941) HL

Cooper, an estate agent, was engaged to find a purchaser for four of the principals' cinemas. The principal vendors agreed to pay Cooper a commission of £10,000 if the cinemas were sold for £185,000 or more. Cooper introduced a purchaser who offered £185,000. However, the principals refused the offer and no sale was made. Cooper sued the principals, claiming that they were in breach of an implied term that the principals would not act so as to prevent the agent earning his commission.

Held for the defendant principals, that there was no such implied term in the agency agreement.

Alpha Trading v Dunnshaw Pattern (1981) CA

An agent negotiated a contract for the sale of cement between the seller (P) and the third party. The contract of sale was made but the seller breached the contract in that he failed to deliver. Consequently, the price was never paid and no commission was paid to the agent.

Held there was an implied term in the agency agreement that the principal seller would not breach the sale contract so as to deprive the agent of his commission. The principal was in breach of this term and so liable to the agent.

Sellers v London Counties Newspapers (1951) CA

Sellers (A) was employed by the defendants (P) to obtain orders for advertising space in their newspapers. The terms of the agreement were that Sellers would be paid £3 per week, plus a commission on orders obtained payable when the advertisements appeared in the newspapers. The defendants terminated Sellers' employment and Sellers claimed commission in respect of orders which he had obtained during his employment, but which was not payable until the respective advertisements appeared in the newspapers after his employment ended.

Held (2:1) the defendants had to account to Sellers for commission that became payable after the ending of his employment.

Note ───

On the subject of commission continuing after termination of the agency, see Powell, *The Law of Agency*, 2nd edn, 1964, p 364.

6.2.6 Indemnity

Read v Anderson (1884) below, 6.3.3.

Barron v Fitzgerald (1840)
An agent was instructed to take out life insurance on the principals, in the names of the principals or in his own name. The agent took out insurance in the name of himself *and* another and claimed an indemnity.

Held as the agent had exceeded his actual authority he was not entitled to an indemnity.

Bayliffe v Butterworth (1847)
A broker (A) in Liverpool was instructed by his principal to sell shares. He did so to a second broker, but failed to deliver them. The second broker sued for his loss and the first broker claimed an indemnity from his principal on the basis that it was a custom among Liverpool brokers to be responsible to each other for such breaches. The principal argued that by failing to deliver the shares, their agent exceeded his authority, and secondly, that the custom was unreasonable and so not a matter for the principal.

Held principals are bound by a reasonable trade custom. However, if they are aware of a custom, it matters not if it is reasonable or unreasonable – they are bound by it and are liable to their agent.

Rhodes v Fielder, Jones & Harrison (1919)
A firm of country solicitors (P) employed a firm of London solicitors (A) to brief counsel. After the case, the country solicitors instructed the London solicitors to withhold counsel's fees. Nevertheless, the London solicitors paid the fees even though counsel cannot sue for his fees, and claimed to be entitled to an indemnity.

Held the London solicitors were employed as solicitors. To fail to pay counsel would have been a case of professional misconduct. Therefore, they were entitled to go against their principal's instructions in order to act properly. In the circumstances they were entitled to be indemnified.

Adams v Morgan (1924)
By carrying out his principal's instructions, the agent incurred supertax. He claimed an indemnity from his principal.

Held in the absence of a term to the contrary, a term will be implied that the agent is entitled to an indemnity against the supertax incurred.

6.2.7 Agent's lien

See, further, unpaid seller's lien below, 14.3.

Houghton v Matthews (1803)

Matthews (A), who were brokers, sold in their own name two parcels of goods to Jackson. However, Jackson never paid for them. Later, Jackson asked Matthews to sell one of the parcels for him. So now Jackson was a principal employing Matthews as agent. Jackson delivered the parcel to Matthews but before it was sold Jackson became bankrupt. His assignees offered to pay for the parcel in Matthews' possession but he declined to hand it over, claiming a lien against the debt for *both* parcels formerly sold to Jackson.

Held Matthews had no lien on the parcel because the debt in question had arisen before an agency agreement between Matthews and Jackson existed.

Taylor v Robinson (1818)

An agent negotiated a contract whereby the principal purchased a quantity of staves from the third party seller but this seller would store them for the time being at his own yard for rent. Later, the seller asked the agent to remove the staves. So the agent, without authority from his principal, moved the staves to his own premises. Then the principal became bankrupt and the question arose whether the agent had a lien on the staves.

Held the original agreement was that the agent would not take possession of the staves. He took possession without authority and so unlawfully; for the agent to enjoy a lien he must have *lawful* possession.

Bryans v Nix (1839)

A principal employed a carrier to transport goods to his agent in Dublin. He delivered the cargo to the carrier together with documents which indicated clearly that the carrier held the goods for the agent.

Held for an agent to have a lien on the goods he must be in possession of them. However, constructive possession is enough. For this purpose, the agent had possession enough for his lien.

Re Bowes, Earl of Strathmore v Vane (1886)

A life insurance policy was deposited with a banker with instructions that it should be used as security on overdrafts over £4,000. Normally, a banker enjoys a customary general lien on the insurance policy against any debts on the account.

Held the terms of the agreement may expressly or *impliedly* exclude a lien. In this particular agreement, the terms impliedly excluded the banker's customary general lien.

6.2.8 Loss of lien

Forth v Simpson (1849)

Forth was a racehorse trainer who kept stables. Worley sent horses to him to be kept and trained, but could retake possession of them at any time for the purpose of putting them in a race. Forth claimed a lien on the horses against unpaid stabling charges.

Held where the owner can remove the horses at any time the trainer has no right of continuing possession and so has no lien.

> Note ───────────────────────────────
> Although this is not a case of agency, the principle is of general application.

Sweet v Pym (1800)

An agent shipped some bales of cloth to the principal and at the principal's expense and risk.

Held where the agent parts with possession he will lose his lien. Here the agent was held unable to recall his lien by stopping the goods in transit.

6.3 Termination by the parties

Commercial Agents (Council Directive) Regulations 1993 SI 1993/3053

14 Conversion of agency contract after expiry of fixed period

An agency contract for a fixed period which continues to be performed by both parties after that period has expired shall be deemed to be converted into an agency contract for an indefinite period.

15 Minimum periods of notice for termination of agency contract

(1) Where an agency contract is concluded for an indefinite period either party may terminate it by notice.

(2) The period of notice shall be:

(a) one month for the first year of the contract;

(b) two months for the second year commenced;

(c) three months for the third year commenced and for the subsequent years; and the parties may not agree on any shorter periods of notice.

(3) If the parties agree on longer periods than those laid down in para (2) above, the period of notice to be observed by the principal must not be shorter than that to be observed by the commercial agent.

(4) Unless otherwise agreed by the parties, the end of the period of notice must coincide with the end of a calendar month.

(5) The provisions of this regulation shall also apply to an agency contract for a fixed period where it is converted under reg 14 above into an agency con-

tract for an indefinite period subject to the proviso that the earlier fixed period must be taken into account in the calculation of the period of notice.

16 Savings with regard to immediate termination

These Regulations shall not affect the application of any enactment or rule of law which provides for the immediate termination of the agency contract:

(a) because of the failure of one party to carry out all or part of his obligations under that contract; or

(b) where exceptional circumstances arise.

6.3.1 The general rule

Campanari v Woodburn (1854)

The agent agreed to try to sell the principal's picture for a commission of £100 should he succeed. However, before the picture was sold the principal died. The agent then sold the picture and the administratrix confirmed the sale although she knew nothing of the agency agreement. The agent then sued the administratrix for his £100 commission.

Held the agreement was one which could be terminated at any time before the painting was sold. In the event, the agency terminated with the death of the principal. The administratrix's confirmation did no more than confirm the sale, it did not confirm the old agreement nor did it establish a new one between the agent and herself. The commission was not, therefore, payable.

Rhodes v Forewood (1876) HL

The agent was employed by the owner of a colliery as sole agent for the sale of coal for seven years or as long as the principal carried on his business in a certain town. The agreement contained a provision for notice of termination if the principal could not supply, or the agent could not sell, a certain amount per year. After four years, the principal sold the colliery and the agent sued for breach of contract.

Held the principal was only bound to supply coal while he carried on his business. The construction of the contract was that the seven year period was subject to prior termination.

Turner v Goldsmith (1891)

The agent was employed to sell such shirts 'as from time to time be forwarded or submitted by sample or pattern'. The agency was for a period of five years. After two years the principal's factory burnt down and he did not resume business; he attempted to terminate the agency agreement.

Held the agent could recover damages for loss of commission for the rest of the five year period. The agreement was for five years and it was not performed if the principal failed to supply shirts. The principal was not excused because the factory burnt down.

Page v Combined Shipping and Trading Co (1996) CA

Mr Page (A) acted for CST (P), buying and selling commodities. Their written agency agreement was to last four years, and it provided that CST could dictate the amount of business conducted by Page. However, five months into the agreement CST terminated it. Page claimed damages under the Commercial Agents Regulations 1993 SI 1993/3053, which provides, in reg 17(6), 'the commercial agent shall be entitled to compensation for the damage he suffers as a result of the termination of the agency where', and (reg 17(7)(a)) 'that termination deprives the agent of the commission which proper performance of the agency contract would have procured for him'. CST argued that they were entitled under the agreement to vary the business given to Page; accordingly, they were entitled to reduce that business to nil. That being the case, CST argued, it was not possible for Page to show that he had suffered 'damage' because of the termination: he could have suffered equally had CST reduced the business to nil, which would have been 'proper performance'. They further argued that the Commercial Agents Regulations had not altered English law and so *Rhodes v Forewood* (above) applied. Before the full trial, Page sought a *Mareva* injunction (this has the effect of restraining a defendant from disposing of his assets so as to frustrate any judgment that may made against him). In order to get the injunction, Page had to show that he had a 'good arguable case'.

Held the Commercial Agents Regulations provided for damages where the agent had been deprived of the commission which 'proper performance' of the agreement would have given him. In this case, it was arguable that 'proper' meant 'normal'. So reducing the business to nil would not be proper – or normal – performance. Hence, Page had a good arguable case and the injunction was granted.

Notes

1 Unless the parties settle, the case will go to full trial, where the issues will be finally decided.

2 See Saintier [1997] JBL 77.

3 In *King v Tunnock* [1996] SCLR 742 (Sheriff's Court) it was held that a seller of bakery products was entitled to three months' notice under reg 15(2)(c) of the Commercial Agents Regulations 1993.

6.3.2 Irrevocable agency

Gaussen v Morton (1830)

A principal owed money to William Forster (A). So it was agreed that the agent would sell land belonging to the principal and recover the debt from the proceeds. Later, the principal tried to terminate the agreement.

Held he could not do so because the object of the agreement was to discharge the debt – it was authority coupled with an interest. This was an irrevocable agency.

Smart v Sandars (1848)

Corn-factors (A) were in possession of their principal's goods for the purpose of sale. Later, the factors loaned money to the principal. The principal defaulted on the repayment and revoked the factors' authority to sell the goods in their possession. The factors claimed that this was authority coupled with an interest and so the authority to sell was irrevocable.

Held the authority to sell was revocable. This was not an authority coupled with an interest; but an independent authority and an interest subsequently arising. *Per* Wilde CJ:

> This is what is usually meant by an authority coupled with an interest, and which is commonly said to be irrevocable. But we think this doctrine applies only to cases where the authority is given for the purpose of being a security, or … as part of the security; not to cases where the authority is given independently, and the interest of the donee of the authority arises afterwards, and incidently only.

Frith v Frith (1906) PC

Reginald Frith (A) was appointed by Elizabeth Frith (P) to enter in possession of and manage the family's estate. The estate was mortgaged to Astwood and Reginald undertook personally to pay off the mortgage debt. Neither the mortgage debt nor the personal undertaking were expressed in any documents relating to the appointment. Later, Elizabeth revoked the appointment and demanded that Reginald give up possession. Reginald claimed that his authority was coupled with an interest and so the appointment was irrevocable.

Held as the documents relating to the appointment contained no reference to the special interest the appointment and authority had no connection with it. Therefore the authority was revocable and the agent had to give up possession.

6.3.3 Executed authority

Hampden v Walsh (1876)

The principal gave a sum of money to his agent to lay a wager as to whether the earth was curved. The wager was lost but before the sum was paid the principal demanded it back. The agent settled the wager from his own purse and refused to hand back the money to his principal.

Held the principal had revoked in time and so could recover the sum from his agent. Cf *Read v Anderson* (1884) (below).

Read v Anderson (1884)

The agent was authorised to place bets and settle if they were lost. The agent placed bets and settled because they were lost. The principal tried to revoke the agency without indemnifying the agent for his expense.

Held as the agent had incurred personal liability carrying out his authority, the agency was not revocable.

Note

Under the Gaming Act 1892, this case would be decided differently; however, the principle remains. Cf *Hampden v Walsh* (1876) (above).

7 Relationship between agent and third party

7.1 Warranty of authority

Yonge v Toynbee (1910)

A solicitor (A) acted for a client (P) of unsound mind (one incompetent to create legal relations). The solicitor was unaware of these circumstances and did not act negligently.

Held the solicitor was ordered to pay the opposing side's costs. He represented to them that his client was a competent person. The client's solicitor is in the best position to establish his client's credibility.

Babury v London Industrial (1989)

A landlord (T) sought to levy distress for rent arrears against the tenant company (P), unaware that the tenant company had ceased to exist. Nonetheless, a director of the tenant company instructed solicitors (A) to bring an action for wrongful distress. They did so in good faith and judgment was entered. Then the landlord discovered that the tenant company did not exist and got the judgment for wrongful distress set aside. Further, he requested that his costs be met by the solicitors of the tenant company.

Held the solicitors would have to pay the landlord's costs because they represented to the landlord that the tenant company did exist. The fact that the solicitors were unaware of this and acted *bona fide* was no defence – they could have conducted a company search into the status of their client; the court would not expect the other side to make such investigations. The solicitors made a representation to the landlord which was relied upon.

Penn v Bristol and West Building Society (1997) CA

Mr and Mrs Penn (P) were joint owners of their home. Mr Penn, who had business debts, decided to raise money by executing a mortgage fraud. He used a Mr Wilson to help. Mr Penn planned to 'sell' his – and his wife's – house to Mr Wilson. Mr Wilson, in order to 'buy' the property, would raise the money with the Bristol and West Building Society (T). Throughout, Mrs Penn knew nothing of this.

Mr Penn instructed a solicitor (A) to handle the 'sale'. In all correspondence with the solicitor, Mr Penn forged the signature of Mrs Penn, so the solicitor was unaware that Mrs Penn had not consented to the sale. Accordingly, in due course, the solicitor warranted to the Building Society that he was acting for Mr *and* Mrs Penn. When the sale was executed, the proceeds went to pay off Mr Penn's debts as planned.

When the fraud was discovered the building society became aware that they no longer had a security over the house: Mrs Penn (a joint owner), not being party to the sale contract, was still the owner. The issue for the Court of Appeal was whether the solicitor could be liable to the building society for breach of warranty of authority. The solicitor argued that this could not be so where the third party has not been induced to *deal with the principal* (here, Mrs Penn).

Held the solicitor was liable to the building society for any losses flowing from the breach of warranty of authority. It made no difference that the loss did not stem from a dealing with the principal. In support, the following passage from *Bowstead and Reynolds on Agency*, 16th edn, 1996, para 9-057, was cited:

(i) Where a person by words or conduct, represents that he has authority to act on behalf of another, and a third party is induced by such representation to act in a manner in which he would not have acted if that representation had not have been made, the first mentioned person is deemed to warrant the representation is true, and is liable for any loss caused to such a third party by a breach of that warranty, even if he acted in good faith, under a mistaken belief that he had such authority.

7.2 Contractual liabilities of the agent – the general rule

Lewis v Nicholson (1852)

Lewis (T) had a charge on a bankrupt's (P) property. Solicitors (A) of the bankrupt made an agreement on behalf on the bankrupt with Lewis to sell the property and pay the debt owed to Lewis from the proceeds. In fact the solicitors had no authority to make such an agreement. In the event the property was sold but Lewis remained unpaid. He brought an action against the solicitors for breach of the agreement.

Held both Lewis and the solicitors intended that the agreement be between the bankrupt (principal) and Lewis (third party). Therefore they could not be liable on a contract to which they were not a party; it made no difference that the solicitors acted without authority.

Wakefield v Duckworth (1915)

A solicitor, acting as agent for his client (a defendant in a criminal case), employed a photographer (T). The photographer sued the solicitor for his fees.

Held the solicitor, as agent, was not liable. The correct person to sue was the principal (client).

7.2.1 Liability for misrepresentation

Resolute Maritime v Nippon Kaiji Kyokai, *The Skopas* (1983)

The plaintiffs (T) purchased a ship from one of the defendants (P). The sale was negotiated by O'Keefe (A), as agent for the seller. The plaintiffs alleged that the sale was induced by misrepresentations made by O'Keefe in respect of maintenance, repairs and a survey. A preliminary issue for the court was whether an agent could be liable under s 2(1) of the Misrepresentation Act 1967 ('negligent' misrepresentation).

Held the Act was concerned with the contracting parties. As the agent was not a party to the contract which he negotiated (on behalf of his principal) he could not be liable under the Act.

7.3 Contractual liabilities of the agent – exceptions to the general rule

7.3.1 Contracts in writing

Gadd v Houghton (1876)

Fruit brokers (A) signed a contract without qualification. However, the body of the contract explained that the transaction was with the principal, not the agent.

Held the agent was not liable on the contract.

Note ────────────────────────────────

In *Punjab National Bank v De Boinville* (1992) (a similar case concerning insurance contracts) Hobhouse J said: 'A decision on similar ... words used by a fruit broker is scarcely any authority for the meaning of words used in an insurance contract in 1983.'

────────────────────────────────

Universal Steam Navigation Co v James Mckelvie (1923) HL

Agents signed a contract 'For and on behalf of James Mckelvie & Co (as agents). JA Mckelvie'. The agents were sued for breach of the contract but claimed to have been acting only as agents on behalf of an Italian company.

Held the agents would have been liable had they signed the contract without qualification. By adding the words 'as agents' they clearly indicated that they were acting for another and had no intention of being bound by the contract.

The Swan, Bridges & Salmon v *The Swan* (1968)

A fishing boat was owned by Mr JD Rodger (A). He formed a company called 'JD Rodger Limited' (P) to hire the boat from him and operate it. Mr Rodger ordered repairs to the boat orally and on the company's notepaper which he signed 'JD Rodger, director'. The repairers knew that Mr Rodger was both an agent for the company and the owner of the boat. The repairers sent their bill to the company, which became insolvent before it was settled. So they sued Mr Rodger personally on the contract.

Held the liability of the agent depends upon an objective view of the intention of the parties, which may be taken from the written contract and surrounding circumstances. Where a person contracts as agent for a company and does no more than add the word 'director' or 'secretary' to his signature he will be liable on that contract. Although the repairers sent their bill to the company, it was still reasonable to expect Mr Rodger, as owner, to be liable unless he made it clear that this was not to be the case.

7.3.2 Negotiable instruments

Durham Fancy Goods v Michael Jackson (Fancy Goods) Ltd (1968)

The Companies Act 1948 (now s 349(4) of the Companies Act 1985) requires an officer of a company to state the exact title of the company on negotiable instruments to avoid liability. A bill of exchange drawn on a company called 'Michael Jackson (Fancy Goods) Ltd' was signed on behalf of 'M Jackson (Fancy Goods) Ltd'.

Held this was not an accurate or exact description of the company and so the person signing could be held personally liable on the bill.

7.3.3 Contracts under seal

Hancock v Hodgson (1827)

The directors (A) of a company contracted under seal to make payments from the shareholders' (P) subscriptions.

Held where an agent contracts under a seal, he will be liable personally, even where he describes himself as acting as an agent. The directors were liable for the payments.

7.4 The contractual rights of the agent – general rule

Fairlie v Fenton (1870)

A cotton broker (A) placed the word 'broker' by his signature and the contract stated that the agent was acting on behalf of the (named) principal.

Held the agent could not sue for non-delivery. The general rule is that the agent has no rights on the contract made on behalf of his principal.

7.5 The contractual rights of the agent – exceptions to the general rule

7.5.1 Auctioneers

Chelmsford Auctions v Poole (1973)

An auctioneer (A) sold goods to the highest bidder (T) and received commission out of the buyer's deposit. Later, the auctioneer sued the third party for the price.

Held the auctioneer had a right to sue, not on the contract made on behalf of his principal, but on a collateral contract between him and the highest bidder.

7.5.2 Agent the true principal

Bickerton v Burrell (1816)

Bickerton employed an auctioneer to sell a lease for the benefit of Mrs C Richardson. So the auctioneer understood the position to be that Bickerton was the agent, Mrs C Richardson the principal and he the third party. The auctioneer collected the ground rent but failed to hand it over to Bickerton. Bickerton sued and the auctioneer defended by stating that he was only liable to the principal – Mrs C Richardson. It was then that Bickerton revealed the truth: the deal was only for the benefit of Mrs C Richardson, who was his housekeeper and had no interest in the sale. Bickerton was the true principal.

Held Bickerton had no right to sue; the 'agent' could not shift his position.

7.6 Doctrine of election

Thomson v Davenport (1829)

Thomson (T) sold goods to M'Kune. Thomson knew that M'Kune was an agent, but did not know who the principal was. So this was a case of unnamed principal. Thomson sent a bill to M'Kune and later discovered one Davenport to be the principal. So he abandoned any action against M'Kune and sued Davenport. It was argued that the action against Davenport was barred because of the election to sue the agent, M'Kune.

Held if the principal is undisclosed and the third party makes the agent the debtor, he may change his mind when the principal is disclosed. However, if the principal is known to the third party then he cannot change his mind once he has elected. The instant case fell between these two propositions. As the third party had not the power at the time to choose, he could change his mind in the case of the unnamed principal.

Clarkson Booker Ltd v Andjel (1964) CA

An agent purchased airline tickets from Clarkson Booker (CB) on behalf of an undisclosed principal and failed to pay for them. Having discovered the agency agreement, CB issued a writ against the principal. Then, the principal became insolvent, so CB sued the agent. The agent's defence was that CB had elected to sue the principal and so he could not change his mind; this was an unequivocal act which amounted to election.

Held that it was not an unequivocal act so as to constitute election. Hence CB remained free to sue the agent.

Part 2 Contracts generally

8 Contract classification

8.1 Sale of goods within the Sale of Goods Act 1979

8.1.1 Goods – s 61(1):

... personal chattels other than things in action and money; and in particular 'goods' includes emblements, industrial growing crops, and things attached to or forming part of the land which are agreed to be severed before sale or under the contract of sale; and includes an undivided share in goods.

Moss v Hancock (1899)
A thief stole a £5 gold coin and sold it to a curiosity shop for its face value. In fact the coin had been presented to the owner as a gift and was worth considerably more than its face value, although it was good tender. The thief was caught and convicted; under the Larceny Act 1861 stolen money could be returned to its original owner provided that it had not passed into general circulation. So the court had to decide whether the thief had spent the coin as money, or sold it as a good.

Held the coin was sold as a good. Thus, money, where sold as a curiosity, can be a good.

Toby Constructions Products v Computa Bar Ltd (1983) Aus
The defendant sold to the plaintiff a computer system, comprising of hardware and software. There were two items of software: a business management package and a word processing package. The plaintiff buyer alleged breaches of conditions and warranties implied by the (Australian) Sale of Goods Act. The issue was whether the computer system was 'goods' within the meaning of that Act, which carried a similar definition of 'goods' as the English Sale of Goods Act (SGA).

Held the computer system, comprising of hardware and software, was 'goods' for the purposes of the SGA. *Obiter*, it was a debatable question whether or not a sale of software by itself could be a sale of goods.

St Albans City Council v International Computers (1996) CA

The local authority purchased a computer software system from the defendants for the purpose of managing the collection of the Community Charge (a local tax). However, the system failed and the local authority sued the defendants for breach of the statutory implied term as to merchantable quality (s 14 of the SGA). One issue raised was whether computer software was 'goods' within the definition given by s 61 of the SGA. If not, the statutory implied term would not apply. At first instance it was held that computer software was 'goods'. The only judge in the Court of Appeal to discuss the point was Sir Iain Glidewell.

Held obiter:

(i)   computer disks clearly were 'goods' within the meaning of s 61 of the SGA. But, just as clearly, computer software was not 'goods';

(ii)   however, where disks are sold with programs encoded on to them, those programs are part of the disk and so 'goods'. That was analogous to the text within an instruction manual;

(iii)   where programs are supplied separately from disks, those programs are not 'goods' and so the SGA would not apply. However, the common law would imply a term into the contract that the programs were reasonably fit for the intended purpose. Thus, if the SGA could not assist the local authority, the common law would.

Note ───

Liability in this case turned on the effectiveness of an exclusion clause. See below, 9.7.2.

8.1.2   Existing and future goods – s 5

Howell v Coupland (1876) CA

A farmer contracted to sell 200 tons of potatoes yet to be grown in a specified field. Only 80 tons were yielded because of an unpreventable disease. The buyer sued for non-delivery of the balance. The farmer argued that his non-performance should be excused under the common law rules of frustration, which require that the contract was for specific goods.

Held this was a contract for future and specific goods and the non-performance would be excused.

Note ───

Since this case, the SGA was passed which provided a narrower definition of specific goods (see s 61(1): 'goods identified and agreed on at the time the contract is made'). Clearly, this contract would now fall outside of the statutory definition. In *Re Wait* (1927) CA, Atkin LJ suggested that this case is now covered by s 5(2) (contract dependent on a contingency).

8.1.3 Money consideration and part-exchange

Aldridge v Johnson (1857)

Aldridge supplied 32 bullocks in exchange for 100 quarters of barley. The parties valued the bullocks at £192 and the barley at £215. It was agreed that Aldridge would pay the difference of £23 in cash. A dispute arose over the passing of the property in the barley.

Held in this case, there were two separate contracts of sale, and not a single contract of barter or exchange.

Dawson Ltd v H & G Dutfield (1936)

Dawson contracted to sell to Dutfield two lorries for a combined price of £475. Against this price Dawson allowed £225 for two Leyland vehicles owned by Dutfield. Dutfield paid the balance of £250 but then, because of a dispute over one of the lorries, they refused to hand over their two Leyland vehicles. Dawson sued for the allowance (£225) in cash, in other words he sued for price. This assumed that the contract to sell the two lorries to Dutfield was a sale of goods contract and not a contract of barter or exchange, otherwise Dawson would have no action for price.

Held this was a sale of goods contract and so Dawson could recover the price. Delivery by Dutfield of the two Leyland vehicles would have satisfied the purchase price to the extent of £225, but as they failed to deliver £225 was payable.

Flynn v Mackin (1974) Ire

A car dealer agreed to supply a car in part-exchange for the customer's car plus £250 cash. No value was accredited to either car.

Held this was a contract of barter or exchange, and not a contract of sale.

Note

Customs & Excise require (for VAT purposes) car dealers to give each part-exchange motor car a money value and to record in their books part-exchange deals as two individual sales.

8.1.4 Transfer of property

See, further, below, 10.1.

Rowland v Divall (1923) CA

The plaintiff purchased a car from the defendant. Two months later it was discovered that the car was stolen property and the plaintiff had to give it up to the police. The car was stolen before it came to the defendant and both parties were innocent. Nonetheless, the defendant had no title to pass on and so the plaintiff sued the defendant for the *whole* of his money back. This was despite the fact that he had had two months use of the car.

Held the whole object of a sale of goods is to transfer the property from the seller to the buyer. No property had been transferred here; there was a total failure of consideration and the buyer was entitled to his money back.

8.1.5 Sale of goods or contract for work and materials?

Clay v Yates (1856)
A printer was employed to print a book, the manuscript being supplied by the employer.

Held the manuscript is the important material; the printer merely converts it into a printed form. This was a contract for work and materials.

Dixon v London Small Arms Co (1876) HL
Under a contract to make rifles, the purchasers supplied the stocks (in rough) and the steel barrels.

Held to determine if a contract is of sale or for work or materials the court should look to see which party supplies the principal materials. To decide which are the principal materials the court should look to all the circumstances of the case and not just their comparative value. This contract was held to be one of sale.

Lee v Griffin (1861)
This case involved a contract to make a set of dentures. At issue was whether this was a sale of goods.

Held (per Blackburn J) the test is: does the labour end up in nothing which can become the subject of a sale? For instance, where a solicitor draws up a deed there is a contract for work and materials. The test is not whether the value of the work exceeds the materials used; for instance, a sculptor's labour may exceed the value of the marble, yet the statue would be sold under a sale contract. Accordingly, a contract to make a set of dentures is a contract for the sale of goods.

Robinson v Graves (1935) CA
An artist was commissioned to paint a portrait. The issue arose as to the application of the SGA and whether this was a contract of sale or for work and materials.

Held the test is whether the substance of the contract is the production of something to be sold (sale of goods), or the materials which pass to the customer are only ancillary to the substance, which is the skill and labour employed. Hence this was a contract for work and materials.

Q Can you reconcile this case with *Lee v Griffin* (above)? See *Benjamin's Sale of Goods*, 5th edn, 1997, para 1-047.

Lockett v Charles (1938)

The plaintiff ordered a meal in a restaurant. The meal included whitebait, which gave her food-poisoning. She sued the restaurant for damages.

Held this was a contract for the sale of goods and the SGA applied.

Dodd v Wilson (1946)

A farmer employed a veterinary surgeon to inoculate his herd of cattle. Afterwards, some of the cattle became sick because the toxoid used for the inoculation was defective. The farmer sued the vet.

Held this to be a contract for work and materials and the SGA did not apply.

Marcel (Furriers) Ltd v Tapper (1953)

The plaintiffs made an oral agreement to supply a mink coat, made to the customer's order. The customer selected the skins and gave instructions as to the design. However, when the coat was made the customer rejected it. The plaintiffs sued for £950. As the law then stood, a sale contract (for over £10) was enforceable only if it was reduced to writing. The customer claimed that this was a sale of goods and not a contract for work and materials.

Held although care and skill was required this was a sale of goods and the customer was not liable beyond £10 because the contract was not in writing.

Head v Showfronts (1970)

A contract was made where carpets were to be supplied, and then stitched together and fitted. One issue was whether the SGA applied to the contract.

Held Mocatta J approved this passage from Chalmers:

> ... if the main object of a contract is the transfer from A to B, for a price, of the property in a thing ... then the contract is a contract of sale, but if the real substance of the contract is the performance of work by A for B, it is a contract for work and materials ...

Applying this to the facts, there was a contract for the sale of goods and the SGA applied.

Note ──────

For further details of this case, see below, 10.2.1.

Parsons v Uttley Ingham Ltd (1978) CA

The defendant contracted to supply and instal a hopper for storing pignuts and feeding them to the swine. The defendant failed to ensure that a ventilator was open with the result that the pignuts became mouldy. Consequently, 254 pigs died.

Held this was a contract of sale and the SGA applied.

Hyundai Heavy Industries v Papadopoulos (1980) HL

Hyundai contracted to build and deliver a ship. Payment was to be made in five instalments, the dates of which were to be ascertained by reference to stages in the construction of the ship.

Held this was a contract for services and not a contract of sale. This is because from the moment the contract was made, the ship builder was obliged to incur expenses in preparation, for example, the cost of design.

Note ——————————————————————————————
For further details of this case, see below, 14.1.2.

8.1.6 Sales, conditional sales and hire-purchase

Lee v Butler (1893) CA

Furniture was supplied to Lloyd on a 'hire and purchase' agreement: Lloyd would pay 'rent' for the goods over a three month period and property would only pass when all the payments had been made. The issue arose as to whether that was a contract of sale of one of hire.

Held although described as a 'hirer', Lloyd was bound to buy the goods from the outset; the buyer paid by instalments and property passed when the price was fully paid. Both parties were committed to the sale from the outset, so it was a contract of sale and the SGA applied.

Note ——————————————————————————————
For the relevance of this distinction, see below, 12.5.1.

Helby v Mathews (1895) HL

Brewster agreed to hire a piano from Helby on terms that if Brewster paid 36 monthly instalments the piano would become his property. Brewster could, however, return the piano at any time during the hire period. The issue arose as to whether Brewster had 'bought or agreed to buy' the goods or had only 'hired' them.

Held Brewster had not agreed to buy the piano from the outset; he only had an option to buy. Therefore he had not 'bought or agreed to buy' the goods: this was a 'hire-purchase' contract and not covered by the SGA.

Note ——————————————————————————————
For the relevance of this distinction, see below, 12.5.1.

Forthright Finance Ltd v Carlyle Finance Ltd (1997), see below, 12.5.1.

8.1.7 Gifts

Esso Petroleum v Commissioners of Customs & Excise (1976) HL
'World Cup Coins' (to celebrate the England football team's appearance in the 1970 World Cup Finals) were given free by Esso with every four gallons of petrol. The issue for the court was whether the coins attracted purchase tax (now VAT) under a contract of sale.

Held the garage was bound to supply a coin to every customer who purchased four gallons; so this was not a gift. However, the consideration given by the customer was not money, but the act of contracting to buy four gallons of petrol. So this was not a sale of goods either (see above, 8.1.3) and purchase tax was not applicable.

Q Do you think that there was a collateral contract, or perhaps a barter? (Either would be covered by SGSA 1982.)

8.2 Contracts of bailment

South Australian Insurance Co v Randell (1869) PC
A farmer left corn with a miller on terms that he could claim at any time the return of the same quantity of corn or its market value. The corn was mixed with other corn deposited with the miller. The mill and its contents were destroyed in a fire. The miller's insurance company refused to pay out in respect of the deposited corn. They claimed that it belonged to the farmer and so the mill held it under a contract of bailment.

Held there was no stipulation that the farmer should be entitled to have returned the actual corn deposited, only the same amount, or its value. Therefore there was a transfer of property to the mill owner and this was not a contract of bailment. The insurance company were liable to pay out in respect of that corn.

Mercer v Craven Grain Storage Ltd (1994) HL
A farmer, Mercer, stored 2,200 tonnes of grain with Craven on terms that the property remained with the farmer. The grain was mixed with grain stored by other farmers. The bulk was continually being drawn on (when grain was sold on behalf of a particular farmer) and replenished (as more grain was added). Mercer called for the return of his grain, but Craven only returned 107 tonnes. Mercer sued Craven in conversion. To succeed, Mercer would have to show that the property in the grain was his. Craven argued that despite the agreement, Mercer's grain became indistinguishable once mixed with the other grain.

Held Craven were bailees on behalf of Mercer. Craven could not have acquired any title to the grain and so the property remained with Mercer.

Q Is this case distinguishable from *South Australian Insurance Co v Randell* (above)?

8.3   Auctions

Warlow v Harrison (1859) Ex Ch (CA)

A horse was advertised to be sold by auction 'without reserve'. The plaintiff made the highest bid, but in an attempt to prevent the horse being sold too cheaply, the horse's owner out-bid the plaintiff. The plaintiff refused to make a higher bid and demanded the horse at 'his' price.

Held the owner of goods for sale by auction 'without reserve' is not making an offer able to be accepted and so bind him in contract. However (3:2), the owner was in breach of a *collateral contract* that the sale would be without reserve and that the owner would not therefore bid for his own goods. Thus the plaintiff could recover damages. The minority came to the same result by holding that the auctioneer *warranted* that he had authority to sell without reserve.

9 Terms of the contract

9.1 Innominate terms

Hong Kong Fir Shipping v Kawasaki Kisen Kaisha (1962) CA

A ship was chartered (hired to a party) for a period of 24 months. Upon delivery, the ship was unseaworthy because she had old engines and an inefficient engine-room crew. By the time the ship was made seaworthy, only 17 months were left for the charterers to use the ship. Meanwhile, the freight market had collapsed from 47 s (£2.35) per ton to 13 s 6 d (68p) per ton. The charterers purported to terminate the charter, arguing that there had been a breach of a *condition* that the ship would be delivered seaworthy.

Held there was an *innominate* term (not a condition) that the ship would be delivered seaworthy. Whether a breach of that term allowed the innocent party to terminate depended on the seriousness of the breach: did it go to the root of the contract? Here, the charterers still had 17 months of use. They could recover damages for the other period, but they could not terminate the contract.

Diplock LJ stated:

> ... the shipowner's undertaking to tender a seaworthy ship has, as a result of numerous decisions as to what can amount to 'unseaworthiness', become one of the most complex contractual undertakings. It embraces obligations with respect to every part of the hull and machinery, stores and equipment and the crew itself. It can be broken by the presence of trivial defects easily and rapidly remediable as well as by defects which must inevitably result in the total loss of the vessel.

> Consequently, the problem in this case is, in my view, neither solved nor soluble by debating whether the owners' express or implied undertaking to tender a seaworthy ship is a 'condition' or a 'warranty'. It is, like many other contractual terms, an undertaking, one breach of which may give rise to an event which relieves the charterer of further performance of his undertakings if he so elects, and another breach of which may not give rise to such an event but entitle him only to monetary compensation in the form of damages ...

The Mihalis Angelos (1970) CA

A term of a charterparty (hire contract) stated that a ship would be ready to load about 1 July. By 17 July the ship was still not ready and the char-

terer terminated the contract. The shipowners claimed that the term was
not a condition, but merely an innominate term.

Held the term was a condition. Three reasons were given for that decision. First, certainty in the law. Where justice did not require flexibility it
was better to be rigid, especially in commercial cases. Secondly, if the
shipowner could not deliver in time he should not have agreed to the term.
Thirdly, the term 'ready to load' had always been treated as a condition in
sale of goods contracts and it was, therefore, better to avoid an anomaly
between the two branches of law.

Cehave NV v Bremer, *The Hansa Nord* (1976) CA

A contract for the sale of citrus pulp pellets for £100,000 contained the
express term: 'shipment to be made in good condition.' In fact, not all of
the goods were shipped in good condition. The buyers rejected the whole
consignment and the sellers resold it. Eventually, the buyers purchased the
whole consignment on the open market for just £34,000; further, as the pellets were more or less of the required standard they used them for their
original purpose. It was argued that the buyers rightfully rejected the
goods because the express term was a condition.

Held the express term was an innominate term, a serious breach of
which would allow the buyer to reject the goods. Clearly, in the circumstances, this was not a serious enough breach to allow rejection. The buyers could claim damages only.

Note

See, also, *Rearden Smith Line v Yngvar Hansen-Tangen* (1976) HL (description), below, 9.3.2 and *Bunge Corporation v Tradax Export SA* (1981) HL
(time), below, 13.1.3.

9.2 Implied terms – title – s 12 of the Sale of Goods Act (1979)

(Goods supplied with services – s 2 of the Supply of Goods and Services
Act 1982; hire-purchase – s 8 of the Supply of Goods (Implied Terms) Act
1983. See, also, 16.2.1)

Section 12 of the SGA 1979:

(1) In a contract for sale, other than one to which sub-s (3) below applies, there
is an implied [condition] on the part of the seller that in the case of a sale
he has the right to sell the goods, and in the case of an agreement to sell, he
will have such a right at the time when the property is to pass.

(2) In a contract of sale, other than one to which sub-s (3) below applies, there
is also an implied [warranty] that:

(a) the goods are free, and will remain free until the time when the property is to pass, from any charge or encumbrance not disclosed or known
to the buyer before the contract is made; and

(b) the buyer will enjoy quiet possession of the goods except so far as it may be disturbed by the owner or other person entitled to the benefit of any charge or encumbrance so disclosed or known.

(3) This sub-section applies to a contract of sale in the case of which there appears from the contract or is to be inferred from its circumstances an intention that the seller should transfer only such title as he or a third person may have.

9.2.1 Sellers' right to sell – s 12(1) of the SGA

Rowland v Divall (1923), see above, 8.1.4.

Butterworth v Kingsway Motors Ltd (1954), see below, 16.2.1.

Niblett v Confectioners' Materials (1921) CA

A contract was made for the sale of 3,000 cases of condensed milk, to be shipped from New York to London. About 1,000 of the cases arrived in London bearing the labels 'Nissly' brand. This infringed the trade mark of another company, Nestlé, and so the buyers had to strip the cans of their labels and sell them for the best price obtainable. They sued the sellers for breach of the condition implied by s 12(1).

Held s 12 implies a condition that the seller has the right to sell the goods. Here the seller could have been restrained by an injunction from selling the goods for infringement of a trade mark. Clearly, he had no right to sell. (It was also held that the labels rendered the goods unmerchantable, see below, 9.4.3.)

9.2.2 No incumbrances and quiet possession – s 12(2)(a)(b) of the SGA

Mason v Burningham (1949)

The plaintiff purchased a second-hand typewriter and then (reasonably) had it overhauled. Subsequently, she discovered it to be stolen and had to return it to the true owner. She sued the sellers under s 12(2)(b).

Held the plaintiff was entitled to a refund and compensation for the cost of the overhaul.

Microbeads AG v Vinhurst Roadmarkings (1975) CA

Road-marking machines were sold to the buyers, but later a third company obtained a patent over the machines, and so the machines infringed the patent.

Held as at the time of the sale no patent had been published, there was no breach of s 12(1). However, there was an infringement of the warranty implied by s 12(2)(b) that the buyers shall enjoy quiet possession and they could recover damages from the sellers.

Empressa Exportadora de Azucar v Industria Azucarera National SA, *The*
Playa Larga **(1983)**

The Cuban state sugar-trading enterprise sold sugar to a private buyer in
Chile, to be dispatched by ship. After the ship had unloaded some of its cargo
in Chile there was a *coup d'état* and a military dictatorship came to power.
Cuba broke off trading links and instructed the ship to leave Chile without
unloading any more sugar, even though the property had passed to the buyer.

Held this was a breach of the warranty implied by s 12(2)(b) that the
buyer will enjoy quiet possession and the buyer was entitled to damages.

9.3   Implied terms – description – s 13 of the Sale of Goods Act 1979

(**Goods supplied with services – s 3 of the SGSA 1982; Hire – s 8 of the
SGSA 1982; Hire-purchase – s 9 of the SG(IT)A 1983. See, also, 16.2.2**)

Section 13 of the SGA:

(1)   Where there is a contract for the sale of goods by description, there is an
implied [condition] that the goods will correspond with the description.

(2)   If the sale is by sample as well as by description it is not sufficient that the
bulk of the goods corresponds with the sample if the goods do not also correspond with the description.

(3)   A sale of goods is not prevented from being a sale by description by reason
only that, being exposed for sale or hire, they are selected by the buyer.

9.3.1   Sale by description

Varley v Whipp (1900)

The buyer agreed to purchase a second-hand reaping machine that was
stated to be 'new the previous year, and only used to cut 50 or 60 acres'.
He had not seen the machine and relied upon that description. The
machine turned out not to be 'new the previous year' and so it did not correspond with the description. However, the term will only be implied
where there is a sale by description. So one issue was whether there could
be a sale by description of a specific good.

Held there was a sale by description in all cases where the purchaser had
not seen the goods but was relying on the description alone. Hence, this
was a sale by description.

Note ────────────────────────────────
The reaping machine was in poor condition. However, the buyer could
not use s 14 of the SGA (merchantable quality) because the sale was not
in the course of a business: the seller was not a dealer in agricultural
machinery. This case is a reminder that, unlike s 14, s 13 can apply to private sales.

Wren v Holt (1903)

The defendant's public house was tied to Holden's brewery and sold only Holden's beer. The plaintiff visited that public house because he preferred Holden's beer. However, the beer contained arsenic and the plaintiff fell ill as a result. He sued for breach of an implied condition that the beer was of merchantable quality. At this time for the term to apply, there had to be a sale by description.

Held this was a sale by description. The plaintiff knew that the tied house would sell only Holden's beer.

Grant v Australian Knitting Mills (1936) PC

A customer chose some woollen underpants (a specific good) from a display on the counter of a retail shop. They contained sulphur and gave him dermatitis. He sued for breach of an implied term that the goods would be of merchantable quality. At this time for the term to apply, there had to be a sale by description.

Held there was a sale by description even though the buyer was buying something before him on the counter. It did not matter if it was a specific good, as long as it was sold not as a specific thing, but as a thing corresponding to a description.

Note

See, now, s 13(3) of the 1979 Act (above).

Beale v Taylor (1967) CA

Beale saw a car advertised in a newspaper as a 'Herald 1961'. He visited the seller and inspected the car. He noticed a badge on the car which read: '1200'. This indicated that the car was made after 1961, as no 1200's were made before then. Beale bought the car believing it to be a 1961 model. However, when driving home the car handled badly and Beale discovered later that the car was in fact a mixture: the rear being from a 1961 model, and the front being (welded on) from an earlier model. Beale could not sue under s 14 of the SGA (merchantable quality) as this was a private sale. Instead, he sued under s 13 (which applies to private and business sales). However, for s 13 to apply there had to be a sale by description.

Held this was a sale by description; the newspaper advertisement and the badge combined to describe the car as a 1961 model.

Hughes v Hall (1981)

The defendants, who were car dealers, sold a second-hand car, giving to the purchaser a document which included the phrase 'sold as seen and inspected' as a term of the transaction. The defendants were charged with furnishing to a consumer a document which included a statement made void by s 6(2) of the Unfair Contract Terms Act 1977, contrary to Art 3(d) of the Consumer Transactions (Restrictions on Statements) Order 1976.

Held prima facie where the phrase 'sold as seen and inspected' was included in a contract, there was not a sale by description and so s 13 of the SGA did not apply. But that was subject to other express terms of the contract. (In any event, the purchaser would lose some of his rights, so that inclusion of the phrase in the contract would constitute an offence.)

Q Do you think that in non-consumer cases (where such a clause is not automatically void) the phrase 'sold as seen' could exclude s 13? Compare this case with *Cavendish Woodhouse Ltd v Manley* (below).

Speedway Safety Products v Hazell (1982) Aus
After inspecting the goods in question (motor-cycle spares) on several occasions the buyer agreed to purchase, by a written contract: 'The stock situated at the premises 74–78 Wentworth Avenue'.

Held this was not a sale by description.

Cavendish Woodhouse Ltd v Manley (1984)
A customer bought a suite of furniture from the defendant company. The cash sale invoice given to him at the time contained the statement 'bought as seen'. The defendant company was charged under Arts 3 and 4 of the Consumer Transactions (Restriction on Statements) Order 1976 for making a statement made void by s 6(2) of UCTA 1977.

Held that the statement 'bought as seen' was not a void statement by virtue of s 6(2) of UCTA 1977, because it did not purport to exclude the implied terms in ss 13 and 14 of the SGA 1979. All the phrase did was to confirm that the purchaser has seen the goods he had bought.

Note ————————————————————————————————
Compare this case with *Hughes v Hall* (above).

Harlingdon & Leinster v Christopher Hull (1989) CA
Hull (an art dealer) approached Harlingdons (also art dealers) stating that he had a painting by Münter for sale. Hull made it plain that he was not an expert on Münter. Harlingdons relied on their own judgment and bought the painting for £6,000, only to discover later that it was a forgery and worth £50 to £100. Harlingdons sued alleging, *inter alia*, breach of the term implied by s 13. For s 13 to apply, there had to be a sale by description.

Held (2:1) as the seller denied expert knowledge the buyer could not have relied upon the description given, therefore this was not a sale by description and s 13 did not apply.

Nourse LJ said:

In theory, it is no doubt possible for a description of goods which is not relied on by the buyer to become an essential term of the contract for their sale. But in practice it is very difficult, and perhaps impossible, to think of facts where that would be so ... For all practical purposes, I would say that there cannot be a contract for the sale of goods by description where it is not within the reasonable contemplation of the parties that the buyer is relying on the description.

However, Stuart-Smith LJ (dissenting) said:

For my part, I have great difficulty understanding how the concept of reliance fits into a sale by description. If it is a term of the contract that the painting is by Münter, the purchaser does not have to prove that he entered into the contract in reliance on this statement. This distinguishes a contractual term or condition from a mere representation which induces a purchaser to enter into a contract. In the latter case the person to whom the representation was made must prove that he relied on it as a matter of fact.

Notes

1 There is no definition of a 'sale by description' in the SGA. Do you think the introduction of the 'reliance' ingredient by the courts is more to do with policy than strict statutory interpretation? After all, this encourages business buyers to buy with caution (*caveat emptor*) whilst allowing scope to protect consumers: if the buyer of the painting were a consumer, a court could hold that that buyer – having no expertise – relied on the description.

2 See, also, under s 14 of the SGA, below, 9.4.3.

9.3.2 Goods must correspond with the description

Re Moore and Landauer (1921) CA

A contract for the sale of 3,000 tins of canned fruit stipulated that the consignment would be packed in cases, each containing 30 tins. In fact about half of the consignment was packed in cases, each containing 24 tins. The buyers rejected the whole consignment.

Held the stipulation as to the number of tins per case was part of the description and so the sellers were in breach of the condition implied by s 13. That entitled the buyers to reject the whole consignment.

Pinnock Bros v Lewis (1923)

Copra cake was sold to be used as cattle feed. The copra cake supplied was adulterated with caster beans, which was poisonous to cattle.

Held the feed did not correspond with the description. See, further, *Ashington Piggeries v Christopher Hill* (below).

Arcos v Ronaasen (1933) HL

A sale contract for wooden staves (to be used for making cement barrels) stipulated that the staves should be half an inch thick. Most of the staves were too thick, although they were still suitable for making cement barrels and merchantable. Nevertheless, the buyers rejected the consignment.

Held the staves did not correspond with the contract description and so the buyers could reject. Lord Atkin stated:

> A ton does not mean about a ton, or yard about a yard. Still less when you descend to minute measurements does half an inch mean about half an inch.

See, further, *Ashington Piggeries v Christopher Hill* and the Note to *Rearden Smith Line* (below).

Ashington Piggeries v Christopher Hill (1971) HL

A contract of sale was made for 'King Size', which was herring meal to feed to minks. During shipment, the herring meal reacted with its preservative and this rendered the feed poisonous to minks. The minks were injured and the buyers sued contending, *inter alia*, that the feed did not correspond with the description.

Held (4:1 on this point, Lords Guest, Wilberforce, Hodson and Diplock, with Viscount Dilhorne dissenting) the feed did correspond with its description. The key to s 13 was identification. The reaction may have affected the quality of the feed, but it did not alter its identity as 'herring meal'. *Pinnock v Lewis* (1923) was distinguished on the basis that in that case there was a 'substantial addition' to the commodity.

Q Do you think that the courts in *Re Moore and Landauer* and *Arcos v Ronaasen* (above) would have found a breach of s 13 if those cases were heard after *Ashington Piggeries*? If so, would they grant the right to reject in light of s 15A of the SGA (recently inserted by the Sale and Supply of Goods Act 1994) which provides (in non-consumer cases) that there is no right to reject if the 'breach is so slight that it would be unreasonable ... to reject' the goods?

Rearden Smith Line v Yngvar Hansen-Tangen (1976) HL

A contract to charter (not a sale contract) a ship not yet built described the vessel to be built by Osaka; it was designated 'Yard No 354'. In fact it was built elsewhere and designated 'Yard No 004'. When the ship was ready for delivery the market had collapsed and the charterers rejected it, claiming that it did not correspond with the contract description.

Held those descriptive words merely helped a party locate a ship for the purpose of a sub-charter. They could be distinguished from words which state (or identify) an essential part of the description of the goods. Thus there was no breach of a condition and the buyers could not reject the ship.

Note ————————————————————————————————————

Although this is not a sale of goods case, the principle is a general one. Further note that Lord Wilberforce described earlier cases on s 13 (such as *Re Moore and Landauer* and *Arcos v Ronaasen* (above)) as 'excessively technical and due for fresh examination in this House'.

Toepfer v Warinco AG (1978)
Under a contract for the sale of 'fine-ground' soya bean meal, the sellers supplied coarse-ground meal. The buyers rejected it.

Held the word 'fine-ground' was a word of description and so the buyers were entitled to reject for breach of the implied condition that the goods would correspond with the description.

Raynham Farm v Symbol Motor Corporation (1987)
Raynham purchased a new Range Rover car from Symbol, who were motor dealers. However, the particular Range Rover delivered had, before the sale, been seriously damaged by fire and restored to 'as new' condition. When Raynham discovered this, they tried to reject the car, claiming that it did not correspond with the description of 'new'.

Held as there would always be a lurking doubt as to the soundness of the car after the damage and repair, it could not properly be described as 'new'. Thus there was a breach of the condition implied by s 13 of the SGA and Raynham were entitled to reject.

9.4 Implied terms – quality – s 14 of the Sale of Goods Act 1979

(Goods supplied with services – s 4 of the SGSA 1982; hire – s 9 of the SGSA 1982; hire-purchase – s 10 of the SG(IT)A 1973. See, also, 16.2.3)

Section 14 of the SGA:

(2) Where the seller sells goods in the course of a business, there is an implied [condition] that the goods supplied under the contract are of satisfactory quality.

(2C) The term implied by sub-s (2) above does not extend to any matter making the quality of the goods unsatisfactory:

(a) which is specifically drawn to the buyer's attention before the contract is made;

(b) where the buyer examines the goods before the contract is made, which that examination ought to reveal; or

(c) in the case of a contract for sale by sample, which would have been apparent on a reasonable examination of the sample.

9.4.1 Course of a business

Havering LBC v Stevenson (1970)
The defendant ran a car hire business and once his cars were two years old he sold them. On one occasion, he sold a car with a false description as to its mileage. The defendant was prosecuted under the Trade Descriptions Act 1968 which carries the same qualifying phrase as s 14 of the SGA, that

is, 'course of a business'. The defendant argued that as his business was the hiring of cars a *sale* of a car fell outside of the Act.

Held the selling off of the cars was a regular and normal practice by the defendant and therefore an integral part of his business. Thus, the sale was 'in the course of business' for the purposes of the Trade Descriptions Act.

Davies v Sumner (1984) HL

The defendant was a self-employed courier who transported films around Wales for Harlech Television. In June 1980, he purchased a new car, which he sold about a year later with a false mileage. The defendant was prosecuted under the Trade Descriptions Act 1968 which carries the same qualifying phrase as s 14 of the SGA, that is, 'course of a business'.

Held where there was a degree of regularity, so that the sale was a part of the seller's normal business, the sale was in 'the course of business'. Here, the sale was not integral to the courier's business and so the Trade Descriptions Act did not apply.

Devlin v Hall (1990)

The defendant sold a Peugeot car with a false mileage reading. He was prosecuted under the Trade Descriptions Act 1968 which carries the same qualifying phrase as s 14 of the SGA, that is, 'course of a business'. This was his first sale in two years as a self-employed taxi proprietor. However, he had offered a choice of two cars to the customer, taken a car in part-exchange and made two subsequent sales before the trial. He had used the Peugeot car for business and private purposes. The court had to decide if the sale of the Peugeot was in the 'course of a business'.

Held sales in the course of a business can be: (i) a one-off adventure in the nature of a trade carried through with a view to profit; (ii) a transaction which is an integral part of the business carried on, that is to say, part of its normal practice; or (iii) a transaction which is merely incidental to the carrying on of the relevant business that is carried on with some degree of regularity.

This was not a one-off adventure within (i). As this was the first sale in two years of business, it was not integral within (ii): *Havering LBC v Stevenson* (above) was distinguished. Although the sale was incidental to the business, there was not a sufficient degree of regularity to come within (iii). The two subsequent sales could not be taken into account, but even if they could be, the number of transactions was still insufficient to establish the necessary regularity. Hence, the defendant was acquitted.

Note

See, also, *R & B Customs Brokers v UDT* (1988) (below, 9.7.1) as to 'dealing as a consumer' under UCTA and *Boyter v Thomson* (1995) (above, 5.1) on s 14(5).

9.4.2 Goods supplied

Geddling v Marsh (1920)

Mineral water was sold in bottles which were returnable to the manufacturer, who retained ownership of them throughout. A defective bottle burst and injured the plaintiff buyer.

Held the bottle was 'supplied' under the contract of sale and so s 14(2) applied to the bottle as well as the water. Hence, it was an implied term of the contract that the bottle supplied was of merchantable quality.

Wilson v Rickett (1954) CA

A bag of 'Coalite' sold contained an explosive detonator. When the coal was burning on the fire the detonator exploded; the buyer sued the seller for breach of the term implied by s 14(2) of the SGA.

Held the consignment as a whole was unmerchantable, even though the coal in itself was merchantable (and there was nothing wrong with the detonator!). Thus, the buyer would succeed.

9.4.3 Satisfactory or merchantable quality

Section 14 of the SGA:

(2A) For the purposes of this Act, goods are of satisfactory quality if they meet the standard that the reasonable person would regard as satisfactory, taking account of any description of the goods, the price (if relevant) and all other relevant circumstances.

(2B) For the purposes of this Act, the quality of goods includes their state and condition and the following (among others) are, in appropriate cases, aspects of the quality of goods:

(a) fitness for all the purposes for which goods of the kind in question are commonly supplied;

(b) appearance and finish;

(c) freedom from minor defects;

(d) safety; and

(e) durability.

Note

This definition was inserted by Sale and Supply of Goods Act 1994. The following cases were all decided under the old merchantable quality definition, which was less generous to buyers. However, cases from 1987 on may have been influenced by the Law Commission's 1987 Final Report, Sale and Supply of Goods, which recommended these amendments. Hence, these later cases may reflect the new definition and serve as a useful guide.

Niblett v Confectioners' Materials Ltd (1921) CA

A contract was made for the sale of 3,000 cases of condensed milk. However, about 1,000 of the cases had labels which infringed the trade mark of another company.

Held the labels rendered the goods unmerchantable.

Note ———

The infringement of the trade mark also raised an issue of the sellers' right to sell, see above, 9.2.1.

Aswan v Lupdine (1987) CA

Aswan bought a consignment of liquid waterproofing compound, which was supplied in plastic buckets. The pails were stacked on a quayside in Kuwait, and, in the extreme heat, they melted and collapsed. Aswan claimed that the goods were not of merchantable quality.

Held multi-purpose goods could be merchantable even if they were not fit for all of their purposes. Thus the buckets were merchantable because in most conditions they would not have melted.

Note ———

Section 14(2B) of the SGA (inserted by SSGA 1994) now provides that goods must be fit for *all* their common purposes. The Law Commission, Final Report, *Sale and Supply of Goods*, 1987, para 3.36, intended that the new s 14(2B)(a) would reverse *Aswan v Lupdine*. For a contrary view, see Atiyah, *The Sale of Goods*, 9th edn, 1995, pp 142–43.

Kendall v Lillico (1969) HL

Brazilian groundnut extract was used as an ingredient in an animal feed. The plaintiff used the feed on his pheasant farm, but it proved poisonous to poultry.

Held the feed was merchantable because it was fit for most of its purposes, that is, feed for cattle and pigs.

Note ———

Section 14(2B) of the SGA (amended by SSGA 1994) now provides that goods must be fit for *all* of their common purposes. See Atiyah, *The Sale of Goods*, 9th edn, 1995, pp 142–43. Also note that the buyers succeeded under s 14(3) of the SGA, see below, 9.5.2.

Wormell v RHM Agriculture East Ltd (1987) CA

A farmer purchased a herbicide but failed to follow the instructions when using it. The herbicide failed to work and the farmer sued.

Held the weed killer would have worked if it had been used in accordance with the instructions. Therefore it was merchantable.

Q Here the instructions rendered otherwise unsatisfactory goods satisfactory. Does it follow that poor or absent instructions could render otherwise satisfactory goods unsatisfactory, for example, erroneous instructions attached to a perfectly good electrical plug?

Lutton v Saville Tractors (Belfast) Ltd (1986) NI

A three year old Ford Escort XR3 car with 30,000 recorded miles was sold by a dealer to a consumer with a three month warranty. The car had or developed many minor faults: excessive blue smoke; engine hesitating at high speeds; worn brakes; faulty oil warning light; water loss from the radiator; a complete electrical failure causing breakdown; faulty seat belt; poor battery; scratched roof; and a faulty distributor causing breakdown. After seven weeks and having covered 3,000 to 4,000 miles, the buyer rejected the car claiming, *inter alia*, that it was not of merchantable quality.

Held although this was a second-hand car, it was unmerchantable. Emphasis was placed on the issue of the warranty, which was evidence that the parties expected a period of trouble-free motoring from the car. See, also, right to reject, below, 15.1.2.

Rogers v Parish (Scarborough) Ltd (1987) CA

A new Range Rover car purchased by Rogers from the defendant car dealers for £16,000 suffered the following problems: defective oil seals; a noisy gearbox; an engine misfire; and defects (rust) in the bodywork (caused by poor storage). Rogers sued claiming that the Range Rover was unmerchantable. The defendants argued, *inter alia*, that as all the defects would be repaired under the manufacturers' warranty, the vehicle was merchantable.

Held the following factors (from the old s 14(6)) should be taken into account:

(i) The purpose for which goods of that kind are commonly bought. This included an appropriate degree of comfort, ease of handling, reliability and pride in the vehicle's appearance;

(ii) The description: the car was new and it was a Range Rover, which suggested a certain level of performance, handling, comfort and resilience;

(iii) The price: at £16,000 the car was at the higher end of the market.

In the circumstances the Range Rover was not of merchantable quality.

On the effect of a warranty or guarantee it was held that: (i) can it really be said that the buyer should expect less of his new car without a warranty than with one?; (ii) a warranty was an addition to the buyer's rights, not a subtraction from them; and (iii) if the defendants were correct, then the buyer would be advised to leave the warranty in the showroom. This cannot have been the intention of the manufacturer, dealer or the customer.

Shine v General Guarantee Corp (1988) CA

A new Fiat X-19 sports car was sold in 1981 with a manufacturer's anti-rust guarantee. A year later, while in a garage for servicing, it was submerged in water for 24 hours; for some of this time the water was frozen.

The insurance company wrote off the car (it costing more to repair than its value) and the manufacturer would no longer entertain an anti-rust guarantee. Sometime later the car was sold from a garage forecourt for £4,400 to Shine, who was told by the garage: 'nice car, good runner, no problems'. When Shine discovered the truth, he sued for breach of an implied term (by s 14(2)) that the goods were of merchantable quality.

Held the car was described as a second-hand Fiat, a make that tended to rust, which could normally be protected by the manufacturer's warranty. It was an enthusiasts' car and described as a 'nice car, good runner, no problems'. The price paid was appropriate for a car of that age and mileage without the problems. Shine's car was worth £2,800–3,400. In the circumstances, the car was unmerchantable.

Business Applications Specialists v Nationwide Credit (1988) CA

The plaintiff took on hire-purchase a second-hand Mercedes car for £14,850; it was two and a half years old and had covered 37,000 miles. After 800 miles it became apparent that there was serious wear to the engine and this cost £635 to repair. The plaintiff sued claiming that the car was unmerchantable.

Held the court must consider the purpose for which the car was bought, not only for driving it from one place to another but of doing so with the appropriate degree of comfort, ease of handling and pride in its appearance. Nevertheless, the buyer of a second-hand car must expect that defects will develop sooner or later. Thus, the car was merchantable.

Harlingdon & Leinster v Christopher Hull (1989) CA

Hull (an art dealer) approached Harlingdons (also art dealers) stating that he had a painting by Münter for sale. Harlingdons bought the painting for £6,000, only to discover later that it was a forgery and worth £50–100. Harlingdons sued alleging, *inter alia*, that the painting was not of merchantable quality and so there was a breach of the term implied by s 14.

Held (2:1) the claim would fail. *Per* Nourse LJ, paintings are commonly bought for the purpose of aesthetic appreciation and 'merchantable quality' does not relate to anything beyond the physical qualities of the goods; so the actual artist is immaterial. As to the price, the question of 'merchantable quality' cannot depend upon a resale at a profit.

Q Do you think that this case would be decided differently under the new 'satisfactory quality' requirements of s 14?

Note ───────────────

This case also concerned 'correspondence with description' (s 13 of the SGA), see above, 9.3.1. The case has been noted by Bridge [1990] LMCLQ 455; Brown (1990) 106 LQR 561; Lawrenson (1991) 54 MLR 122.

Thain v Anniesland Trade Centre (1997)

Ms Thain purchased a Renault 19 car from a dealer, Anniesland. The car was about 5–6 years old and had covered about 80,000 miles. Ms Thain paid

£2,995 for the car. She declined an option to buy a three month warranty. After two weeks she discovered that a gearbox bearing was worn and later tried to reject the car, a repair being uneconomic. The dealer offered Ms Thain a number of alternative cars, but she insisted upon a refund, claiming that the car was not of satisfactory quality. The dealer refused.

Held the relevant aspects of s 14 were 'fitness for purpose' (s 14(2B)(a)) and 'durability' (s 14(2B)(e)). The gearbox bearing was not faulty at he time of the sale and so the car was, at that time, fit for its purpose. The defect could have emerged at any time because of normal wear and tear, given the age and mileage of the Renault. Therefore the car's durability 'was a matter of luck'. The price was reasonable – much less than a new model. In the circumstances a reasonable person would accept that there was a risk of expensive repairs. Ms Thain could have covered the risk by purchasing the warranty. Thus the car was of satisfactory quality.

Q Do you think that the reasonable person, buying a car for £3,000, *from a dealer*, accepts a risk that it might be useless after two weeks? If so, why not buy a similar car *privately*, for less money?

9.4.4 Defects specifically drawn to buyer's attention before the contract was made – s 14(2C) of the SGA

Bartlett v Sydney Marcus Ltd (1965) CA

In negotiations for the sale of a second-hand Jaguar car, the seller, a dealer, informed Bartlett that the clutch was defective. The dealer offered to repair the clutch, or to sell the car at £25 discount. Bartlett purchased the car at the discount, intending to get the repair done himself. However, the defect turned out to be worse than expected and cost Bartlett £84 to repair. He sued claiming that the car was not merchantable.

Held the car was merchantable.

9.5 Implied terms – goods fit for a particular purpose – s 14(3) of the Sale of Goods Act 1979

(Goods supplied with services – s 4 of the SGSA 1982; hire – s 9 of the SGSA 1982; hire-purchase – s 10 of the SG(IT)A 1973)

Section 14(3) of the SGA:

(3) Where the seller sells goods in the course of a business and the buyer, expressly or by implication, makes known:

(a) to the seller; or

(b) where the purchase price or part of it is payable by instalments and the goods were previously sold by a credit broker to the seller, to that credit broker, any particular purpose for which the goods are being bought, there is an implied [condition] that the goods supplied under the contract are reasonably fit for that purpose, whether or not that is a purpose for which such goods are commonly supplied, except where the circumstances show that the buyer does not rely, or that it is unreasonable for him to rely, on the skill or judgment of the seller or credit broker.

9.5.1 Purpose made known impliedly

Wallis v Russell (1902) IRE

Boiled crabs were supplied under a contract of sale. The buyer sued claiming that they were not fit for the particular purpose and although that purpose (eating) was not stated, it was implied because food has no other purpose.

Held with single purpose items, the purpose need not be stated expressly. It can be implied.

Priest v Last (1903) CA

A customer went into a shop and asked for a hot-water bottle. Later, the bottle burst, causing injuries. The customer sued under what is now s 14(3) of the SGA.

Held this was a single purpose item and so the customer did not need to state the purpose. In buying it, he relied upon the skill and judgment of the seller.

Frost v Aylesbury Dairy Co (1905) CA

Milk was supplied by the dairy to a family for their consumption. Some contained germs of typhoid fever and this led to the death of the plaintiff's wife. An action was brought under what is now s 14(3).

Held in buying milk the plaintiff relied upon the skill and judgment of the dairy.

Griffiths v Peter Conway (1939)

A lady bought a Harris Tweed Coat and contracted dermatitis because of her unusually sensitive skin. She sued the sellers under s 14(2) (merchantable quality) and (what is now) s 14(3) (goods fit for the purpose).

Held the coat was merchantable so the action under s 14(2) would fail. As for the action under s 14(3) the coat was for a *special* purpose (to be worn by someone with sensitive skin) and this should have been stated *expressly* to the seller for s 14(3) to apply. Thus the action under s 14(3) would fail as well.

9.5.2 Reasonable reliance upon the skill and judgment of the seller

Bristol Tramways v Fiat Motors (1910) CA

The plaintiffs ordered seven buses for burdensome passenger work in heavy traffic in Bristol, a hilly district. The buses proved not to be robust enough and had to be reconstructed.

Held the buses were not fit for the particular purpose stated by the plaintiffs.

Manchester Liners v Rea (1922) HL

Coal was ordered for the 'steamship *Manchester Importer'*. The coal supplied was unsuitable for that particular ship and the buyers sued under (what is now) s 14(3).

Held the sellers were told expressly what ship the coal was for. Thus the buyers relied on the skill and judgment of the seller. The seller was liable.

> Note _____
>
> Compare this case with *Teheran-Europe v Belton* (1968) (below) where Lord Denning MR said that it had been given 'a knock-out blow' by Lord Reid's dictum in *Kendall v Lillico* (1969) (also below).

Cammell Laird v Manganese Bronze & Brass Co (1934) HL

Cammell Laird employed Manganese to construct two ship propellers. Cammell Laird provided certain specifications but left other matters (the thickness and shape of the blades) to Manganese. The propellers were useless and Cammell Laird sued under (what is now) s 14(3).

Held the defects were related to matters outside of the specification given by Cammell Laird. Thus it was reasonable for Cammell Laird to have relied on the skill and judgment of Manganese in these matters. Manganese were liable.

Dixon Kerby Ltd v Robinson (1965)

Robinson ordered a yacht to be built to the sellers' untried design. He stated that he wanted to use the yacht for sea-cruising and cross-channel trips. The yacht did not perform as well as had been hoped although it was not defective.

Held the sellers gave no warranty that the vessel would be suitable for the stated purposes.

Teheran-Europe v Belton (1968) CA

The buyers bought a consignment of portable air compressors; they made it known to Belton, the sellers, that they were for resale in Persia (now Iran). However, the compressors proved unsuitable for sale in Persia and the buyers sued claiming that the goods were not fit for the stated purpose.

Held the buyers did no more than make the purpose known. To come within (what is now) s 14(3) they must do more: they must show reliance on the skill and judgment of the sellers. Here the sellers knew nothing of the conditions in Persia; however, the buyers did. The buyers relied upon *their own* skill and judgment.

Kendall v Lillico (1969) HL

An importer sold Brazilian groundnut to wholesalers knowing that it would be used to make feed for cattle and poultry. The feed proved toxic to poultry.

Held (4:1) the importer was liable under (what is now) s 14(3).

Note

In this case Lord Reid stated, *obiter*, that *Manchester Liners v Rea* (above) was not authority for the view that if the seller knows the purpose for which the buyer wants the goods it will be presumed that the buyer relied on his skill and judgment.

Ashington Piggeries Ltd v Christopher Hill (1972) HL

The buyers were experts in mink farming. They ordered from the sellers mink feed to be manufactured to an agreed formula. The feed proved toxic to minks because one of the ingredients, herring meal, had reacted with its preservative and become poisonous. The buyers sued the sellers, who in turn sued their suppliers.

Held the sellers and suppliers were liable under (what is now) s 14(3), who ought to have foreseen that the herring meal would be used to make animal feed. Thus their skill and judgment was being relied upon.

Slater v Finning (1996) HL(Sc)

Slater owned a fishing ship, *Aquarius II*. In order to increase its fish carrying capacity, they had the length of the vessel increased. In due course Slater asked Finning to overhaul the ship's engine. Finning did this and fitted – among other things – a new, redesigned, camshaft. The camshaft failed. After several replacements had failed also, Slater fitted an altogether different sort of engine. This engine gave no trouble. However, the old engine was fitted to another vessel, and that gave no further trouble. It was found as fact that the camshaft failure was caused by an external factor peculiar to the *Aquarius II* (possibly the lengthening). Neither party knew of this peculiarity at the time that the camshafts were fitted. Slater sued Finning under s 14(3) of the SGA.

Held although s 14(3) of the SGA imposes a strict liability upon the seller, if he is unaware of any peculiar use for the goods, the seller's obligation is no more than to supply goods which are fit for their normal purpose. Thus Finning was not liable.

9.5.3   Section 14 and agency

Boyter v Thompson (1995), see above, 5.1.

9.6   Implied terms – sale by sample – s 15 of the Sale of Goods Act 1979

(Goods supplied with services – s 5 of the SGSA 1982; hire – s 10 of the SGSA 1982; hire-purchase – s 11 of the SG(IT)A 1973)

Drummond v Van Ingen (1887) HL

Cloth was sold by sample to Van Ingen for the known purpose of making into clothes. The cloth in every way corresponded to the sample. However, a latent fault in the cloth caused the manufactured clothes to part at the seams under moderate strain. The buyers sued, claiming that the cloth was not fit for the purpose. The sellers argued that as the cloth corresponded with the sample there was no case to answer.

Held the question is how far does the examination of the sample exclude the warranty that goods will be fit for the purpose. The purpose of the examination is to confirm the subject matter of the contract and not to make scientific tests to reveal every aspect of the article's construction, latent defects included. Thus the warranty that the goods would be fit for the purpose was not, in this case, excluded because the goods corresponded with the sample.

Steels & Busks Ltd v Bleecker Bik & Co (1956)

By a contract for the sale of five tons of pale crepe rubber it was agreed: 'quality as previously delivered'. The buyers used the rubber to make corsets. In the event this consignment proved unsuitable because it contained an invisible preservative, which stained the fabric of the corsets.

Held this was a sale by sample: the sample being the previously delivered rubber. There was no breach under s 15(2)(a) (goods will correspond with sample) because by any visual inspection the consignment accorded with the sample. Further, there was no breach under s 15(2)(c) (latent defects rendering goods unmerchantable) because the preservative did not affect the quality of the rubber; it could be washed out, leaving the rubber usable.

Godley v Perry (1960)

A retailer purchased plastic catapults from a wholesaler. He tested a sample by pulling back the elastic; they proved satisfactory. However, in normal use they snapped; this was because of a latent defect in the plastic. The buyer sued under s 15(2)(c) which provides that the goods should be free from defects (rendering them unmerchantable) not apparent on reasonable examination.

Held s 15 provides for a 'reasonable' examination, not a 'practicable' one. The buyer had made a reasonable examination and so he succeeded.

9.7   Unfair Contract Terms Act 1977

9.7.1   Dealing as a consumer

R & B Customs Brokers v United Dominions Trust (1988) CA

By a conditional sale, UDT supplied to a small company of two partners (who were husband and wife) a Colt Shogun car, which was for business and private use. The car proved to be unmerchantable and the buyers sued for breach of contract. UDT sought to rely on an exemption clause in the contract, which would be void (s 6(2)) if the buyers dealt as consumers, but only subject to the test of reasonableness (s 6(3)) if they had not. Section 12 provides that a party deals as a consumer where: he does not make the contract in the course of his business; the other party does; and the goods are the type ordinarily supplied for private use.

Held the buyers dealt as consumers and so the exemption clause was void. Where a person buys goods for private and business use *and* uses a company to buy the goods, that person may still be 'dealing as a consumer'.

9.7.2 The reasonableness test and the supply of goods

Section 11 of UCTA:

(1) In relation to a contract term, the requirement of reasonableness for the purposes of this part of the Act [and s 3 of the Misrepresentation Act 1967] ... is that the term shall have been a fair and reasonable one to be included having regard to the circumstances which were, or ought reasonably to have been, known to or in the contemplation of the parties when the contract was made.

Schedule 2:

'Guidelines' for Application of Reasonableness Test

(a) the strength of the bargaining positions of the parties relative to each other, taking into account (among other things) alternative means by which the customer's requirements could have been met;

(b) whether the customer received an inducement to agree to the term, or in accepting it had an opportunity of entering into a similar contract with other persons, but without having to accept a similar term;

(c) whether the customer knew or ought reasonably to have known of the existence and extent of the term (having regard, among other things, to any custom of the trade and any previous course of dealing between the parties);

(d) where the term excludes or restricts any relevant liability if some condition is not complied with, whether it was reasonable at the time of the contract to expect that compliance with that condition would be practicable;

(e) whether the goods were manufactured, processed or adapted to the special order of the customer.

Note ───────────────────────────────────────

These guidelines are stated to be relevant in particular to clauses which exempt liability for breach of the statutory implied terms regarding the description and quality of goods (for example, ss 13–15 of the SGA) in non-consumer cases. However, they can be used in other contexts: see *Singer v Tees*, below, 9.7.5.

Green v Cade Bros Farms (1978)

The buyers purchased seed potatoes on a standard form contract negotiated between the National Association of Seed Potato Merchants and the National Farmers Union. It contained the following terms: (i) any complaint must be made within three days of delivery; (ii) damages are limited to the price of the goods. After several weeks it was discovered that the potatoes were infected by the virus 'Y', which was undetectable at the time of delivery. The buyers refused to pay and the sellers sued for price; the buyers counter-claimed for breach of contract claiming loss of profits. The issue for the court was the reasonableness of the terms.

Held the virus 'Y' was not quickly discoverable and so clause (i) was unreasonable (see Sched 2(d) of UCTA). As to clause (ii), the bargaining positions were fair because the contract was negotiated by respective trade associations (see Sched 2(a) of UCTA) and the buyers knew of the terms (see Sched 2(c) of UCTA). Therefore the limitation clause was reasonable and damages were limited to the contract price of the goods.

Mitchell v Finney Lock Seeds (1983) HL

A sale contract for 'Dutch Winter Cabbage (late) Seed', contained a clause which limited liability to replacement of the seeds or a refund of the price (£201.60). The plaintiff buyers planted 63 acres and incurred expense in doing so. However, the crop failed because the seeds were not 'Winter (late)' but an 'Autumn' variety; in any case they were of an inferior quality. The buyers' loss amounted to £60,000. The issue for the court was whether the limitation clause was reasonable (under SG(IT)SA 1973).

Held factors which counted in favour of the clause were: (i) the buyers were aware of the limitation clause (see Sched 2(c) of UCTA); and (ii) the damages were out of proportion to the price. However, factors against the clause were (i) the buyers had no opportunity to pay extra for more favourable terms (see Sched 2(b) of UCTA); (ii) the sellers could have insured against such big losses at a relatively low cost (see s 11(4)(b) of UCTA); (iii) the sellers were negligent in supplying the wrong kind of seed; and (iv) the sellers stated that it was their practice to settle complaints by paying compensation in excess of the limitation clause. Their Lordships found that this practice was evidence that the trade itself did not consider such clauses to be reasonable. All factors considered it was held that the clause was unreasonable.

Stag Line v Tyne Ship Repair Group, *The Zinnia* (1984)

The plaintiffs put their ship in for repairs with the defendants, who used inferior materials which caused a major casualty in the engine room. The plaintiffs sued and the defendants sought to rely on a limitation clause.

Held in the circumstances, especially that the parties were of equal bargaining power, the clause was reasonable. However, more interestingly, Staughton LJ stated *obiter* that he would have been tempted to hold that all the conditions are unfair and unreasonable for two reasons:

First, they are in such small print that one can barely read them; secondly, the draftsmanship is so convoluted and prolix [lengthy and tedious] that one almost needs an LLB to understand them.

However, as counsel never argued this point, the matter was dropped.

Note
The case illustrates that a judge may be willing to attack the 'small print' under the reasonableness test.

St Albans City Council v International Computers (1994)

The local authority purchased a computer system from the defendants for the purpose of managing the collection of the Community Charge (a local tax). However, the system failed costing the local authority over £1 million. They sued the defendants for the losses who relied upon a clause limiting liability to £100,000.

Held the clause would be subjected to the reasonableness test under UCTA. (i) The company had great resources being part of a group worth £2 billion (s 11(4)). (ii) The company were insured for losses up to £50 million (s 11(4)). (iii) The local authority were in an unequal bargaining position because the defendant's competitors dealt on similar standard terms and the council, in contrast to the defendants, were not businessmen (Sched 2(b)). (iv) It would be better for the loss to fall on a multi-national company, who are able to insure, than the local taxpayers. Hence it was held that the clause was unreasonable.

Note
That decision was affirmed by the Court of Appeal, although the amount of damages was reduced.

Lease Management Services Limited v Purnell Secretarial Services Limited (1994) CA

Canon (South West) Ltd supplied a photocopier through a typical triangular arrangement: they sold it to Lease Management Services (LMS) who in turn leased it to Canon's customer, Purnell. The photocopier was delivered directly from Canon to Purnell. However, it did not function as the demonstration model had. Purnell tried to reject the machine for breach of a collateral warranty. However LMS sought, *inter alia*, to rely on the exclusion clause in the lease agreement, which provided that LMS would not liable for: (i) any express or implied conditions or warranties; (ii) any loss or damage arising in connection with the photocopier; (iii) any representations or warranties (express or implied) given by the supplier (Canon) or any other person.

Held the clause was unreasonable because: (i) it nullifies any express warranty given and which would be relied upon by the customer; (ii) it nullifies implied terms (as to quality and fitness for purpose) which were fundamental to the transaction; (iii) under the clause, acquisition by hire from a finance company rather than by purchase from a supplier is a trap: a customer would not expect his rights regarding defects to differ according to which of these two acquisition routes he chooses to follow.

Note ——————————————————————————————————

See, also, dealer as agent, below, 16.5.

Sovereign Finance v Silver Crest Furniture and Others (1997)

Sovereign let on hire purchase a shrinkwrap machine to Silver Crest, a kitchen furniture manufacturer. The machine was manufactured by TMS and delivered directly to Silver Crest. Silver Crest dealt on Sovereign's standard terms. One clause provided:

> As the goods have been selected by the hirer and have not been inspected by the company, the company does not make or give any representation, warranty, stipulation or undertaking, express or implied, by statute, common law or otherwise, as to the age, state, quality or performance of the goods or their correspondence with description, merchantable quality or their fitness for any particular purpose.

Silver Crest claimed that Sovereign were in breach of terms as to satisfactory quality and fitness for purpose implied by the Supply of Goods (Implied Terms) Act 1973. Sovereign sought to rely on their exclusion clause and argued that it was reasonable, *inter alia*, because they had merely financed the transaction and were not involved in the manufacture or delivery of the machine.

Held the clause was so wide as to be unreasonable. *Lease Management Services Limited v Purnell* (above) followed.

9.7.3   Other contract liability

Section 3 of UCTA:

(1) This section applies as between contracting parties where one of them deals as a consumer or on the other's written standard terms of business.

(2) As against that party, the other cannot by reference to any contract term:

(a) when himself in breach of contract, exclude or restrict any liability of his in respect of the breach; or

(b) claim to be entitled:

(i) to render a contractual performance substantially different from that which was reasonably expected of him; or

(ii) in respect of the whole or any part of his contractual obligation, to render no performance at all, expect in so far as (in any of the cases mentioned above in this sub-section) the contract term satisfies the requirement of reasonableness.

Stewart Gill Ltd v Myer (1992) CA

Gill agreed to supply, install and test a conveyor system for Myer, who agreed to pay by instalments. A clause of the contract stated that Myer 'shall not be allowed to withhold payment ... by reason of any payment, set-off, counterclaim, allegation of incorrect or defective goods or for any other reason whatsoever which [Myer] may allege ... '. Myer failed to pay the final two instalments; they alleged breach of contract and claimed a set-off against the instalments. Gill sued for price, relying on the 'no set-off' clause (above). Three issues arose: (i) did UCTA apply to the clause? (ii) if so, could the clause be severed to omit its more draconian aspects in order to render it reasonable for this case? (iii) if not, was it, as a whole, reasonable?

Held: (i) the clause fell within s 3 of UCTA (above) by reason of s 13, which extends to Act to cover '(1)(a) making liability or its enforcement subject to onerous conditions; (b) excluding or restricting any right or remedy ... ; (c) excluding or restricting rules of evidence or procedure ... '. The clause in this case fell within s 13(1)(b) and (c); (ii) s 11(1) (above, 9.7.2) included the phrase 'the term shall have been a fair and reasonable one to be included ... when the contract was made'. That means 'the whole term and nothing but the term'; further, its reasonableness must be determined at the time that the contract was made, without regard to what use it is subsequently put to. Thus, severance was not possible; (iii) the clause was unreasonable because it was drafted so wide so as to include, say, credit or overpayments in Myer's favour. That was unreasonable.

Notes

1 If the more draconian aspects of that clause were drafted as separate terms, a mere 'no set-off' clause may have been held to be reasonable. See *Schenkers Ltd v Overland Shoes* (below) and *WRM Group v Wood* (below, 9.7.4).

2 The effect of s 13 of UCTA is to extend the Act to cover unfair terms which are not, strictly speaking, exclusion clauses.

3 Under the Unfair Terms in Consumer Contracts Regulations 1994 the assessment of the fairness of a term must be made 'at the time of the conclusion of the contract' (reg 4(2)). Following the reasoning in *Stewart Gill*, severance of terms will not be possible under the Regulations (although the Regulations allow for the severance of a (whole) *term* from the contract (reg 5) so that the contract can persist without the offending term). The Regulations are set out on pp 97–101.

Schenkers Ltd v Overland Shoes Ltd (1998) CA

Overland contracted with Schenkers, a worldwide freight carrier, to carry a consignment of shoes from China to Britain. They dealt on Schenkers' standard form contract, which incorporated the standard conditions of the British International Freight Association. One of those conditions provided: 'the customer [Overland] shall pay to the company [Schenkers] in cash or as otherwise agreed all sums immediately when due, without reduction or deferment on account of any claim, counterclaim or set-off.' Overland claimed that Schenkers owed them VAT payments and sought to set this off against the freight charges. Schenkers relied on the clause that excluded the right of set-off and claimed for the freight charges in full. The case turned on the reasonableness under UCTA of that clause.

Held the condition was reasonable because: (i) it had been negotiated by all parties in the freight business; (ii) it was well known in the trade; (iii) there was an equality of bargaining power; Overland have a wide choice of carriers in the Far East; and (iv) the clause did not seek to exclude or limit any liability.

Note

See, also, *WRM Group Ltd v Wood*, below, 9.7.4.

9.7.4 The reasonableness test and misrepresentation

Section 3 of the Misrepresentation Act

If a contract contains a term which would exclude or restrict:

(a) any liability to which a party to a contract may be subject by reason of any misrepresentation made by him before the contract was made; or

(b) any remedy available to another party to the contract by reason of such a misrepresentation,

that term shall be of no effect except in so far as it satisfies the requirement of reasonableness as stated in s 11(1) of the Unfair Contracts Terms Act 1977 ...

Walker v Boyle (1982)

During negotiations for the sale of a house the buyer asked the purchaser if the property was subject to any boundary disputes. By mistake and innocently, the vendor stated that it was not. The buyer then discovered the truth and refused to complete the sale. The vendor sued for specific performance and relied on the clause in the National Conditions of Sale which provided that 'no misdescription can annul the sale'.

Held the clause was unreasonable; it was not negotiated by the parties themselves, or their representatives.

South Western General Property Co v Marton (1982)

An auction catalogue described a lot as 'long leasehold building land'. It also contained a statement that any details given were: (i) without responsibility; (ii) statements of opinion only; and (iii) that it was up to the intending purchasers to satisfy themselves as to their accuracy. In fact the land in question was subject to planning restrictions and the plaintiff would never had bought the land if he had known this.

Held the exemption clause was unreasonable under UCTA because the matter of planning restrictions was of vital importance to the buyer. Also, many prospective buyers attend auctions at short notice and they would have no opportunity to confirm the details.

WRM Group Ltd v Wood and Others (1997) CA

WRM contracted to buy the share capital in two companies, Wood Distribution Ltd and Chelquest Ltd, for £7.5 million. Payment was to be by £732,277 in cash and the issue by WRM to the sellers of loan notes for the remainder. The agreement contained a clause which restricted a right of set off by WRM to £300,000. The sale went ahead, but then WRM made a claim for misrepresentation amounting to £5.56 million. Meanwhile, the sellers were claiming the accrued interest on the loan notes. WRM refused to pay this, arguing that their misrepresentation claim could be used as a set-off against the interest payments due as the limitation clause was unreasonable under s 3 of the Misrepresentation Act 1967 (set out above) and s 11(1) of UCTA (set out above, 9.7.2).

Held (i) the limitation clause, although not a standard exclusion clause, was caught by s 3(b) of the Misrepresentation Act; (ii) the clause was reasonable because: (a) the agreement was a carefully drawn document and sought to balance, as the result of a bargain at arms length, the competing interests of the sellers and purchaser; (b) under the agreement, the purchaser obtained complete control of the two companies on the conclusion of the contract but was only required to pay about 10% of the price immediately; (c) there was no exclusion of liability for misrepresentation nor rescission; (d) if it feared that the sellers might dissipate their assets in order to frustrate the misrepresentation claim, WRM could seek a *Mareva* injunction to freeze the sellers' assets. In those circumstances, it was fair and reasonable to require the purchaser to pay the deferred price when due without any deduction for what was at that stage a mere claim, however arguable, even if for fraud.

9.7.5 The reasonableness test and 'negligence'

Section 2 of UCTA:

(1) A person cannot by reference to any contract term or to a notice given to persons generally or to particular persons exclude or restrict his liability for death or personal injury resulting from negligence.

(2) In the case of other loss or damage, a person cannot so exclude or restrict his liability for negligence except in so far as the term or notice satisfies the requirement of reasonableness.

Section 11 of UCTA

(3) In relation to a notice (not being a notice having contractual effect), the requirement of reasonableness under this Act is that it should be fair and reasonable to allow reliance on it, having regard to all the circumstances obtaining when the liability arose or (but for the notice) would have arisen.

Note ——————————————————————————————————————

'Negligence' is given a particularly broad definition by s 1 of UCTA. As well as common law negligence (for example, *Donoghue v Stevenson, Hedley, Byrne v Heller*) it includes any contractual obligation to take reasonable care and skill (for example, s 13 of the SGSA 1982) and the duty of care imposed by the Occupiers' Liability Act 1957.

——

Woodman v Photo Trade Processing (1981)

A film processing company included a limitation clause in their terms of dealing with consumers which restricted damages to the price of a new film.

Held as all developers at the time included a similar clause, there was little opportunity to contract elsewhere on better terms. In the circumstances, the limitation clause was not reasonable and so void.

Waldron-Kelly v British Railways Board (1981)

Whilst carrying the plaintiff's suitcase on 'owner's risk' terms British Railways lost it. A clause in the contract limited liability by reference to the weight of the luggage, in this case, £27. It was worth £320 and the plaintiff sued.

Held the limitation clause was unreasonable under UCTA.

Phillips v Hyland and Hampstead Plant Hire (1984) CA

Phillips hired from Hampstead an excavator with a driver to carry out some work on their factory. However, the factory was damaged because of the driver's negligence. Phillips sued Hampstead, who sought to rely on an exclusion clause in the hire agreement which provided that Phillips were responsible for the operation of the excavator by the driver. This clause was held to be subject to the reasonableness test under s 2(2) of UCTA (see below, 9.7.6).

Held Phillips were not in the plant hire business and dealt on Hampstead's standard terms. They could not negotiate the terms and had no choice in the driver. In fact, Phillips had no control over the driver, he being the master of his machine. The hire was for a short period, which made it difficult for Phillips to arrange insurance. In these circumstances, the clause was unreasonable.

Singer Co v Tees and Hartlepool Port Authority (1988)

Singer employed Bachman to send machinery to Brazil. Bachman crated the machinery and delivered it to the Port Authority for loading onto a ship. The machinery was damaged during loading. Singer sued in negligence and the Port Authority relied on an exclusion clause.

Held the clause was subject to the reasonableness test under ss 2(2) and 3(2) of UCTA and although the guidelines in Sched 2 do not strictly apply to negligence cases, they may be considered. Here the bargaining positions of the parties was equal and the exclusion clause was well known to the plaintiffs. Therefore the clause was reasonable.

Smith v Bush (1990) HL

Smith had agreed to buy a house. Whilst arranging her mortgage, the building society employed the defendants, a firm of surveyors, to carry out a valuation survey on the property in question. The mortgage agreement between the building society and Smith contained a notice exempting the surveyor from liability in negligence. Although the building society employed the surveyor, the cost of the survey was passed on to Smith in her mortgage agreement. During the survey, the surveyor noticed that two chimney breasts had been removed, but he failed to check whether the chimneys were left adequately supported and made no comment in his report. Smith relied on the report and completed the purchase. Some 18 months later, a chimney collapsed, fell through the roof and settled in the main bedroom. Smith sued the surveyor in negligence, who relied upon the exemption notice. It was held that the surveyor was negligent; the other issue was the reasonableness of the exemption notice (see s 2(2) of UCTA).

Held the following factors were considered: (i) the bargaining power of the parties; (ii) whether there were there alternative sources of advice; (iii) the difficulty of the task (if it was very difficult with a high risk of failure it may be reasonable to exclude liability); (iv) the consequences of the court's decision, especially the costs and adequacy of the surveyor's insurance. This was a modest house bought for domestic purposes involving a simple valuation survey, which ought to be covered by the surveyor's insurance. Thus the surveyor was liable.

Omega Trust Company Ltd and Another v Wright Son and Pepper (1996) CA

Omega were arranging to loan £350,000 to a company. The company put up some commercial property as security. Before granting the loan, Omega commissioned a survey of the property from the defendant surveyors, Barker and Co. Barker did this and valued the property at £945,000. Their valuation report carried the following exclusion clause. 'This report shall be for private and confidential use of the clients for whom the report is undertaken and should not be reproduced in whole or in part or relied upon by third parties for any use whatsoever without the express written authority of the surveyors.' Omega then agreed with another bank, Finindus, jointly to loan the money to the company. Both Omega and Finindus relied on Barker's valuation before loaning the money, although Barker knew nothing of Finindus. In the event, both Omega and Finindus lost money because the property was valueless. Finindus sued Barker in negligence. One issue was the reasonableness, under UCTA, of the exclusion clause.

Held the clause was reasonable. The court applied the guidelines from *Smith v Bush* (above): (i) the parties were of equal bargaining power. *Smith v Bush* was distinguished because *both* parties were commercial entities; (ii) it would have been reasonably practicable for Finindus to have obtained a survey elsewhere, or to have asked Barker permission to rely on the survey; (iii) the valuation was a straightforward, easily duplicated, one; there would have been no difficulty in obtaining one; (iv) the obvious purpose of the disclaimer was to limit the assumption of responsibility to Omega and to no one else. It was made clearly to assure clarity, transparency and certainty.

Monarch Airlines v London Luton Airport Ltd (1996)

In April 1992 a contract was made allowing Monarch to use Luton Airport. It contained the following clause: ' ... the airport company ... shall [not] be liable for loss or damage to the aircraft arising or resulting directly or indirectly from any act, omission, neglect or default on the part of the airport company ...' In September 1992, as one of Monarch's aircraft was turning, some runway paving blocks came loose and struck the aircraft, causing damage to it. Monarch sued in negligence and/or under s 2 of the Occupiers' Liability Act 1957. The airport company relied on the exclusion clause.

Held (i) as a matter of construction the words in the clause 'act, omission, neglect or default' cover a negligent act by the airport company; (ii) s 11(1) of UCTA (set out above, 9.7.2) provided that a contractual term should be 'fair and reasonable ... having regard to the circumstances ... when the contract was made'. In this case that was before the incident, in April 1992. The exclusion clause was reasonable under UCTA for two reasons: (a) it was a clause generally accepted in the market by airlines and airports; (b) it was possible for any airline to have insured against such a risk.

Note

The judge noted that an assessment of the reasonableness of the clause under s 11(3) – 'at the time that liability arose' (that is, September 1992) – might produce a different decision.

9.7.6 Indemnity clauses and UCTA

Section 4 of UCTA:

(1) A person dealing as consumer cannot by reference to any contract term be made to indemnify another person (whether a party to the contract or not) in respect of liability that may be incurred by the other for negligence or breach of contract, except in so far as the contract term satisfies the requirement of reasonableness.

(2) This section applies whether the liability in question:

(a) is directly that of the person to be indemnified or is incurred by him vicariously;

(b) is to the person dealing as consumer or to someone else.

Phillips v Hyland and Hampstead Plant Hire (1984) CA

Phillips hired from Hampstead an excavator with a driver to carry out some work on their factory. However, the factory was damaged because of the driver's negligence. Phillips sued Hampstead, who sought to rely on an exclusion clause in the hire agreement which provided that Phillips alone were responsible for the operation of the excavator by the driver and all claims arising from it. Hampstead argued that this clause was not subject to UCTA because it did not purport to *exclude* liability, rather it merely allocated the risk of liability between the two parties.

Held s 2(2) of UCTA provides that a person cannot 'by reference to' a contract term exclude liability for negligence unless that term is reasonable. Here, the *effect* of the clause is to exclude liability for negligence. Therefore, it is caught by s 2(2) and must be assessed for reasonableness.

Notes

1 For the application of the reasonableness test in this case, see above, 9.7.5.

2 Section 4 of UCTA provides that indemnity clauses are subject to a reasonableness test, but in *consumer* cases only. Hence, s 4 did not apply in this case.

Thompsom v Lohan (Plant) Ltd (1987) CA

Lohan hired out an excavator and driver to Hurdiss Ltd. A term of the standard form contract provided that Hurdiss alone were responsible for the operation of the excavator by the driver and all claims arising from it. Mrs Thompson's husband was killed because of the fault of the driver. Mrs Thompson sued Lohan for negligence; Lohan sought indemnification from Hurdiss. The issue was whether Lohan or Hurdiss were liable to Mrs Thompson. Lohan argued that the term (above) had allocated the risk onto Hurdiss. Hurdiss argued that the term was within the scope of s 2 of UCTA and as it related to death it was void.

Held the clause did *not* purport to exclude liability. It merely allocated the risk of liability between the parties. *Phillips v Hyland* (above) was distinguished because in that case there was a exclusion of liability which would have left the victim with no remedy.

Notes————————————————————————————————————

1   Section 4 of UCTA provides that indemnity clauses are subject to a reasonableness test, but in *consumer* cases only. Hence, s 4 did not apply in this case.

2   It seems that the only difference between *Thompson v Lohan* and *Phillips v Hyland* (above) was the status of the victim: in *Phillips* the victim was a party to the contract, in *Thompson* she was not. See Treitel, *The Law of Contract*, 9th edn, 1995, p 235.

9.7.7   Unfair Terms in Consumer Contracts Regulations 1994 SI 1994/3159

2   Interpretation

(1)   In these regulations:

'business' includes a trade or profession and the activities of any government department or local or public authority ...;

'consumer' means any natural person who, in making a contract to which these Regulations apply, is acting for purposes which are outside his business ...;

'seller' means a person who sells goods and who, in making a contract to which these Regulations apply, is acting for purposes relating to his business; and

'supplier' means a person who supplies goods or services and who, in making a contract to which these Regulations apply, is acting for purposes relating to his business.

3   Terms to which these Regulations apply

(1)   Subject to the provisions of Sched 1, these Regulations apply to any term in a contract concluded between a buyer or supplier and a consumer where the said term has not been individually negotiated.

(2)   In so far as it is in plain, intelligible language, no assessment shall be made of the fairness of any term which:

(a) defines the main subject matter of the contract; or

(b) concerns the adequacy of the price or remuneration, as against the goods or services sold or supplied.

(3)   For the purposes of these Regulations, a term shall always be regarded as not having been individually negotiated where it has been drafted in

advance and the consumer has not been able to influence the substance of the term.

(4) Notwithstanding that a specific term or certain aspects of it in a contract has been individually negotiated, these Regulations shall apply to the rest of the contract if an overall assessment of the contract indicates that it is a pre-formulated standard contract.

(5) It shall be for the seller or supplier who claims that a term was individually negotiated to show that it was.

4 Unfair terms

(1) In these Regulations, subject to paras (2) and (3) below, 'unfair term' means any term which contrary to the requirement of good faith causes a significant imbalance in the parties' rights and obligations arising under the contract to the detriment of the consumer.

(2) An assessment of the unfair nature of a term shall be made taking into account the nature of the goods or services for which the contract was concluded and referring, as at the time of the conclusion of the contract, to all the circumstances attending the conclusion of the contract and to all other terms of the contract or of another contract on which it is dependent.

(3) In determining whether a term satisfies the requirement of good faith, regard shall be had in particular to the matters specified in Sched 2 to these Regulations.

(4) Schedule 4 to these Regulations contains an indicative and non-exhaustive list of the terms which may be regarded as unfair.

5 Consequence of inclusion of unfair terms in contracts

(1) An unfair term in a contract concluded with a consumer by a seller [or] supplier shall not be binding on the consumer.

(2) The contract shall continue to bind the parties if it is capable of continuing in existence without the unfair term.

6 Construction of written contracts

A seller or supplier shall ensure that any written term of the contract is expressed in plain, intelligible language, and if there is any doubt about the meaning of a written term, the interpretation most favourable to the consumer shall prevail ...

Regulation 3(1)

Schedule 1

Contracts and particular terms excluded from the scope of these Regulations

These Regulations do not apply to:

(a) any contract relating to employment;

(b) any contract relating to succession rights;

(c) any contract relating to rights under family law;

(d) any contract relating to the incorporation and organisation of companies or partnerships; and

(e) any term incorporated in order to comply with, or which reflects:

(i) statutory or regulatory provisions of the United Kingdom; or

(ii) the provisions or principles of international conventions to which the Member States or Community are party.

Regulation 4(3)

Schedule 2

Assessment of good faith

In making an assessment of good faith, regard shall be had in particular to:

(a) the strength of the bargaining positions of the parties;

(b) whether the consumer had an inducement to agree to the term;

(c) whether the goods or services were sold or supplied to the special order of the consumer, and

(d) the extent to which the seller or supplier has dealt fairly and equitably with the consumer.

Regulation 4(4)

Schedule 3

Indicative and illustrative list of terms which may be regarded as unfair

1   Terms which have the object or effect of:

(a) excluding or limiting the legal liability of a seller or supplier in the event of the death of a consumer or personal injury to the latter resulting from an act or omission of that seller or supplier;

(b) inappropriately excluding or limiting the legal rights of the consumer vis à vis the seller or supplier or another party in the event of total or partial non-performance or inadequate performance by the seller or supplier or any of the contractual obligations, including the option of offsetting a debt owed to the seller or supplier against any claim which the consumer may have against him;

(c) making an agreement binding on the consumer whereas provision of services by the seller or supplier is subject to a condition whose realisation depends on his own will alone;

(d) permitting the seller or supplier to retain sums paid by the consumer where the latter decides not to conclude or perform the contract, without providing for the consumer to receive compensation of an equivalent amount from the seller or supplier where the latter is the party cancelling the contract;

(e) requiring any consumer who fails to fulfil his obligation to pay a disproportionately high sum in compensation;

(f) authorising the seller or supplier to dissolve the contract on a discretionary basis where the same facility is not granted to the consumer, or permitting the seller or supplier to retain the sums paid for services not yet supplied by him where it is the seller or supplier himself who dissolves the contract;

(g) enabling the seller or supplier to terminate a contract of indeterminate duration without reasonable notice except where there are serious grounds for doing so;

(h) automatically extending a contract of fixed duration where the consumer does not indicate otherwise, when the deadline fixed for the consumer to express this desire not to extend the contract is unreasonably early;

(I) irrevocably binding the consumer to terms with which he had no real opportunity of becoming acquainted before the conclusion of the contract;

(j) enabling the seller or supplier to alter the terms of the contract unilaterally without a valid reason which is specified in the contract;

(k) enabling the seller or supplier to alter unilaterally without a valid reason any characteristics of the product or service to be provided;

(l) providing for the price of goods to be determined at the time of delivery or allowing a seller of goods or supplier of services to increase their price without in both cases giving the consumer the corresponding right to cancel the contract if the final price is too high in relation to the price agreed when the contract was concluded;

(m) giving the seller or supplier the right to determine whether the goods or services supplied are in conformity with the contract, or giving him the exclusive right to interpret any term of the contract;

(n) limiting the seller's or supplier's obligation to respect commitments undertaken by his agents or making his commitments subject to compliance with a particular formality;

(o) obliging the consumer to fulfil all his obligations where the seller or supplier does not perform this;

(p) giving the seller or supplier the possibility of transferring his rights and obligations under the contract, where this may serve to reduce the guarantees for the consumer, without the latter's agreement;

(q) excluding or hindering the consumer's right to take legal action or exercise any other legal remedy, particularly by requiring the consumer to take disputes exclusively to arbitration not covered by legal provisions, unduly restricting the evidence available to him or imposing on him a burden or proof which, according to the applicable law, should lie with another party to the contract.

2   Scope of sub-paragraphs 1(g), (j) and (l)

(a) Sub-paragraph 1(g) is without hindrance to terms by which a supplier of financial services reserves the right to terminate unilaterally a contract of indeterminate duration without notice where there is a valid reason, provided that the supplier is required to inform the other contracting party or parties thereof immediately.

(b) Sub-paragraph 1(j) is without hindrance to terms under which a supplier of financial services reserves the right to alter the rate of interest payable by the consumer or due to the latter, or the amount of other charges for financial services without notice where there is a valid reason, provided that the supplier is required to inform the other contracting party or parties thereof at the earliest opportunity and that the latter are free to dissolve the contract immediately. Sub-paragraph 1(j) is also without hindrance to terms under which a seller or supplier reserves the right to alter unilaterally the conditions of a contract of indeterminate duration, provided that he is required to inform the consumer with reasonable notice and that the consumer is free to dissolve the contract.

(c) Sub-paragraphs 1(g), (j) and (l) do not apply to:

transactions in transferable securities, financial instruments and other products or services where the price is linked to fluctuations in a stock exchange quotation or index or a financial market rate that the seller or supplier does not control;

contracts for the purchase or sale of foreign currency, traveller's cheques or international money orders denominated in foreign currency;

(d) Sub-paragraph 1(l) is without hindrance to price indexation clauses, where lawful, provided that the method by which prices vary is explicitly described.

9.8   Exclusion clauses and the criminal law

Hughes v Hall (1981), see above, 9.3.1.

Cavendish Woodhouse v Manley (1984), see above, 9.3.1.

9.9 Consumer Protection Act 1987

European Commission v United Kingdom (1997) ECJ

The European Directive on Product Liability (85/374/EEC), which was adopted to make producers strictly liable to consumers for defective products, included a 'development risk' defence. Article 7(1) provided that a producer would not be liable if he proves that '... (e) the state of scientific and technical knowledge when he put the product into circulation was not such as to enable the existence of the defect to be discovered'. When the Directive was implemented in the UK by Pt I of the Consumer Protection Act 1987, this defence was transposed as 'the state of scientific and technical knowledge at the relevant time was not such that *a producer of products of the same description as the product in question might be expected to have discovered* the defect if it had existed in his products while they were under his control' (s 4(1)(e), emphasis added). The different wording caused the European Commission to think that the UK had introduced a subjective element and thus widened the defence for producers. In other words, a producer could argue that, although knowledge of the defect existed, he did not know of it; whereas the wording of the Directive indicates that the defence would only succeed if such knowledge did not exist. The Commission thought that the UK version, in effect, would reduce strict liability to mere negligence liability, which defeats the object of the Directive. The Commission brought Art 169 proceedings against the UK.

Held the UK defence is in accordance with the Directive because: (i) it places the burden of proof on the producer; (ii) it places no restriction on the state and degree of scientific and technical knowledge at the material time which is to be taken into account; (iii) it does not suggest that the availability of the defence depends on the subjective knowledge of a producer taking reasonable care in the light of the standard precautions taken in the industrial sector in question; (iv) there is no evidence to suggest that UK courts would not interpret the UK version in the light of the wording and the purpose of the Directive. The ECJ also noted that it was implicit in Art 7(1)(e) that the knowledge of the defect had to be 'accessible'; and this raised difficulties of interpretation which would have to be resolved in the national courts, or if necessary, by the ECJ (under Art 177 proceedings).

Note

For an analysis of the differently worded defences see Newdick's lengthy commentary on the development risk defence in [1988] CLJ 455. For a general commentary on Part I of the Consumer Protection Act, see Clark (1987) 50 MLR 614.

Part 3 Sale of goods

10 Passing of property

10.1 Section 17 of the Sale of Goods Act 1979 – property passes when the parties intend

Dennant v Skinner (1948)

A rogue, calling himself King, purchased a Standard car at an auction. King procured a cheque and requested that he may take possession immediately. The auctioneer agreed to this, but only after King signed a document stating that the property in the car passed only when the cheque cleared. Naturally, the cheque was dishonoured but not before King had resold the car; eventually it came to the hands of the (innocent) defendant, who was sued for its return or value (conversion) by the auctioneer. The auctioneer based his claim upon s 17 of the SGA, that property passed when the parties intended it to. As the cheque had not cleared, no property had passed to King to feed good title down the line to the defendant.

Held the auctioneer lost his claim. The sale was made on the fall of the auctioneer's hammer. According to s 18, r 1, property passes at the time of sale, unless there is a contrary intention. Here any 'contrary intention' (evidenced in the document) was formed *after* the sale. This was too late, as property had already passed to King.

Ward v Bignall (1967) CA

Bignall contracted to buy two cars from Wards, but then later refused to accept delivery. One issue was whether property in the cars had passed (under s 18, r 1), thus enabling Wards to sue for price.

Held obiter the governing rule is s 17, and in modern times very little is needed to give rise to the inference that the property in specific goods is to pass only on delivery or payment, as opposed to the earlier time, when the contract was made.

Note ————————————————————————
This case was decided on other grounds, see below, 14.5.

10.2 Section 18 of the Sale of Goods Act 1979 – rules for ascertaining intention

10.2.1 Deliverable state

Section 61 of the SGA

(5) Goods are in a deliverable state within the meaning of this Act when they are in such a state that the buyer would under the contract be bound to take delivery of them.

Pritchet v Currie (1916) CA

Pritchets contracted with the defendants to sell and install a large battery as part of an electrical installation. In accordance with the contract the battery was sent by rail to a designated station and collected by the defendants. However, the battery acid was to be supplied after installation. Before this occurred the defendants went into liquidation. The issue was whether the property in the battery had passed.

Held this was a contract for unascertained goods and s 18, r 5, would apply. Despite the fact that the battery was without acid it was in a deliverable state and property had passed upon delivery to the station.

Underwood v Burgh Castle (1921) CA

A contract was made for the sale FOR (free on rail) of a horizontal tandem condensing engine weighing 30 tons. The engine had to be removed from its concrete bed, dismantled and loaded on rail: a process which cost £100. During loading it was accidentally damaged and the court had to decide at whose risk the goods were at the time of the accident.

Held s 18, r 1, was not applicable here because when the contract was made (before any removal from the concrete bed) the machine was not in a deliverable state. Consequently the property in the goods did not pass at the time of the contract. As, by s 20, risk normally passes with property, the risk did not pass either. Under the contract the sellers had agreed to deliver the machine on rail; this they had not done at the time of the accident. As the sellers had not discharged all of their duties at that time, they retained risk.

Head (Phillip) v Showfronts (1970)

Following a contract to supply and fit a large carpet, the sellers delivered the carpet to the premises where it was to be laid. However, before it was laid, it was stolen. For the property, and so the risk of the loss (s 20), to have passed to the buyers, the carpet had to be in a deliverable state under s 18, r 5(1).

Held as the carpet was very large and heavy, and had not yet been laid, it was not in a deliverable state. Therefore, property and risk had not passed when it was stolen.

10.2.2 Rule 3 – goods to be weighed, measured, etc

Hanson v Meyer (1805)

Meyer agreed to sell the buyers a quantity of starch, which was lying in a warehouse of a third party. The starch had to be weighed before delivery. The buyers directed the warehouse keeper to weigh the starch. After part of the starch had been weighed and delivered the buyers became bankrupt. Their assignees sued Meyer claiming that the property in *all* of the starch (including the unweighed starch) had passed to the buyers.

Held the property in the goods vested in the buyers only after it had been weighed and delivered. Consequently, the starch remaining in the warehouse belonged to the sellers.

Turley v Bates (1863)

Turley contracted to sell to Bates a heap of fireclay lying on Turley's land. The priced was agreed at two shillings per ton and it was to be carted away and weighed by Bates. Bates took and paid for 270 tons, but left the remainder – about 1,000 tons. Turley sued for damages, claiming that the property in the whole heap had passed to Bates at the time of the contract. Bates relied on the rule that property does not pass where goods need to be weighed or measured to ascertain the price.

Held the rule only applied where the *seller* was bound to weigh or measure the goods. In this case the *buyer* had agreed to weigh the fireclay and so in the absence of the rule the court will look to the intention of the parties. On the evidence, it was clear that it was intended by the parties that property in the whole heap should pass at the time of the contract.

Note ───

This common rule is now codified in s 18, r 3.

Nanka Bruce v Commercial Trust (1926) PC

Laing agreed to buy cocoa at 59 s per 60 lbs. The arrangement was that Laing would resell the cocoa to other merchants, who would weigh it before reselling it to ascertain the amount owed by Laing to the seller.

Held the arrangement for weighing and payment was *not* a condition which suspended the passing of property because s 18, r 3, only applied to acts required of the *seller* by the contract. Hence, property could pass to the merchant sub-buyers before the cocoa was weighed.

10.2.3 Rule 4 – goods on approval or sale or return

Section 18, r 4, of the SGA

When goods are delivered to the buyer on approval or on sale or return or other similar terms the property in the goods passes to the buyer:

(a) when he signifies his approval or acceptance to the seller or does any other act adopting the transaction;

(b) if he does not signify his approval or acceptance to the seller but retains the goods without giving notice of rejection, then, if a time has been fixed for the return of the goods, on the expiration of that time, and, if no time has been fixed, on the expiration of a reasonable time.

Elphick v Barnes (1880)

A horse taken on approval for eight days died on the third day through no fault of the buyer.

Held the transaction had not become a sale when the horse died and so an action for price would fail.

Kirkham v Attenborough (1897) CA

Winter took some jewellery from the plaintiff on a sale or return basis. However, he pledged the jewellery to Attenborough. Kirkham claimed that the jewellery was still his property.

Held the act of pledging the goods was an 'act adopting the transaction' under s 18, r 4(a), and so the property had passed to Attenborough.

Note

Contrast this case with *Weiner v Gill* (below).

Weiner v Gill (1906) CA

Huhn took goods from Weiner on approval. However, the terms of the agreement stated that the goods were on sale, that either the cash or the goods should be returned and that the goods would remain the property of Weiner until they were paid for. Huhn was defrauded of the goods by Longman who pledged them to Gill. The issue for the court was, had the property in the goods passed to Huhn?

Held that s 18, r 4, did not apply here because a contrary intention was expressed in the agreement between Weiner and Huhn; the property in the goods had not passed to Huhn to feed Gill good title.

Poole v Smith Car Sales (1962) CA

At the end of August 1960, Poole was due to go on holiday and wanted his Vauxhall Wyvern car sold quickly to avoid the effects of depreciation. So he supplied the car to Smiths on a sale or return basis. By October, Poole had returned but the car had not been sold and there was a falling market. Poole telephoned Smiths on several occasions requesting the return of the car. Finally, he wrote stating that if the car was not returned by 7 November he would assume that it had been sold to Smiths. Some time after 7 November, the car was returned in poor condition and having been driven some 1,600 miles. Poole sued for price, stating that property had passed because the goods had been retained beyond (i) a fixed time; or (ii) a reasonable time (s 18, r 4(b)).

Held in the circumstances – quick sale, falling market, holiday arrangement, requests for return – a reasonable time had elapsed and the property had passed to the defendants; consequently Poole was entitled to the price. *Obiter* had the property not passed, Smiths could have been liable for the deterioration of the car as bailees.

Atari Corporation v Electronics Boutique (1977) CA

Atari sold computer games on a sale or return basis. Electronics Boutique (EB), a chain of retail outlets, agreed to take games from Atari 'on full sale or return until 31 January 1996'. On 19 January 1996, EB faxed Atari stating that they no longer wished to stock the Atari Jaguar game and that when all the stock was gathered at their central warehouse they would submit a complete list for return. Atari argued that the property in the Jaguar games had passed to EB because this was not a valid notice of rejection. They contended that the notice: (i) did not identify the goods precisely enough; and (ii) did not make the goods available for immediate collection.

Held (i) in the circumstances – many outlets and continuing sales – it was unnecessary to identify the stock other than generically; (ii) in any case, a notice of rejection of goods on sale or return did not have to give an immediate right to possession to be effective. It may give a right to possession at some reasonable notice. (Whether or that notice may extend beyond 31 January was not at issue and remained undecided.) Thus, EB's notice was effective. *Obiter*, a notice of rejection need not be in writing.

10.3   Unascertained goods and s 18, r 5(1)

Section 18, r 5(1) of the SGA

> Where there is a contract for the sale of unascertained or future goods by description, and the goods of that description and in a deliverable state are unconditionally appropriated to the contract, either by the seller with the assent of the buyer or by the buyer with the assent of the seller, the property in the goods then passes to the buyer; and the assent may be express or implied, and may be given before or after the appropriation is made.

10.3.1   Appropriation

Healey v Howlett (1917)

Healy agreed to sell Howlett 20 boxes of bright mackerel, to be delivered by train. Healy dispatched 190 boxes, with instructions to the railway company to designate 20 boxes for Howlett and divide the remaining boxes for two other customers. The train was delayed and all of the fish went bad. Howlett refused to take delivery and Healy sued for the price. The issue was, when did the property (and so risk, s 20) pass?

Held the action for price failed; the property could only pass to the buyer when the 20 boxes were designated; until then the goods remained unascertained. Section 16 of the SGA provided that property in unascertained goods could not pass. Avery LJ justified the decision using the following example:

> Suppose that in the present case 20 boxes only had become bad, it is quite impossible to say ... which of the various purchasers would have been bound to take the 20 bad boxes ...

Carlos Federspiel v Twigg (1957)

Twigg agreed to sell bicycles (FOB) to Federspiel, a trader in Costa Rica. In accordance with the FOB contract, Twigg was obliged to transport the bicycles to Liverpool and load them on the designated ship. In the event, after the bicycles were packaged and labelled for Federspiel, Twigg became bankrupt. Federspiel claimed that the property in the bicycles had passed to them.

Held usually, but not necessarily, the appropriating act is the last act to be performed by the seller. Here, the seller had yet to transport the goods to Liverpool and load them on the ship. The property had not passed.

Warder's v Norwood (1968) CA

A contract was made to sell 600 boxes of frozen kidneys from a bulk of 1,500 boxes lying in a cold store. It was agreed that the buyer would send a lorry to collect the goods. When the lorry arrived at 8 am, 600 boxes had already been removed from the cold store for the buyers. The driver handed the delivery note to the porter and loading began. However, the driver did not switch on the lorry's refrigeration unit until 10 am. The loading continued under hot sunshine and was completed at midday. The buyer refused to accept the kidneys because they were defrosted. The seller claimed the price.

Held when the driver gave the delivery note to the porter the goods were appropriated to the contract and property (and so risk, s 20) in them passed to the buyers. Hence the kidneys defrosted after they became the property of the buyers and they would have to pay the price.

Q How would you distinguish this case from *Carlos Federspiel v Twigg* above?

10.3.2 Appropriation must be unconditional

Mitsui v Flota Mercante Grandcolumbiana SA (1989), see below, 19.5.

National Coal Board v Gamble (1959)

In pursuance to a bulk contract for coal, lorries were loaded with coal from a hopper and then driven on to a weighbridge to ascertain the exact weight and price. The issue arose of whether the property passed when the lorry was loaded, or later when it was weighed.

Held the property in the coal did not pass when the coal was loaded on to the lorry. The Coal Board's employee, the weighbridgeman, could insist that a lorry return to unload any excess before allowing it to leave.

Unconditional appropriation could not happen until after the lorry had been weighed and released.

Edwards v Ddin (1976)

For this prosecution under the Theft Act 1968 it was necessary to prove that the property in a quantity of petrol passed at the time the accused intended his fraud. The fraud involved filling a tank of petrol at a self-service station and driving off without making payment.

Held the property in the petrol passed as soon as it entered the car's fuel tank; the appropriation was unconditional. So, if the accused formed the intent to defraud after he filled the car's tank, the prosecution would fail.

10.3.3 Assent after appropriation

Godts v Rose (1854)

The plaintiff agreed to sell five tons of rape-oil to the buyer on terms of payment on delivery. The rape-oil was stored at a wharf of a third party. The plaintiff directed the wharf owner to transfer the rape-oil into the buyer's name and then offered the transfer order to the buyer in exchange for payment. However, the buyer took the transfer order but refused to pay. He then took delivery of the rape-oil from the wharf. The plaintiff sued the buyer for conversion.

Held although the goods had been appropriated to the contract by the buyer, there was no assent to this by the seller, who (rightly) expected payment at delivery.

Rohde v Thwaites (1827)

Thwaites agreed to buy from Rhode 20 hogsheads of sugar out of a bulk. Twenty hogsheads were filled and Thwaites took delivery of four and promised to take the other 16. Thwaites failed to collect the remainder and Rhodes sued for price.

Held the property in the sugar had passed and so Thwaites was liable for the price. The act of filling the 20 hogsheads was an appropriation by the seller, while Thwaites's promise to collect the remaining 16 hogsheads was an assent to that appropriation.

Pignataro v Gilroy (1919)

In pursuance to a contract for the sale of 15 bags of rice, the sellers wrote to the buyers on 28 February that the rice was ready to be collected from '50 Long Acre'. The sellers received no reply. On 6 and 12 March, the sellers wrote twice more to the buyers. There was no reply to these letters either. At the end of March, the rice was found to have been stolen. The court had to decide if the property in the goods had passed to the buyers.

Held the goods were appropriated to the contract when they were placed at 50 Long Acre and the buyers were informed of this. The buyers' failure to respond for a month amounted to *implied* assent to that appropriation.

10.3.4 Assent before appropriation

Mucklow v Mangles (1808)
Royland contracted to build a barge and the whole of the price was advanced as work proceeded. The buyer's name was painted on the barge, but before it had been completed Royland became bankrupt. The issue was whether the property in the barge had passed to the buyer before the bankruptcy.

Held no property in the barge could have passed to the buyer until it had been completed, which was too late for the buyer. As the barge was incomplete at the time of bankruptcy, it had not been appropriated to the contract. Secondly, there was no assent; advance payment had the effect only of obliging Royland to finish the barge.

Aldridge v Johnson (1857)
Aldridge inspected a heap of 200 quarters of barley and agreed to buy 100 quarters from the heap. Aldridge then sent 200 of his own sacks to be filled with the barley. After 155 had been filled, the sellers were declared bankrupt and the trustee in bankruptcy claimed the barley which was in the sacks. Aldridge argued that the property in all of the barley had passed to him.

Held when the barley was separated from the heap and loaded into a sack, it was unconditionally appropriated to the contract by the seller. The sending of the sacks by the buyer was an express assent to that appropriation *in advance*. Therefore the property in the barley *in the 155 sacks only* had passed to Aldridge before the declaration of bankruptcy.

Langton v Higgins (1859)
Mrs Langton agreed to buy all the oil distilled from a peppermint crop grown on the seller's land. She sent bottles to the seller who filled them with the oil. However, the seller then sold some of the bottles of oil to Higgins. Langton sued Higgins in conversion, arguing that the property in the oil had already passed to her.

Held the filling of the bottles was the appropriation which was assented to in advance by the sending of the bottles.

Noblett v Hopkinson (1905)
The buyer ordered half a gallon of beer, to be delivered the next day – a Sunday. The beer was drawn into a bottle and placed aside overnight; the buyer paid for it then. Delivery was made the next day (Sunday) and the publican was charged with selling beer on a Sunday. The justices found that property passed on the Saturday and so no offence was committed. The prosecution appealed.

Held there was no appropriation assented to by the buyer on the Saturday. If the bottle had broken during Saturday night, other beer would have been supplied to the buyer.

10.4 Ascertainment without s 18

10.4.1 Ascertainment by exhaustion

Wait and James v Midland Bank (1926)

Wait and James owned wheat lying in a warehouse. They sold various amounts of the wheat to a number of buyers. A firm called Redlers bought two consignments of 250 quarters each and one of 750 quarters under three respective contracts. Redlers collected 400 quarters and pledged the remaining 850 quarters to the Midland Bank. The other buyers all collected their wheat leaving 850 quarters in the warehouse. Wait and James remained unpaid and claimed that the property in the wheat had not passed because while it was subject to two or three separate contracts it was not ascertained.

Held when all the other buyers' wheat was removed from the warehouse, leaving only wheat subject to the Redlers' contracts, that wheat had been ascertained by exhaustion; it did not matter that the wheat was subject to separate contracts, as long as they were for one buyer. The property in the wheat passed to Redlers and, accordingly, the bank was entitled to it.

Note
This case has since been put on a statutory footing: see s 18, r 5(3) and (4) of the SGA 1979.

Re London Wine Co (1975)

The company had contracted to sell wine to a number of customers which was stored in warehouses and remained unascertained. Before any wine had been delivered the company's bank took a charge over its property. The court considered several representative cases. In one a customer had bought the company's total stock of particular wine. In a second, two or more customers had bought the company's total stock of a particular wine. It was argued, relying on *Wait & James v Midland Bank* (see above), that the property had passed because the wine became ascertained by exhaustion.

Held rejecting the argument, in both cases the company was not obliged to fulfil the orders with wine from their own stocks; they could have supplied wine from other sources. Thus, the goods subject to contract were never ascertained. Further, the second case could be distinguished from *Wait & James v Midland Bank* because in that case there was only *one* buyer with several contracts.

Note
For further arguments in equity in this case, see below, 10.5.

Karlshamns v Eastport Navigation Corp, *The Elafi* (1982)

The buyer contracted to purchase 6,000 tons of copra, which was part of a cargo of over 20,000 tons being shipped aboard *The Elafi*. The buyer then purchased another quantity of the copra on board the ship from Fehr, who had bought it from the seller. The ship then called at various ports, discharging its cargo until all that was left were the two consignments which were the subject of the buyer's two contracts. When this cargo was being unloaded it was damaged by water. The issue for the court was, had the goods, originally unascertained, been ascertained 'by exhaustion'.

Held the parties intention was that property in the goods should pass as soon as possible (s 17). The goods were ascertained 'by exhaustion'. Once ascertained, the property passed even though there was no unconditional appropriation to each contract.

Note

This case has since been put on a statutory footing: see s 18, r 5(3) and (4) of the SGA 1979.

10.4.2 Ascertainment by segregation

In re Goldcorp Exchange (1994) PC

Two groups of persons entered into contracts with Goldcorp for the sale of bullion. The first group purchased bullion 'for future delivery' at seven days' notice. The bullion was not appropriated to any of these contracts. However, Goldcorp promised to store and insure the bullion. The second group had purchased bullion from W, a company later taken over by Goldcorp. Goldcorp unlawfully mixed the W bullion with their own stocks and then sold off bullion from the mixed stock. Before any bullion was delivered under the contracts, Goldcorp went into receivership and a floating charge over Goldcorp's assets crystallised in favour of the Bank of New Zealand. The receivers asked the court for directions as to the disposal of the bullion.

Held the subject matter of the contracts was unascertained and so the property could not have passed to the purchasers. The collateral promises of storage, insurance and delivery at seven days' notice could not overcome this. There was no trust in favour of the purchasers because the subject matter, being unascertained, was uncertain. Even if Goldcorp were estopped by their promises from denying the purchasers title to the bullion, this would not affect the bank's title. However, the bullion from W had been sufficiently ascertained to pass title to the second group and their shared interest could be traced to Goldcorp's bullion although their recoveries could not exceed the lowest balance held by Goldcorp at any time.

Note ──────────────────────────────────────

Since these two cases the Sale of Goods (Amendment) Act 1995 inserted
s 20A into the SGA 1979. Broadly speaking, it provides that where a buyer
has paid for undivided shares ('unascertained goods') forming part of an
identifiable bulk, the property in the undivided share will pass to the buyer,
who owns the share as a tenant in common. See Bradgate and White [1994]
LMCLQ 35; Atiyah, *The Sale of Goods*, 9th edn, pp 293–97; and Dobson, P,
'Sale of goods forming part of a bulk' (1995) 16 SLR 11, pp 11–13.

Re Stapylton Fletcher Ltd, Re Ellis & Vidler (1994)

Two wine merchants went into receivership. At the time they held stocks of
wine ordered and paid for by customers, who had also paid storage
charges. The receivers applied for directions on whether the property in the
wine had passed to the customers before their appointment. Among others,
three representative cases were considered. (i) Where the customers' wine
was separated from the trading stock, although it had not been allocated to
individual customers. This wine was not on record as part of the merchant's assets. However, much of this wine later became mixed with the
merchant's trading stock. (ii) Where wine was held in a bonded warehouse
(under the charge of HM Customs & Excise until duties were paid). Here,
again, customers' wine was separated from the trading stock, although not
allocated to individual customers. (iii) Where the customers' wine was held
in a bonded warehouse but not separated from the trading stock.

Held in cases (i) and (ii), wine which was separated from the trading
stock (thus distinguishing *Re London Wine*, above, 10.4.1) was ascertained
for the purposes of s 16 of the SGA, even though not appropriated to each
individual customer. Consequently, s 18, r 5, did not apply; property passed
by common intention. The fact that in case (i) the wine became mixed with
trading stock after property had passed could not affect that finding.
Hence, the property in the wine had passed to the customers, who held the
stock as tenants in common. In case (iii), the wine was not separated from
the trading stock and so was not ascertained for the purposes of s 16.
Hence, the property had not passed to the customers; *Re London Wine* was
followed.

10.5 Equitable interest in unascertained goods

Re Wait (1927) CA

Wait agreed to buy 1,000 tons of wheat on board a ship and due to unload
in England. He contracted to sell 500 tons of this wheat to Humphries, who
paid in advance. Before the ship arrived Wait became bankrupt. At (common) law the property in the wheat belonged to Wait (or his trustee in
bankruptcy). Humphries claimed in equity to have a proprietary interest
in the unascertained goods.

Held (2:1) there was no equitable assignment giving Humphries a beneficial interest in the goods. The SGA 1893 (which provided the rules for the passing of property) was drafted at a time when all the principles of equity were established. Equitable remedies were not included in the rules and so it must be taken that they were not applicable to the passing of property.

Re London Wine Co (Shippers) Ltd (1986)

The company had contracted to sell wine to a number of customers which was stored in warehouses and remained unascertained. Before any wine had been delivered the company's bank took it as charge over its property. The customers had paid for the wine and were given in return documents, each entitled 'Certificate of Title', which described the holder as 'sole and beneficial owner' of the wine in question. The customers were charged for storage and insurance until the wine was delivered or resold. Three representative cases were considered. First, where a customer had bought the company's total stock of a particular wine. Secondly, where two or more customers had bought the company's total stock of a particular wine. Thirdly, where a customer had purchased just some of the total stock of a particular wine and pledged it to a finance company. In this third case, the warehouseman acknowledged to the customer *and* the finance company that the wine subject to the contract was being held to the customer's order. The first argument covered all three cases; it was that the company held the wine on trust for the customers. The second argument put forward in case (iii) was that the acknowledgments of the warehouseman created, by estoppel, proprietary interests in favour of the customer and his pledgee.

Held both arguments were rejected. The company were not obliged to fulfil the orders with wine from their own stocks; they could have supplied wine from other sources. Therefore, although there may have been an intention to create a trust in particular stocks (evidenced by the certificates of title), the trust must fail for uncertainty of the subject matter, as the goods were unascertained. On the second argument, it was clear that no property in the goods had actually passed and so that action must fail. However, *obiter,* an action for damages in conversion based on estoppel may lie against the warehouseman.

Note

For a further argument that the wine was ascertained by exhaustion, see above, 10.4.

10.6 Reservation of title clauses

Aluminium Industrie Vaassen BV v Romalpa Aluminium (1976) CA

The plaintiffs (AIV) sold foil to Romalpa on terms that until all debts owed by Romalpa to AIV were met: (i) the property in the foil would not be transferred to Romalpa; and (ii) the foil would be stored in such a way that it was clearly the property of AIV. There was a further (implied) term that Romalpa were entitled to sell the foil to sub-buyers. Before full payment was made Romalpa went into receivership. AIV claimed the foil which they had supplied (worth £50,000) and the proceeds from sub-sales (£35,000) by Romalpa. Romalpa conceded that they held the foil as bailees.

Held the property in the remaining unsold foil had not passed to Romalpa and so AIV were entitled to recover that foil. On the issue of the proceeds from sub-sales, as Romalpa held the foil as bailees they owed AIV a fiduciary duty, and so AIV were entitled to trace the proceeds of the sale of their property. The defendants' contention that after resale the relationship between the parties was no more than that of debtor and creditor was rejected.

Re Bond Worth Ltd (1980)

Fibre was supplied to Bond Worth on terms that until the price was paid equitable and beneficial (but not legal) ownership of the fibre, any products made from the fibre and any proceeds of resale, would remain with the suppliers.

Held these terms had the effect of creating a charge over the buyer's assets and such a charge should be registered under the Companies Act (to alert, for example, banks offering credit for security); the terms were void for want of such registration. The *Romalpa* case was distinguished. First, because there the clause reserved *legal* title and the relationship of bailment was conceded; the clause referred to a fiduciary relationship. Secondly, the foil was stored separately as the property of the seller. Thirdly, the proceeds of the sub-sales were held in a separate account and so identifiable.

Borden v Scottish Timber Products (1981) CA

Borden sold resin to Scottish Timber which was to be mixed with hardeners, emulsion and wood-chippings to produce chipboard (an irreversible process). The contract contained a clause which stipulated that property in the resin would pass only when all goods supplied by Borden were paid for. Scottish Timber went into receivership owing Borden £300,000. Relying on *Romalpa*, Borden claimed that they could trace ownership of any chipboard manufactured with their resin or any proceeds from sales of such chipboard.

Held the manufacturing process had amalgamated the resin with the other ingredients. As such the resin had lost its identity and ceased to exist. It would be impossible to trace the resin into the chipboard.

Re Peachdart Ltd (1984)

Leather was supplied to Peachdart to be made into handbags. The contract provided that the property in the leather, and handbags made with it, remained with the supplier until the price was paid; it also provided that a fiduciary relationship existed between the parties and so the supplier was entitled to trace any proceeds of sub-sales of the leather or handbags. (Although there was no stipulation that the goods or proceeds should be kept separately.)

Held the parties could not have intended that the property remained with the supplier after the leather was used for making the handbags. There was no more than a charge on the manufactured handbags and that would be void for want of registration under the Companies Act.

Hendy Lennox v Puttick (1984)

Diesel engines were supplied by Lennox for the purpose of fitting into generator sets, which were resold. The contract provided that the property in the engines would remain with the supplier until the price had been paid; there was 30 days credit; and in the case of default the supplier could repossess engines not paid for. The buyers went into receivership with three engines on their premises. All three engines had been fitted to the generator sets; the property in two sets had passed to sub-buyers. Lennox claimed to be entitled to the unsold engine and the proceeds from the two resold engines.

Held the claim to the unsold engine would be allowed. Although it had been mixed with other goods in the construction of a generator set, it could easily be unbolted and become separate again; thus, *Re Bond Worth, Borden v Scottish Timber* and *Re Peachdart* (all above) were distinguished. The claim to proceeds of the sub-sales would be refused because there was no fiduciary relationship and the fact that the contract gave 30 days credit and allowed repossession for default implied that the buyers were entitled to keep the proceeds of any sub-sales.

Re Andrabell, Airborne Accessories v Goodman (1984)

Airborne Accessories sold travel bags to Andrabell on terms of 45 days credit and that property would not pass until the goods were paid for. Andrabell went into liquidation and as Airborne were left unpaid they claimed (relying on the *Romalpa* case, above) to be entitled to proceeds from the resale of the bags.

Held the *Romalpa* case was distinguished on the grounds that: (i) there was no provision that the travel bags should be separately stored so as to indicate Airborne's ownership; (ii) there was no expression of a fiduciary relationship in the contract; (iii) there was no requirement to keep the proceeds of resale separate as would be the case where there was a duty to account stemming from a fiduciary relationship and; (iv) the 45 day credit period implied that Andrabell were entitled to keep the proceeds of any sub-sales.

Thus, in the absence of a fiduciary relationship, the parties were to be treated simply as debtor and creditor and Airborne were not entitled to the proceeds nor were they entitled to recover the bags from sub-buyers.

Clough Mill v Martin (1985) CA

Clough Mill sold yarn to Heatherdale to make into fabrics. The contract included a 'simple clause' which provided that property in the yarn remained with the seller until it was paid for or resold. Clough Mill claimed to be entitled to the unused yarn at the time Heatherdale went into receivership.

Held the plain words of the 'simple clause' were effective and Clough Mill were entitled to their (unused) yarn.

Four Point Garage v Carter (1985)

Carter ordered and paid for a Ford Escort XR3i car from Freeway Ltd, who located and ordered the required model from Four Point. Four Point delivered the car directly to Carter, understanding that Carter was leasing the car. Freeway went into liquidation without paying Four Point for the car. Four Point claimed the car from Carter on the basis, *inter alia,* that a reservation of title clause in the contract between Freeway and Four Point meant that, Four Point remaining unpaid, title never vested in Freeway to pass to Carter.

Held the clause was subject to an implied term that Freeway were authorised to resell the car. Thus, the claim against Carter was defeated.

Tatung v Galex Telesure (1989)

Tatung sold electrical video goods to Galex, who retailed the goods by sale, rental or hire-purchase. The contract included terms which provided (i) that property remained with Tatung until all debts were settled; and (ii) that the proceeds of resale or hire should be kept in a separate account for the benefit of Tatung.

Held a charge had been created over the proceeds of sale and was void for want of registration under the Companies Act. As Tatung's interest in the proceeds ceased when they were paid what was due from Galex, the rights over those proceeds were by security rather than ownership.

Pfeiffer v Arbuthnot Factors (1988)

The plaintiffs sold wine to Springfield Wine Importers Ltd on terms that: (i) the property in the wine would remain with the plaintiffs until it had been paid for; and (ii) the plaintiffs would enjoy an equitable assignment of all debts owed to Springfield by sub-purchasers. Springfield assigned its debts owed by sub-purchasers to the defendants (under a factoring agreement). The result was that both the plaintiffs and the defendants had competing claims to the sub-purchasers' debts. The plaintiffs claimed priority.

Held the assignment to the plaintiffs amounted to a charge and so was void for want of registration under the Companies Act. Even if it were not so the defendants would have priority under the rule in *Dearle v Hall* (1828) as they gave notice first to the sub-buyers.

Armour v Thyssen (1991) HL (Sc)

A German company sold steel on terms that the steel remained the property of the sellers until *all* debts owing under any contract were settled. The buyers (in receivership) argued that the term was a charge under Scottish law and so void.

Held the terms were effective – property in the steel could not pass to the buyer until all debts owing to the sellers were settled. A security (or charge) is property owned by the debtor put at risk in favour of the creditor. In this case the debtor never owned the property to be able to offer it as security. Hence the clause did not resemble a security or charge.

Note
See McCormack [1991] 2 LMCLQ 154.

In re Highway Foods International Ltd (Mills v Harris) (1995), see below, 12.5.7.

11 Risk, mistake and frustration

11.1 Transfer of risk

11.1.1 Risk passes with property – s 20(1) of the SGA

Castle v Playford (1872)

Under a contract for the sale of fresh-water ice to be shipped to the UK, it was agreed that the buyer would take the 'risk and dangers of the sea' upon receipt of the bills of lading (documents of title). However, payment was to be on delivery. The bills of lading were received and then the ship was lost.

Held the property passed upon receipt of the bills of lading and normally the risk passes with the property. In any event the parties agreed that the risk would pass on the receipt of the documents irrespective of time of payment or the passing of property. Therefore, the ice was at the buyer's risk when the ship was lost.

Note ———————————————————————

That the general rule, that risk passes with property, is now embodied in s 20(1) of the SGA.

11.1.2 Risk passing before property

Martineau v Kitching (1872)

Four 'titlers' of sugar, lying in the sellers' warehouse, were sold to the defendant on terms that: (i) the goods had to be weighed before delivery to determine the exact price; and (ii) the goods, whilst in the sellers' warehouse, would be at the seller's risk for two months. After two months had elapsed, a fire broke out and destroyed the contents of the warehouse, including sugar not yet taken by the defendant. The defendant claimed that the risk had not passed to him because the property could not have passed, the goods not having been weighed.

Held as a general rule, risk passes with property. However, the risk can be separated from property by terms of the contract. That was the case here and although the property may not have passed, the risk passed after two months and before the fire. The defendant bore the loss.

Inglis v Stock (1885) HL

The buyer agreed to purchase a quantity of sugar, part of a larger bulk on board a ship. The ship was lost and the issue was whether the buyer had an insurable interest in the sugar.

Held although the property in the goods had not passed (because the goods were unascertained) the buyer did have an insurable interest in an undivided part of the bulk. The House of Lords also said that the risk had passed to the buyer at the time of shipment.

Sterns v Vickers (1923) CA

Sterns agreed to sell 120,000 gallons of white spirit which was stored in a tank (containing 200,000 gallons) belonging to a third party. The buyers obtained a delivery order, which the third party accepted, but decided not to take delivery for the time being. The spirit deteriorated in quality before the buyers eventually took delivery. At issue was whether the risk in an unascertained part of a bulk passed to the buyers.

Held the property in the goods had not passed to the buyers because the goods were unascertained and so not appropriated to the contract. However, in the circumstances – that is: (i) that the sellers had done all that they could on their part; (ii) that the buyers had the right to demand delivery at any time; and (iii) if they had taken delivery earlier they would have got what the sellers had promised them – the risk had passed to the buyers.

Note ——

This decision was approved by the House of Lords in *The Julia* (1949).

Q What if the white spirit was stored in two tanks, and only the spirit in one tank had deteriorated? See Atiyah, *The Sale of Goods*, 9th edn, 1995, pp 301–02.

Horn v Minister of Food (1948)

A farmer agreed in January to sell the Ministry a quantity of potatoes. It was a term of the contract that the farmer should store the potatoes with 'reasonable care' to protect them against frost and winter weather. It was also agreed that the Ministry would give delivery instructions to the buyer in May, June or July and that property would pass upon delivery. However, before delivery the farmer discovered a seam of rot in the potatoes. It was found that the farmer was not at fault. The Ministry refused to take delivery and the farmer sued for price or damages. The Ministry claimed that the contract was frustrated under s 7 of the SGA (goods perishing before the risk passes). They argued that the risk had not passed when the potatoes perished. This was because risk normally passes with property (s 20 of the SGA) and (according to the contract) property was to pass upon delivery. Therefore, as the goods were never delivered the risk remained with the farmer.

Held s 7 did not apply because the risk had passed to the Ministry when the contract was made. The contract stipulated that the farmer should look after the potatoes; therefore any failure on the farmer's part would have been a breach of contract, for which the Ministry could claim damages. Consequently, the risk was always on the Ministry. The farmer could recover damages. See, further, 11.4.

11.1.3 Risk passing after property

Head v Tattersall (1870)

A horse falsely described as having been hunted with the Bicester hounds was sold with a one week warranty. The buyer took possession of the horse and during the first week it was accidentally injured. Then the buyer discovered that it had not been hunted with the Bicester hounds and he returned the horse.

Held the buyer could return the horse and have a full refund. The risk had not passed to him at the time the horse was injured.

11.1.4 Risk and bailment – s 20(3) of the SGA

Bullen v Swan (1907) CA

Some valuable engraved plates belonging to Bullen were stored by Swans at the convenience of both parties. Swans had proper facilities for storing such plates and wished to take some prints from them. While in their custody the plates were stolen. Bullen claimed for their return or their value.

Held Swans were in possession of the plates as gratuitous bailees. Their duty was to take reasonable care, that is, as much care as the prudent owner would use in keeping his own property. Here Swans stored the plates in the normal manner and no want of care was shown. Judgment for Swans.

Wiehe v Dennis Bros (1913)

Wiehe contracted to buy a shetland pony, delivery in a month. While the pony was in the sellers' possession it was taken to an event, mishandled and suffered injuries.

Held the sellers were liable for failing to take reasonable care as bailees of the goods.

Poole v Smith Car Sales (1962) CA

In August 1962 Poole supplied a second-hand car to Smiths on a sale or return basis. However, Smiths never sold the car and despite many requests only returned it (in poor condition) in October.

Held the property had passed to Smiths under s 18, r 4. *Obiter* had the property not passed Smiths would have been liable for the deterioration of the car as bailees.

Note ——

For a fuller account of the case, see above, 10.2.3.

11.1.5   Delay in the delivery of the goods – s 20(2) of the SGA

Demby Hamilton v Barden (1949)
Demby Hamilton sold 30 tons of apple juice to be collected by February 1946. By November 1946 much of the apple juice remained uncollected by the buyer, and this had become putrid.

Held as the delay in the delivery of the goods was through the fault of the buyer, the apple juice was at his risk.

11.1.6   Buyer takes risk necessarily incident to transit – s 33 of the SGA

Mash & Murrell v Emmanuel (1961)
Merchants in Cyprus agreed to sell potatoes to buyers in Liverpool. The potatoes were in good condition when loaded, but rotten when they arrived in Liverpool.

Held although the potatoes were fit for use when they were loaded, they were not fit to travel to Liverpool. Hence the sellers were in breach of an implied condition that the goods would be merchantable.

Note
This decision was reversed on other grounds by the Court of Appeal. See Sassoon [1962] JBL 351.

Q Section 33 of the SGA provides that the buyer takes the risk of deterioration necessarily incident to the transit. Is this section confined to cases only where the goods were fit for the journey?

11.2   Mistake and s 6 of the Sale of Goods Act 1979

Couturier v Hastie (1856) HL
A contract was made for the sale of corn, which was believed by both parties to be aboard a ship sailing from Salonika to London. However, unknown to the parties, before the contract was made the ship's captain had (lawfully) sold the corn at Tunis because it was deteriorating. When this was discovered the buyer refused to pay. The seller sued for price.

Held the seller could not sue for price because on the true construction of the contract the subject matter of the contract was the corn, and as that had not been delivered, the buyer was not bound to pay the price (see s 28 of the SGA).

Note
For many years this case was understood to have been decided on the ground that the contract was void for mistake, and that s 6 SGA (which provides that a contract is void where the goods have perished before the contract was made) was based upon that decision. See Atiyah, *The Sale of Goods*, 9th edn, pp 67–72.

Barrow, Lane & Ballard v Phillip Phillip & Co (1929)

Phillips contracted to sell 700 bags of nuts to Ballards. Unknown to the parties, 109 bags had been stolen. And, after the delivery of 150 bags, the rest went missing. Ballards refused to pay the price on the ground that the sellers were in breach of an implied term that the goods were in existence. Phillips sued Ballards for the price of all 700 bags.

Held when the contract was made 109 bags had already been stolen; hence the parcel of 700 bags had 'perished' within the meaning of s 6 and the contract was void.

McRae v Commonwealth Disposals Commission (1951) Aus

The Commission contracted to sell to McRae a stricken oil tanker lying on 'Jourmand Reef'. At considerable expense McRae set off to recover the tanker. However, he found no tanker or reef at the given location; in fact, the tanker never existed. He sued for the cost of the aborted salvage expedition. The Commission argued that the corresponding Australian section to the English s 6 of the SGA applied and so the contract was void for mistake.

Held the Commission had warranted to McRae that there was a ship for sale at the given location and consequently the non-existence of that ship meant that the Commission were in breach of contract; this was not a case of (statutory) mistake.

Note ———

In this case the goods never existed to 'perish' as the strict words of the statute require; but the court did not base its decision on this point.

11.3 Frustration and s 7 of the Sale of Goods Act 1979

Howell v Coupland (1876) CA

In March 1872, an agreement was made to sell 200 tons of potatoes grown on the seller's land, delivery in September. But in August the crop was struck by disease and only 80 tons were produced. The buyer took delivery of the 80 tons but sued for damages for non-delivery of the remainder.

Held the contract was for specific goods and conditional upon the goods existing when the time came to perform the contract. Consequently, the seller was excused from delivery of the remainder.

Note ———

Section 7 of the SGA was based upon this case (specific goods perishing after the agreement to sell but before the sale).

Also note, however, that that contract would not be subject to s 7 because the Act's definition of specific goods (s 61(1): goods identified and agreed on *at the time* the contract is made) is more restrictive than at common law.

Maritime National Fish v Ocean Trawlers (1935) PC

The defendants owned five fishing ships. One, the *St Cuthbert*, was chartered ('hired') to the plaintiffs. However, it was an offence to operate such ships without a licence from the Minister of Fisheries. The defendants were granted just three licences and allocated them to ships other than the *St Cuthbert*. The plaintiffs sued under the charter and the defendants claimed that the charter was frustrated.

Held the defendants chose not to allocate a licence to the *St Cuthbert* and so the frustration was self-induced; therefore the defendants were not discharged from their obligations under the charter.

Sainsbury v Street (1972)

Sainsbury agreed to purchase 'about 275 tons' of feed barley to be grown on the seller's land. However, without fault on the seller's part, the crop only harvested 140 tons. The market price of feed barley had risen since the contract date and the seller sold the 140 tons to a third party for considerably more than the contract price. Sainsbury sued for damages on the loss of 140 tons. The seller claimed that as the contract was frustrated he was excused from performing it at all.

Held although the seller was excused from performance there was an implied term that Sainsbury had the option to demand part-delivery.

Q If a seller has made several contracts to sell goods from a bulk and part of that bulk is destroyed, which contracts is he obliged to fulfil? See Hudson (1968) 31 MLR 535.

11.4 Perish

Barrow, Lane & Ballard v Phillip Phillip & Co (1929), see above, 11.2.

Asfar v Blundell (1896) CA

A ship carrying a consignment of dates sank and the dates were saturated with seawater and sewage for two days. The question for the court was whether the cargo was a total loss for insurance purposes.

Held the test was: as a matter of business has the nature of the thing altered? Clearly in this case it had and the goods were a total loss.

Horn v Minister of Food (1948)

For the facts, see above, 11.1.2.

Held obiter s 7 of the SGA did not apply because the potatoes had not 'perished' within the meaning of the Act. Although the rotten potatoes were useless, they still answered to the description 'potatoes'.

Note ───

This part of the case has been widely criticised; see, for instance, Atiyah, *The Sale of Goods*, 9th edn, 1995, p 74.

12 Passing of title by non-owner

12.1 The general rule, *nemo dat quod non habet* – s 21 of the Sale of Goods Act 1979

Cundy v Lindsay (1878) HL

Blenkiron were a well-known and respected firm who carried on business at 123 Wood Street, Cheapside. A rogue, called Blenkarn, from 37 Wood Street, impersonated the neighbouring firm and ordered a quantity of linen from Lindsay. Lindsay sent the linen on credit believing that they were dealing with the firm, Blenkiron. Blenkarn (the rogue) then sold some of the linen to Cundy. Lindsay brought a claim in conversion against Cundy.

Held the contract between the rogue and Lindsay was void for mistake. Consequently, the rogue had no title to pass to Cundy and Lindsay would succeed.

Jerome v Bently (1952)

Jerome entrusted a diamond ring to a stranger, Tatham, with authority to sell it for over £550; Tatham could keep any surplus and if he could not sell it within seven days he should return it. After 12 days, Tatham sold the ring to Bently for £175, who took it in good faith believing that Tatham was the owner. Jerome brought an action in conversion against Bently.

Held Tatham, having no authority to convey title in the ring, could not pass good title to Bently, and so Jerome succeeded.

12.2 *Nemo dat* exceptions – s 21 of the Sale of Goods Act and estoppel

Section 21 of the SGA

(1) Subject to this Act, where goods are sold by a person who is not their owner, and does not sell them under the authority or with the consent of the owner, the buyer acquires no better title to the goods than the seller had, *unless the owner is by his conduct precluded from denying the seller's authority to sell*. [Emphasis added.]

12.2.1 Estoppel by words or conduct

Henderson v Williams (1895) CA

A sugar merchant, Grey, sold 150 bags of sugar, which were held in another's warehouse, to a rogue named Fletcher. Upon Grey's instruction, the warehousemen transferred the goods in their books to the order of Fletcher. Fletcher, meanwhile, had agreed a resale to the plaintiff, who was suspicious, and demanded that the sugar be put in his own name before he would pay. So the warehousemen gave the plaintiff written statements confirming that the sugar was held for his order. Then, Grey, not having been paid by the rogue, Fletcher, instructed the warehousemen not to release the sugar. The contract between Grey and Fletcher was void for mistake. Grey contended that as Fletcher never had good title to the sugar, he could not pass title to the plaintiff.

Held both Grey and the warehousemen were estopped from denying the plaintiff's title. Grey represented that Fletcher was the owner by having the goods transferred into his name. The warehousemen represented that they held the goods for the plaintiff (attornment).

Farquharson Bros v King (1902) HL

The clerk of the plaintiff timber company was given limited power to sell to certain customers and general written authority to sign delivery orders on the plaintiffs' behalf (this enabled the warehouse to release timber to the delivery note holders). By abusing his authority, the clerk had timber delivered to himself in the false name of 'Brown'. In that name he sold it to the defendants – who knew nothing of the fraud. When the fraud was discovered the plaintiff timber company sued for the timber back or its value. The defendants argued that the plaintiffs were estopped from claiming the title by having represented that the clerk had authority to sell the timber to them.

Held the defendants did not act on any representation by the plaintiffs about the clerk. In fact the defendants knew nothing of the plaintiff timber company; they dealt with the clerk in his own false name.

Note ——————————————————————————————————

See, also, agent's apparent authority, above, 1.3.1.

Eastern Distributers v Goldring (1957) CA

Murphy owned a Bedford van. He wanted to raise some money. So Coker, a car dealer, suggested that Murphy sold the van to the plaintiff hire-purchase company and repaid the money raised in instalments. In the event, Murphy signed blank (HP) proposal forms and a memo of agreement, and they pretended that Coker was selling the van to Murphy. The hire-purchase company bought the van and let it to Murphy, who then sold it to the defendant – who bought it in good faith. When Murphy defaulted, the hire-purchase company traced the van and sued the defendant for conversion. By the *nemo dat* rule the plaintiffs had no title to assert because they bought the van from a non-owner (Coker).

Held Murphy was estopped by his conduct from denying the plaintiffs' title. Therefore when Murphy sold the van 'again' (to the defendant) he did not have title, it being vested in the plaintiff. Consequently, judgment was entered for the plaintiff hire-purchase company.

Central Newbury Car Auctions v Unity Finance (1957) CA

A rogue offered to buy a Morris car on hire-purchase. He filled in a proposal form and persuaded the plaintiff car dealers to part with possession of the car and its registration document (log book). However, the hire-purchase company refused to finance the deal because the rogue gave a false address. Eventually, the car came into the hands of a dealer who sold the car to a second hire-purchase company (with possession being taken by one Powell) and the fraud was discovered. The plaintiffs claimed the car from the second hire-purchase company under the *nemo dat* rule. In response, the defendants claimed ownership, stating that the plaintiffs were estopped by their conduct, that is clothing the rogue with apparent ownership.

Held (2:1) no estoppel arose because the parting with possession of the goods was not enough to clothe a person with apparent ownership. A car's registration document (log book) was *not* a document of title.

Shaw v Commissioner of Police of the Metropolis (1987) CA

A student, Mr Natalegawa, advertised for sale his Porsche car in a newspaper. A rogue calling himself London replied stating that he had a buyer for the car. Natalegawa gave London possession of the car, its registration document (log book) with the notice of sale slip signed, and a signed disclaimer of legal responsibility for the car. In return London gave Natalegawa a post-dated cheque for £17,250. By doing this, Natalegawa was 'backing both ways': London had agreed to purchase the car himself in the event of the initial deal falling through. However, Shaw, a car dealer, agreed to buy the car from London and gave him a bankers' draft for £10,000; London then gave Shaw possession of the car. London failed to cash the bankers' draft and disappeared. The fraud was discovered and the police impounded the car. Both Shaw and Natalegawa claimed ownership. Natalegawa based his claim on the *nemo dat* rule. Shaw claimed that Natalegawa was estopped by his conduct, that is clothing London with apparent ownership of the car.

Held Natalegawa's conduct amounted to a representation that London was the owner of the car. However, s 21 of the SGA, which puts this estoppel on a statutory basis, states: 'Subject to this Act, where goods are sold by a person who is not their owner ...' In this case there was no 'sale' between London and Shaw, only an agreement to sell: the bankers' draft was never cashed and so no property in the car ever passed to Shaw. Consequently, the car still belonged to Natalegawa.

12.2.2 Estoppel by negligence

Mercantile Credit v Hamblin (1965) CA

Mrs Hamblin wished to raise some money, so she approached a respected car dealer who suggested that the money be raised upon the security of her Jaguar car. She signed some blank forms under the impression that the dealer would use them to discover how much money might be raised. Unbeknown to her, he completed them so as to constitute an offer to sell the Jaguar to the plaintiff hire-purchase company, who accepted the offer. Mrs Hamblin repudiated the agreement. The plaintiff asserted that she was estopped by her negligent conduct (in signing the blank forms) from asserting her title to the car.

Held although Mrs Hamblin owed the plaintiff a duty of care, she was not in breach of that duty because it was reasonable to have trusted a reputable car dealer.

Moorgate Mercantile v Twitchings (1977) HL

McLorg took a car on hire-purchase. The hire-purchase company (Moorgate) were, therefore, the new owners of the car. However, they failed to register the agreement with Hire Purchase Information Ltd (HPI). HPI hold a register upon which hire-purchase companies may record agreements, which enables potential purchasers of a car to check if it actually belongs to a hire-purchase company and not the seller. Nearly all car dealers used this service. McLorg offered the car to the defendant dealer, who checked the HPI register. As the car was not recorded on the register the dealer bought the car. Moorgate then sued the dealer for conversion asserting the *nemo dat* rule. The dealer argued that Moorgate were estopped because they owed a duty of care to car dealers to register all hire-purchase agreements. They were in breach of that duty by their negligent omission to register the agreement.

Held (3:2) that as HPI was a voluntary scheme no duty of care was owed to the defendant by Moorgate. The minority said that as in practice 98% of hire-purchase companies used the HPI register, it was foreseeable the dealer would suffer loss.

12.3 *Nemo dat* exceptions – s 2 of the Factors Act 1889 – sale by mercantile agent

Section 2 of the Factors Act 1889

(1) Where a mercantile agent is, with the consent of the owner, in possession of goods or the documents of title to goods, any sale, pledge, or other disposition of the goods, made by him when acting in the ordinary course of business of a mercantile agent, shall, subject to the provisions of this Act, be as valid as if he were expressly authorised by the owner of the goods to make the same; provided that the person taking under the disposition acts

in good faith, and has not at the time of the disposition notice that the person making the disposition has not authority to make the same.

12.3.1 The seller must be a mercantile agent

Section 1 of the Factors Act 1889 (or s 26 of the SGA)

(1) The expression 'mercantile agent' shall mean a mercantile agent having in the customary course of his business as such agent authority to sell goods or to consign goods for the purposes of sale, or to buy goods, or to raise money on the security of goods.

Weiner v Harris (1910) CA

Fisher had a jewellery shop. He also travelled the country selling jewellery. Weiner entrusted jewellery with him to sell. Fisher instead pledged it to a pawnbroker called Harris, who claimed good title under s 2 of the FA. Weiner contended that Fisher was not a mercantile agent as his main business was running a shop.

Held Fisher travelled the country selling goods on behalf of Weiner – he was a mercantile agent and s 2 applied.

Lowther v Harris (1927)

Colonel Lowther engaged Prior, who owned a shop specialising in glassware, to find purchasers for two tapestries. Prior was given possession of the goods with instructions not to sell without consent. Nevertheless Prior sold the tapestries without Lowther's consent to Harris. Harris claimed good title to the tapestries under the *nemo dat* exception, sale by mercantile agent. One argument put by Lowther was that Prior was not a mercantile agent under the Factors Act: s 1(1) defines a mercantile agent as one '… having in the customary course of his business as such agent authority to sell goods'.

Held the fact that Prior's general occupation was not that of an agent, but a shopkeeper, and that he had only one principal, did not prevent him being a mercantile agent under the Factors Act in this transaction.

Budberg v Jerwood and Ward (1934)

The Baroness Budberg, a Russian refugee, wanted to sell her pearl necklace. So she entrusted it to Dr de Wittchinsky, a lawyer who acted as legal adviser to Russian refugees. Without the knowledge of Budberg, Wittchinsky sold the necklace to Jerwood and kept the proceeds. When she discovered the truth Budberg sued Jerwood for the return of the necklace. Jerwood claimed, *inter alia*, that title had passed to him under s 2 of the Factors Act because Dr de Wittchinsky acted as mercantile agent for Budberg.

Held although a person with just one customer could be a mercantile agent (see *Lowther v Harris* above), he was not a mercantile agent unless he acted in a business capacity. Here there was no suggestion that Dr de Wittchinsky would be paid and it was clear that he acted for Budberg as a friend. Thus it was ordered that the necklace be returned to Budberg.

12.3.2 Possession of the goods must be with the consent of the owner
(See, also, buyer in possession, below, 12.5.3.)

Folkes v King (1923) CA
Folkes entrusted his car to a mercantile agent (a dealer) to obtain offers, but not to sell below £575. The dealer immediately sold the car for £340 and after several sales King bought the car. The dealer's act amounted to 'larceny by trick'. Folkes sued for the return of his car but King claimed that title had passed under s 2 of the Factors Act. *Folkes'* case relied on older cases which held that where there was a larceny by trick there was no consent by the owner to the rogue's possession. Therefore, as the dealer obtained possession by larceny by trick, he did not have possession of the car with the owner's consent, which is a requirement for s 2 to operate.

Held for the purposes of s 2 consent is given if the owner intentionally deposited the goods with the agent, even if this was induced by fraud or trick.

Pearson v Rose and Young (1951) CA
A car was given to a mercantile agent (a dealer) to obtain offers, but not to sell without consent. The dealer obtained possession of the car's registration document by trick where there was no consent: he asked to look at the document for a few moments to check some details and while it was in his hands he was called away to the telephone. On his return he asked the owner to accompany his wife (whom the owner knew) to hospital. The owner obliged, forgetting about the registration book. Meanwhile the dealer sold the car! The buyer claimed that title had passed under s 2 of the Factors Act.

Held s 2 required that the agent had possession of the *goods* with the consent of the owner. Although the dealer had possession of the car with the consent of the owner, there was no such consent to his possession of the registration document. As the registration document was part of the 'goods', the agent did not have possession of the goods with consent. Thus the agent could not pass title under s 2. *Obiter,* where the owner is induced to part with goods by fraud or misrepresentation, that does not negate consent. The owner has clothed the rogue with apparent authority to sell the goods and should not be able to recover them from an innocent purchaser. This dictum was applied in *Du Jardin v Beadman* (1952) a case on s 9 of the FA (s 25 of the SGA), see below, 12.5.3.

Beverley Acceptances v Oakley (1982) CA

A rogue, Oakley, pledged two Rolls Royce cars to Green as security against a loan. Green kept the cars locked in a compound and lent the keys, along with the registration document for one of cars, to Oakley, who falsely said that he needed to show the cars to someone for insurance purposes. In fact Oakley showed the cars and registration document to a potential buyer, Beverley. Over two weeks later Oakley sold the cars to Beverley and gave them a receipt. Beverley sued Oakley for the cars, claiming that Oakley was a mercantile agent for Green and so title had passed to them under s 2 of the FA.

Held (2:1) even if it were said that Green was the owner and Oakley the mercantile agent in possession when he had the keys, that possession had lapsed by the time the sale was made. Possession and disposition must be simultaneous. Thus the buyer was not protected and could not claim title under s 2 of the FA. Also (2:1), the registration book was not a document of title; it contained a warning that the registered keeper is not necessarily the owner.

12.3.3 Where the agent is part-owner of the goods

Lloyds Bank v Bank of America (1938) CA

Strauss & Co pledged a bill of lading (a document of title to goods) with Lloyds as security for a loan. Lloyds then returned the bill to Strauss under a 'letter of trust', which enabled Strauss to sell the goods (under the bill) as mercantile agent and trustee for the bank in order to repay the loan. So Strauss were the legal owners of the bill and equitable owners subject to a prior claim by Lloyds. However, Strauss pledged the bill to the Bank of America for a cash advance. Then Strauss went into liquidation and Lloyds claimed title to the bill arguing that s 2 of the FA could not protect the Bank of America because as the agents were (part) owners of the goods they could not be said to be 'in possession with the consent of the owner' within s 2.

Held where ownership was divided among two or more persons, those persons constituted the 'owner' for the purposes of s 2. Consequently, as Lloyds and Strauss consented to Strauss's possession, that requirement of s 2 was satisfied and title passed to the Bank of America.

12.3.4 Consent must be given *qua* mercantile agent

Staffs Motor Guarantee v British Wagon Co (1934)

Heap was a mercantile agent who dealt in lorries. He sold a Commer lorry to British Wagon, who hired it back to Heap under a hire-purchase agreement. Then Heap, being in possession, fraudulently sold the lorry to Staffs Motor. Later, Heap defaulted on his hire-purchase payments and British

Wagon repossessed the lorry from Staffs Motor. Staffs Motor claimed that they had obtained good title to the lorry under s 2 of the Factors Act.

Held although Heap took possession with the consent of the owner (British Wagon), that consent was given to Heap as a hirer under a hire-purchase agreement, not as a mercantile agent. Thus, s 2 of the Factors Act did not apply.

Astley Industrial Trust v Miller (1968)

A firm called Droylesden ran a self-drive car-hire business and also dealt in second-hand cars. They did not own the hire cars, but took them on hire-purchase. On one occasion, Droylesden took a Vauxhall car on hire-purchase from Astley. However, Droylesden then sold the car to Miller. Later Droylesden defaulted on the hire-purchase payments and Astley sued Miller, claiming title to the car. Miller claimed that he had obtained good title under s 2 of the Factors Act.

Held possession of the car was given to Droylesden as hirers under a hire-purchase agreement, not as mercantile agents. And so Miller was bound to return the car to Astley or pay its value.

12.3.5 The buyer must take in good faith and without notice of a defect in the title

Oppenheimer v Frazer (1907) CA

A mercantile agent obtained possession of some diamonds from Oppenheimer on false pretences. He then sold them to two joint-purchasers and fled the country. Only the first of the two buyers was aware of the fraud. Oppenheimer sued both parties in conversion. The second party claimed title had passed under s 2 of the Factors Act because he, personally, acted in good faith and without notice of the fraud.

Held where one of the joint-purchasers acted in bad faith, the other purchaser would not be protected by s 2.

Heap v Motorists Advisory Agency Ltd (1923)

A rogue called North was in possession of Heap's Citroen car as a mercantile agent (for the purposes of the Factors Act). North sold the car to the defendant car dealers in the following circumstances: (i) North used a friend to sell the car on his behalf; (ii) the sale price was £110 whereas the car was worth about £210; (iii) no registration document was offered with the car; and (iv) North refused a crossed cheque saying that he had no bank account nearby and accepted only an open cheque.

Held that the buyers had notice of a defect in the title of the car and so were not afforded the protection of s 2 of the FA.

Note

It was also held that the buyer bore the onus of proof that he had no notice.

12.3.6 The mercantile agent must be acting in the ordinary course of business

Oppenheimer v Attenborough (1908) CA

A diamond broker was entrusted with diamonds by the plaintiff dealer under the pretence of showing them to customers. The broker pledged them to the defendant pawnbroker instead. The plaintiff claimed that title could not have passed to the pawnbrokers under s 2 of the Factors Act because: (i) it was a custom of the trade that diamond brokers' had no authority to pledge goods; and (ii) the pawnbroker thought that he was dealing with the owner of the diamonds, not an agent, therefore the pledge was not in the 'ordinary course of business' as required by s 2.

Held on point (i), authority conferred by s 2 was a general authority and not limited by a trade custom. On point (ii) Buckley LJ said that 'ordinary course of business' meant: '… within business hours, at a proper place of business and in other respects in the ordinary way in which a mercantile agent would act …' so as not to put the pledgee on notice. Thus, it was irrelevant whether the broker dealt as owner or agent and title could pass to the pawnbroker under s 2.

Stadium Finance v Robbins (1962) CA

Robbins left his Jaguar car with a dealer under a tentative arrangement where the dealer was to find a purchaser. Robbins kept the keys but, unknown to both parties, the registration document was locked in the glove compartment. The dealer sold the car to Stadium Finance. Meanwhile Robbins recovered the car from the dealer. Later Stadium Finance sued Robbins for conversion, arguing that title had passed to them under s 2 of the Factors Act.

Held for s 2 to apply the sale must have been in the ordinary course of business. The sale was made without a registration document or keys. This was not in the ordinary course of business and so Stadium Finance were not protected by s 2 of the Factors Act. Judgment was given in favour of Robbins.

12.4 *Nemo dat* exceptions – s 8 of the Factors Act 1889 (s 24 of the Sale of Goods Act 1979) – seller continues in possession

Section 8 of the Factors Act 1889 (or s 24 of the SGA)

Where a person, having sold goods, continues, or is, in possession of the goods, or of the documents to title of the goods, the delivery or transfer by that person, or by a mercantile agent acting for him, of the goods or documents to title under any sale, pledge or other disposition thereof, [or under any agreement for sale, pledge or other disposition thereof,] to any person receiving the same in good faith and without notice of the previous sale, shall have the same effect as if the person making the delivery or transfer were expressly authorised by the owner of the goods to make the same.

Note ───

The words in brackets appear in the Factors Act only.

12.4.1 Continues or is in possession of the goods

Mitchell v Jones (1905) NZ

The seller sold and gave possession of a horse to the buyer. Later, he took the horse back on lease and wrongfully sold it to a third party.

Held the third party could not obtain title because the seller was not a 'seller in possession'. He had given up possession to the buyer and came back into possession, not as seller, but as bailee (under the lease). He could not, then, pass title to the third party.

Pacific Motor Auctions v Motor Credits (1965) PC

A car dealer called Motordom had in their showroom cars belonging to the plaintiffs, Motor Credits, under a 'display plan' agreement: Motordom would sell their cars to Motor Credits but keep them in their showroom; they would then sell them as agents for Motor Credits. So Motordom had possession of the cars first as owners and then as agents, or bailees, of Motor Credits. Pacific Auctions were owed money by Motordom and 'purchased' and took away 16 cars as security against the debt. However, Motor Credits were also owed money by Motordom and had instructed them not to sell any more of their cars. They demanded the return of the cars from Pacific Auctions, arguing that title could not be passed by a 'seller in possession', because by the display plan agreement as soon as Motor Credits bought a car, Motordom held it not as 'seller', but as agent or bailee. This was unlike the case where the seller might keep possession purely as seller, and fraudulently sell the goods to an innocent third party.

Held the words 'continues in possession' in s 24 mean 'continues in *physical* possession' and where there is a change in the legal status of the seller the section still applies. The section will not apply where there is a *break* in possession; that was not the case here.

Worcester Works Finance v Cooden Engineering Co (1972) CA

Cooden sold a Ford Zephyr car to a rogue dealer called Griffiths. Griffiths then sold the car to the plaintiff finance company (for £450) under the pretence that it was to be let to Millerick. In fact, Griffiths retained possession (without the consent of the finance company) and paid instalments to the finance company. Then Cooden repossessed the car because Griffiths' cheque was dishonoured. Later, Griffiths defaulted on the instalments and the finance company sued Cooden in conversion. Cooden claimed that title had passed under s 8 of the Factors Act because Griffiths was a 'seller in possession'.

Held although Griffiths held the car as seller and then as hirer, he continued in physical possession, and that was enough for s 8 of the FA to apply. Secondly, the repossession of a car, although not a 'sale' amounted to a 'disposition' within s 8. Thirdly, it was not necessary that possession (by Griffiths) was with the consent of the owner (finance company). Hence Cooden obtained good title under s 8.

12.5 *Nemo dat* exceptions – s 9 of the Factors Act 1889 (s 25 of the Sale of Goods Act 1979) – buyer in possession

Section 9 of the Factors Act 1889 (or s 25 of the SGA)

Where a person having bought or agreed to buy goods, obtains with the consent of the seller possession of the goods or the documents of title to the goods, the delivery or transfer, by that person or a mercantile agent acting for him, of the goods or documents of title under any sale, pledge or other disposition thereof, [or under any agreement for sale, pledge or other disposition thereof,] to any person receiving in good faith and without notice of any lien or other right of the original seller in respect of the goods, shall have the same effect as if the person making the delivery or transfer were a mercantile agent in possession of the goods or documents of title with the consent of the owner.

Notes

1 The words in brackets appear in the Factors Act only.

2 A conditional sale within the Consumer Credit Act 1974 is omitted from this *nemo dat* exception (s 9(i) and (ii) of the Factors Act; s 25(2) of the SGA).

12.5.1 Bought or agreed to buy goods

Lee v Butler (1893) CA

Hardy supplied furniture to Lloyd on a 'hire and purchase' agreement (now known as a conditional sale, see above, 8.1.6): Lloyd would pay 'rent' for the goods over a three month period and property would only pass when all the payments were complete. Before all of the payments were made, Lloyd sold the furniture to Butler. Hardy assigned his rights to Lee, who claimed to be entitled to the goods. Lee argued that s 9 of the Factors Act did not apply to pass title to Butler because Lloyd had not 'bought or agreed to buy' the goods as required by the Act; instead she had 'hired' them.

Held although described as a 'hirer', Lloyd was bound to buy the goods from the outset; property would pass at the end of the 'hire' period. Therefore Lloyd had 'agreed to buy' the goods and passed title to Butler under s 9.

Note

Now s 25(2) of the SGA has reversed this decision where the conditional sale falls within the Consumer Credit Act 1974.

Helby v Mathews (1895) HL

Brewster agreed to hire a piano from Helby on terms that if Brewster paid 36 monthly instalments the piano would become his property. Brewster could, however, return the piano at any time during the hire period. Brewster pledged the piano to a pawnbroker, Mathews, who claimed that title had passed under s 9 of the Factors Act.

Held Brewster had not agreed to buy the piano from the outset; he had only an option to buy. Therefore he had not 'bought or agreed to buy' the goods and s 9 did not apply to pass title to Mathews.

Dawber Williamson Roofing v Humberside CC (1979)

A contractor, who had agreed to renovate a building, employed a sub-contractor to supply and fit some roof tiles. The tiles were delivered to the site but then the contractor became bankrupt before paying the sub-contractor. The owner of the building claimed to be entitled to the tiles under s 9 of the Factors Act.

Held the contract to supply and fit the tiles was a contract for *services* and not a contract for the sale of goods and so s 9 did not apply. Therefore title could not have passed to the owner of the building.

Archivent Sales v Strathclyde Regional Council (1984) Sc

Archivent supplied a quantity of ventilators to Robertsons, a contractor engaged in building a school for the regional council, on terms that title to the goods remained with Archivent until payment was made in full. However, the contract between Robertsons and the regional council stipulated that as and when the council made interim payments the property in any building materials at the site would pass to them (the council). Archivent delivered the ventilators to the site, the council made an interim payment and then Robertsons went into receivership, not having paid Archivent. The council claimed title to the ventilators had passed under s 9 of the Factors Act.

Held the contract to supply the ventilators was a sale of goods contract and so s 9 applied. Robertsons had agreed to buy the goods and were in possession. The council had acted in good faith. Therefore, the ventilators became the property of the council when the interim payment was made.

Forthright Finance Ltd v Carlyle Finance Ltd (1997)

Forthright Finance supplied a Ford Cosworth car to Senator Motors under an agreement headed 'Hire Purchase'. However, a term of that agreement stated: 'When the Hirer ... has paid the balance payable and all other sums due to the Owner hereunder the Hirer shall be deemed to have exercised the option to purchase hereby given and the property in the goods shall pass to the Hirer ...' Senator then sold the car to Carlyle. Forthright then sued Carlyle in conversion. Carlyle argued that they acquired good title under s 25 of the SGA. However, s 25 only applies where the 'buyer in possession' (here Senator) has 'bought or agreed to buy' the goods. Therefore, if the agreement between Forthright and Senator was merely a *hire-purchase*, rather than a *sale*, s 25 would not apply.

Held although the agreement was titled 'hire-purchase', in substance, and in form, it was a conditional sale. Therefore, s 25 would operate to pass good title to Carlyle.

Note ───

Conditional sales within the Consumer Credit Act 1974 are exempt from the operation of s 25 of the SGA (see s 25(2)). However, in this case, the agreement was not one within the Consumer Credit Act.

12.5.2 Possession of the goods

Marten v Whale (1917)

Thacker agreed to buy a Renault car from Marten; the sale was dependent upon the completion of a land transaction between the parties, so this was a conditional sale. Meanwhile, Thacker borrowed the car and then sold it to Whale. The land transaction was never completed and Marten sued Whale to recover the car. Whale argued that he had obtained good title under s 9 of the Factors Act.

Held Thacker was in possession having 'agreed to buy the goods' and so s 9 applied and Whale obtained good title against Marten.

12.5.3 Consent of the seller

Du Jardin v Beadman (1952)

Beadman agreed to sell a Standard car to a rogue, Greenaway. Greenaway paid with a cheque and left a Hilman car as security until the cheque cleared. Later, though, Greenaway surreptitiously repossessed the Hilman. The cheque was dishonoured. Greenaway then sold the Standard car to Du Jardin who bought in good faith. Greenaway was later convicted of obtaining property (the Standard car) by false pretences. Beadman claimed title to the car, arguing that s 9 of the Factors Act did not apply because the car was obtained by fraud, not consent.

Held s 9 did apply because 'consent' in s 9 was not negated by fraud. *Dicta* in *Pearson v Rose and Young* (see above, 12.3.2) applied.

12.5.4 Sale has effect as if made by a mercantile agent

Lambert v G & C Finance (1963)

Lambert sold his car to a rogue and on the strength of a cheque reluctantly gave the rogue possession, but retained the car's log book. The cheque was dishonoured and the rogue sold the car to a dealer who resold it to G & C Finance, who claimed that title had passed to them under s 9 Factors Act.

Held (i) the retention of the log book revealed an intention that title should not pass until the cheque cleared; (ii) s 9 provided that the second sale (ie by the rogue) should have effect *as if* made by a mercantile agent. Under s 2 of the FA a mercantile agent can only pass title if he acted in the *ordinary course of business* of a mercantile agent. Thus s 9 did not apply because the car was sold by the rogue without its log book, and this was not a sale in the ordinary course of business of a mercantile agent.

Newtons of Wembley v Williams (1965) CA

Newtons agreed to sell a Sunbeam car to Andrew and on the strength of a cheque they gave Andrew possession of the car. The cheque was dishonoured. Newtons informed the police and HPI (see *Moorgate Mercantile v Twitchings* above, 12.2.2). About a month later, Andrew sold the car to Biss at an established, if unusual, streetside second-hand car market. Biss resold the car to Williams, who claimed good title against Newtons by s 9 of the Factors Act.

Held s 9 provided that the second sale (that is, by Andrew) should have effect *as if* made by a mercantile agent. Under s 2 of the Factors Act a mercantile agent can only pass title if he acted in the *ordinary course of business*. Thus, the sale between Andrew and Biss must have been in the ordinary course of business even if the buyer in possession was not actually a mercantile agent. In this case though, Andrew's sale could be protected by s 9 because on the facts it was in the ordinary course of business of a mercantile agent.

Notes

1 It was also held that Andrew's title was voidable (for fraud) and that when Newtons informed the police and HPI (they could not find the rogue) Andrew's voidable title reverted to Newtons. (See *Car and Universal Finance v Caldwell*, below, 12.6.1.) *However, that did not prevent s 9 of the Factors Act operating to divest Newtons of their title.*

2 This case has been criticised for reducing the protection given by s 9 of the Factors Act (or s 25 of the SGA) to innocent purchasers. See Atiyah, *The Sale of Goods*, 9th edn, 1995, pp 357–59.

12.5.5 'Delivery' of the goods by the non-owner

Gamer's Motor Centre v Natwest Wholesale (1987) Aus

Gamer's, a wholesaler, sold cars to retail dealers. One of those dealers, Evan & Rose Motors, in turn entered into a 'display plan' agreement with Natwest: Evans & Rose would sell their cars to Natwest, but keep them in their showroom and sell them as agents for Natwest. Gamer's supplied some cars to Evans & Rose, who then sold them to Natwest. However, Gamer's remained unpaid and so they seized the cars. Natwest sued Gamer's in conversion, asserting that Evans & Rose had passed title to them under the corresponding Australian legislation to s 25 of the SGA as 'buyers in possession'. However, for the section to operate there had to be a 'delivery' of the goods by the non-owner (that is, from Evans & Rose to Natwest). Gamer's argued that this meant *physical* delivery; and as the cars were never *physically* delivered to Natwest, no title could pass to them under the section. Consequently, Gamer's were entitled to the cars. The case turned then on the meaning of 'delivery' in the Australian SGA.

Held (3:2) 'delivery' for these purposes did not necessarily mean actual *physical* delivery. It could mean a change of possession effected by constructive or symbolic delivery. Hence, here the cars were 'delivered' by Evans & Rose to Natwest even though Natwest never took actual physical possession. Natwest had good title.

Forsythe International v Silver Shipping Co, *The Saetta* (1994)

Shipowners Silver chartered a ship to Petroglobe, who later purchased oil from Forsythe. The oil was sold with a retention of title clause, which provided that title to the oil would not pass until it was paid for. Later, Silver repossessed the ship, with the oil on board, from Petroglobe for non-payment on the charter. However, Forsythe remained unpaid for the oil so they brought an action against Silver for conversion of their oil. Silver argued that title to the oil had passed to them by virtue of s 25 of the SGA.

Held for title to have passed under s 25 there must have been a 'delivery' of the goods to the person claiming title (that is, Silver). 'Delivery' is defined by s 61(1) of the SGA as 'the voluntary transfer of possession'. In this case, Petroglobe did not *voluntarily* transfer the ship, it was taken from them. Therefore there was no delivery and s 25 could not pass title to Silver; the oil remained the property of the sellers, Forsythe.

Note ———————————————————————————
See Skelton [1994] LMCLQ 19.

12.5.6 Stolen goods and s 9 of the Factors Act 1889 (s 25 of the SGA)

National Employers Insurance Association v Jones (1988) HL

A Ford Fiesta car was stolen from Hopkin and after two resales it came to Autochoice who resold it to Mid-Glamorgan Motors who sold it to Jones. Hopkin's insurers claimed the car but Jones argued that he had obtained title under s 9 of the Factors Act. Jones pointed out that s 9 provided that consent to possession (to the 'buyer in possession') must be given by the *seller*, and not necessarily the original owner (that is, Hopkin). In which case Mid-Glamorgan Motors obtained possession with the consent of Autochoice (the 'seller'), and so the sale to Jones was protected by s 9.

Held rejecting that argument, it was clearly not the policy of this *nemo dat* exception to allow title to pass through a thief. Section 9 provided that the second sale (that is, to Jones) should have effect as if made by a mercantile agent. Under s 2 of the Factors Act a mercantile agent can only divest the owner (that is, Hopkin) of title to goods if he was entrusted with the goods by that owner. Accordingly, as Hopkin did not entrust any person with her car (it being stolen) s 9 could not confer a title on subsequent purchasers.

12.5.7 *Romalpa* clauses and s 9 of the Factors Act 1889 (s 25 of the SGA)

Re Highway Foods International Ltd (Mills v Harris) (1995)

Harris sold a large quantity of meat to Highway for £30,000. Highway then sub-sold the meat to Kingfry. Each contract contained a *Romalpa* clause (a clause reserving ownership with the seller until payment is made, see above, 10.6). It is unusual for a sub-sale to include such a clause. Neither Kingfry nor Highway had paid for the meat when Highway went into receivership. Harris claimed title to the meat in Kingfry's possession, arguing that title could not have vested in either Highway or Kingfry because neither had paid for the meat. Thus, the *Romalpa* clauses meant that title remained with Harris. However, it was argued that although Highway were not owners when they sub-sold to Kingfry, they could, as buyers in possession, pass good title under the *nemo dat* exception provided by s 9.

Held: (i) as Kingfry had not paid, title could not pass to them under the sub-sale contract; (ii) in the circumstances, s 9 could not pass title to Kingfry. The judge (Edward Nugee QC) relied on the following passage from *Benjamin's Sale of Goods*, 4th edn, para 5-128:

> ... more difficulty, however, arises, where the buyer in turn agrees to sell the goods to a sub-purchaser subject to a retention of title provision [a *Romalpa* clause], and delivers the goods to the sub-purchaser. In such a case it would seem that, unless and until the sub-purchaser has paid the price of the goods ...

the seller would be entitled to claim the goods as his property in the hands of the sub-purchaser.

Notes

1   This passage does not state an absolute rule that a *Romalpa* clause will prevail over the nemo dat exception, 'buyer in possession' (or the exception 'sale by mercantile agent'). Where the sub-purchaser has paid for the goods, a *nemo dat* exception could divest the original seller of his title. See, now, the fifth edition of *Benjamin's Sale of Goods*, para 5-151.

2   Note that s 9 of the Factors Act differs slightly from s 25 of the SGA in that only s 9 covers 'any *agreement* for sale, pledge or other disposition'. A contract containing a *Romalpa* clause would be an 'agreement for sale' and not a 'sale'.

12.6   *Nemo dat* exceptions – s 23 of the Sale of Goods Act 1979 – voidable title

12.6.1   The voidable contract must be rescinded before the resale

Re Eastgate ex parte Ward (1903)

A rogue fraudulently induced a tradesman, Bowling, to supply some furniture on credit. The rogue then absconded, owing Bowling £11. With the landlord's permission, Bowling broke into the rogue's residence and repossessed the furniture.

Held this was a voidable contract and the repossession amounted to rescission of the contract. Thus title to the furniture reverted to Bowling.

Car and Universal Finance Co Ltd v Caldwell (1965) CA

A rogue called Norris purchased Caldwell's Jaguar car with a cheque which was later dishonoured. As soon as he discovered the fraud Caldwell notified the police and the Automobile Association. Of course he was unable to locate Norris to communicate to him an intention to rescind the contract. At a later time, Norris sold the car to a car dealer called Motobella, and the car eventually came into the hands of the C & U Ltd. Caldwell claimed title to the car.

Held a contract induced by fraud brings the rogue only a voidable title; if the contract is rescinded before the rogue resells the goods the title will re-vest in the original owner. The general rule is that an intention to rescind must be communicated to the other party (in this case Norris) within a reasonable time. However, where that party, by absconding, deliberately makes it impossible to communicate an intention to rescind, the law will allow the innocent party to use other methods. In the circumstances of this case, Caldwell's notice of the fraud to the police and AA effectively rescinded the contract and Norris therefore had no title to pass to Motobella; Caldwell could recover his car.

12.6.2 Good faith and notice

Whitehorn Bros v Davison (1911) CA

A jeweller, Bruford, obtained a pearl necklace by fraud from Whitehorns. So Bruford had a voidable title. Bruford pledged the necklace to Davison, a pawnbroker, before Whitehorns could avoid the transaction. Whitehorns alleged that Davison had notice of the fraud and did not take in good faith, thus they could not have obtained title to the necklace.

Held for title to pass under the 'voidable title' exception, the third party (Davison) must take the goods without notice of the fraud and in good faith; however the onus lies on the original owner (Whitehorn) to prove such notice or bad faith.

> Note ────────────────
> This is the only *nemo dat* exception where such a burden is on the original owner.

12.7 Part III of the Hire Purchase Act 1964

Stevenson v Beverly Bentinck Ltd (1976) CA

Stevenson purchased from Roberts a Jaguar car, which was subject to a hire-purchase agreement with Beverly Bentinck, who, therefore, owned the car. Stevenson dealt in cars during his spare time, but this car was intended for his own private use. Beverly Bentinck claimed the car from Stevenson, who claimed good title under Pt III of the Hire Purchase Act, which confers title upon private buyers of cars subject to a hire-purchase agreement. The Act does not protect a 'trade or finance purchaser', that is, a business which deals wholly or partly in motor vehicles or finance companies who supply motor vehicles on credit.

Held the Act was concerned with the buyer's status and not the capacity in which he made the purchase. Thus, Stevenson was not protected by the Act.

Keeble v Combined Lease Finance plc (1996) CA

John Lay and Paul Murdy were business partners. Combined Lease Finance (CLF) supplied the partnership with a Mercedes-Benz car on hire-purchase terms. Both Lay and Murdy were debtors on the agreement. Later, Murdy left the business and Lay carried on alone. Then Lay sold the car to Keeble, a private purchaser who bought in good faith and without notice of the hire-purchase agreement. However, Lay failed to keep up the payments and CLF traced the car to Keeble and repossessed it. Keeble claimed good title under the *nemo dat* exception provided in Part III of the Hire Purchase Act 1964 (which confers good title upon private buyers of cars subject to a hire purchase agreement). CLF argued that in order for Part III of the Hire Purchase Act to operate, *both* of the debtors to the hire purchase agreement had to be party to the sale to the private purchaser.

Held the word 'debtor' in the Hire Purchase Act meant the persons – or *either* of the persons – who were the debtors under the hire purchase agreement. Accordingly, either of them, acting alone, could confer good title to a private purchaser acting in good faith. Thus the repossession was wrongful, as Keeble had acquired good title from just one of the debtors.

Q If the court had found in favour of CLF, would that have encouraged finance companies to persuade, for example, a debtor's spouse to become a party to a credit agreement, thus reducing greatly the scope of the *nemo dat* exception in the Hire Purchase Act?

13 Performance of the contract

13.1 Delivery

13.1.1 Symbolic delivery

Hilton v Tucker (1888)
Money was lent on the security of certain prints and etchings which, of course, had to be delivered to the lender (pledgee). The pledgor placed the items in a room hired from a third party and informed the lender that the third party held a key to the room 'which I place entirely at your disposal'. However, the pledgor retained a duplicate key for the purpose of cleaning the room and listing the items, but at all times he acknowledged the lender's superior control of the room.

Held the items had been delivered to the lender.

Dublin City Distillery v Doherty (1914) HL
Whisky was kept in a warehouse under the joint control of the distillery company and the Inland Revenue. Each party held a key to respective locks, so that one party could not enter without the other. The distillery company purported to pledge some of the whisky and issued warrants of delivery to the pledgee, although no key was given. The pledgee claimed to be entitled to the whisky under the warrants.

Held the whisky had not been delivered to the pledgee.

13.1.2 Delivery to a carrier by sea – s 32(3) of the SGA

Law and Bonar v British American Tobacco (1916), see below, 20.5.

Wimble v Rosenburg & Sons (1913) CA
Under a contract for the sale of 200 bags of rice FOB (Free on Board, see 19.1) Antwerp the buyer sent instructions for shipping, leaving it to the seller to nominate a ship. On 24 August, the goods were loaded but the buyer was not notified. On 25 August, the ship sailed but the following day it was lost. Neither party had insured the goods. Section 32(3) of the SGA provides that unless otherwise agreed, where the goods are to be sent by sea the seller must give notice to the buyer to enable the buyer to insure. The first issue was whether s 32(3) applied to FOB contracts. The second issue was whether, on the facts, the seller was liable under s 32(3).

Held (2:1) on the first issue that s 32(3) did apply to FOB contracts. Dissenting, Hamilton LJ stated that s 32(3) did not apply to FOB contracts as the seller did not 'send' goods to the buyer, he merely put them on a ship for dispatch to the buyer. On the second issue (2:1) the seller was not liable because, *per* Buckley LJ, on the facts the buyers had enough information for *particular* insurance: although they did not know the name of the ship, they knew what the freight was and the ports of loading and discharge. And as Hamilton LJ thought s 32(3) did not apply at all he held that the sellers were not liable for the loss. Dissenting on this issue, Vaugham Williams LJ stated that sellers should be liable; to hold otherwise would defeat the purpose of the sub-section.

Note

In theory s 32(3) applies to FOB contracts. However, in practice, this is of little consequence because the buyer will normally have enough information to insure.

13.1.3 Time of delivery

Hartley v Hymans (1920)

By a contract for the sale of cotton yarn, delivery was to be made in weekly instalments of 11,000 lbs each between September and November 1918. It was a term of the contract that the deliveries would be punctual. In the event the deliveries were short and late, continuing into March of the following year. During this period the buyer regularly complained and asked for better deliveries. In March the buyer eventually cancelled the contract. The seller brought an action for damages for refusing to take delivery of the remaining yarn.

Held in ordinary commercial contracts for the sale of goods the rule clearly was that time was of the essence with respect to delivery; thus the term requiring punctual delivery was a condition. However, the buyer, by his conduct, had waived his right to treat late deliveries as a breach of a condition. He was also estopped from doing so. In fact, a new agreement was created that delivery may be made within an extended and reasonable period. The seller was entitled to damages.

Bunge Corporation v Tradax Export SA (1981) HL

By a contract for the sale of soya-bean meal, the buyers were obliged to provide a ship and give notice to the sellers by 13 June. This was one of a string of sales for the bean meal. In the event the buyers did not give notice until 17 June. The sellers treated this as a breach of a condition and terminated the contract. The buyers claimed that this was a breach only of an innominate term which was not serious enough to warrant termination.

Held the time stipulation was a condition. The House of Lords then offered some guidelines on the status of stipulations of time:

(i)   consider if the contract is one of a string so that other commercial parties will be affected by delays;
(ii) a time stipulation can only be broken in one way;
(iii) consider if the performance of contractual duties by the innocent party depend upon the other party giving notice in time;
(iv) consider the difficulty of assessing damages if the term is not treated as a condition.

(See Atiyah, *The Sale of Goods*, 9th edn, 1995, pp 60–62.)

13.1.4 Delivery of too little – s 30(1) of the SGA

Champion v Short (1807)

A grocer ordered from the wholesalers quantities of French plums, raw sugar and white sugar. The delivery was short of the white sugar and the grocer accepted the plums but rejected the raw sugar. The wholesalers sued for the price of raw sugar.

Held this was a single contract; whereas the grocer was entitled to reject the whole delivery or accept all of the incomplete delivery, he could not divide his acceptance by rejecting just a portion of the delivery. The grocer was liable for the price of the raw sugar. See Hudson (1976) 92 LQR 506.

Behrend v Produce Brokers (1920)

The buyer agreed to purchase a quantity of cotton which lay aboard the ship *Port Inglis*. Delivery was to be in London. After a small part of the cotton was unloaded, it was discovered that the rest lay under cargo destined for Hull. So the ship went to Hull, unloaded the other cargo, and returned to London to unload the rest of the cotton. Meanwhile, the buyer indicated that he would not accept the second delivery.

Held the sellers were in breach of contract for not discharging all of the cargo before leaving for another port. Section 31(1) provides that unless otherwise agreed the buyer is not bound to accept instalments. Section 30(1) provides the buyer with a choice to either reject the whole or accept the lesser quantity and pay for it at the contract rate. Thus, the buyers should pay for the first delivery of cotton, but they were not bound to accept, or pay for, the remainder.

Gill & Duffas SA v Berger (1983) CA, HL

The sellers had agreed to deliver 500 tons of beans in two loads (445 tons and 55 tons). The buyers rejected both loads insisting that they were unmerchantable. It was found that in fact the first load was merchantable and so (initially) wrongfully rejected. However, the second load was unmerchantable and so that rejection was good.

Held by the Court of Appeal, that the buyers were entitled to reject both loads under s 30(1) (buyer may reject the whole if too little is delivered).

The rejection of the first load, originally wrongful, was retrospectively made good by the rejection of the second load. Once the buyers had rejected the second load, the sellers were guilty of failing to deliver the correct quantity (500 tons).

Note ──

This case was reversed by the House of Lords on a different point: see below, 13.3. It remains unaffected by s 3 of the SSGA 1994 which addresses the buyer's right to *partial* rejection.

───

13.1.5 Delivery of too much – s 30(2) and s 30(3) of the SGA

Hart v Mills (1846)

The defendant ordered 48 bottles of wine. However, 96 bottles were delivered. The defendant chose to keep just 13 bottles. The supplier sued on the original contract for the price of 48 bottles.

Held the seller was entitled to be paid only for the 13 bottles that the buyer retained. Alderson B suggested that as the buyer was entitled to reject the whole delivery (all 96 bottles) because too much had been sent; the retention of the 13 bottles created a new contract for that lesser amount. See Hudson (1976) 92 LQR 506.

Cunliffe v Harrisson (1851)

Under a contract for the sale of 10 hogsheads of wine, 15 hogsheads were delivered. In response to the buyer's complaint (that too much had been delivered) the seller suggested that the buyer keep the wine for several months before making a decision as to whether to buy all 15 hogsheads. The buyer agreed and after several months rejected the whole consignment. The seller sued for goods sold and delivered.

Held the delivery of too much is not performance of the contract at all. It amounts to a new offer which the buyer may accept or reject. The buyer rejected the offer within the time contemplated and so the seller's claim failed. See, now, s 30(2) and s 30(3) of the SGA.

Gabriel, Wade and English v Arcos (1929)

Under a contract for the sale of wood, too much was delivered. The buyer accepted the delivery including the excess.

Held where too much was delivered there were three possibilities: the buyer could reject the whole delivery; he could accept the correct quantity and reject the excess; or he could accept the whole and pay for the excess at the contract rate. This last option operates as a new contract. The sending of too much constituted an offer and the acceptance of the whole was the acceptance of that offer. Hence the buyer could not claim damages for breach of the original contract. See s 30(3) of the SGA.

13.1.6 Delivery of the wrong quantity and *de minimis*

Shipton Anderson v Weil Brothers (1912)

Under a contract for 4,500 tons wheat plus or minus 10%, 4,950 tons and 55 lbs were delivered; an excess of 1 lb in every 100 tons (or 20p in £40,000, which the buyers did not claim).

Held applying the *de minimis* maxim the buyers could not reject for delivery of too much.

Wilensko Slaski v Fenwick (1938)

Slightly less than 1% of timber failed to comply with the contract requirements, which allowed for more or less 10%.

Held that the buyer could reject the whole consignment – the *de minimis* principle was not applicable.

Note ──

The SSGA 1994 has amended s 30 of the SGA which now provides that in *non-consumer* contracts, where the wrong quantity has been delivered, the buyer *may not* reject the goods if the shortfall/excess is so slight it would be unreasonable to do so.

13.1.7 Voluntary transfer of possession

Forsythe International v Silver Shipping Co, *The Saetta* (1994), see above, 12.5.5.

13.2 Instalment deliveries – s 31 of the Sale of Good Act 1979

13.2.1 Severable contracts

Kingdom v Cox (1848)

A contract was made for the supply of 150 tons of cast-iron girders, to be made according to the buyer's drawings. The first set of drawings were to be delivered within three days of the contract. In the event they were delivered four days late and the suppliers (rightfully) terminated the contract. A few days later the buyer requested delivery of 14 tons and a few months after that he requested delivery of 50 tons. No goods were delivered and the buyer sued for damages.

Held the buyer was not entitled to call for delivery by instalments or of a smaller amount than the contract quantity. In any case, the seller's duties were discharged because of the late delivery of the drawings.

Tarling v O'Riordan (1878) Ire

A retailer ordered a quantity of clothes from a supplier; some of the clothes existed, but some were yet to be made. The clothes were delivered in two instalments: the existing clothes in the first and the rest in the second. The first instalment was satisfactory and accepted. The second instalment contained some clothes which did not comply with the contract, and it was rejected.

Held on the facts, the inference was that the goods would be delivered by instalments. Thus the buyer was entitled to reject the second instalment. See Hudson (1976) 92 LQR 506.

Jackson v Rotax (1910) CA

Jackson contracted to sell to Rotax motor car brass horns, 'deliveries as required'. The horns were delivered in 19 boxes by instalments. The buyer accepted one box but rejected all the others on the basis that the horns were dented and poorly polished and so unmerchantable. The sellers sued for the price of all the horns delivered.

Held the words 'delivery as required' showed that this was a contract by instalments. Therefore, the buyers, by accepting one consignment, did not lose their right to reject others.

Montebianco v Carlyle Mills (1981) CA

Carlyle Mills ordered 26,000 kilos of cloth at a cost of £107,947, to be delivered between June and September. Several deliveries were made but the buyers were unhappy with the quality and made numerous complaints until, in September, they purported to reject the goods. The sellers sought to rely on s 11(4) of the SGA which provided that a breach of a condition would be treated as a breach of a warranty where the buyer had accepted the goods. Section 11(4) only applied to non-severable contracts. The buyers contended that this was a severable contract.

Held the fact that delivery of goods under the contract was to be made by instalments, did not automatically mean that the contract was a severable one. This was not a severable contract and so rejection was not possible: the buyers had accepted the goods.

Note ——————————————————————————————————

Section 31(2) provides that where the deliveries are separately paid for, a breach (by either party) may be severable depending on the terms of the contract and the circumstances of the case.

13.2.2 Short deliveries and instalments

Munro v Meyer (1930)

In a contract to deliver 1,500 tons of meat and bone meal in instalments, each of 125 tons, it was found that about half was adulterated.

Held the breach was not severable and so the buyers were entitled to repudiate the whole contract.

Maple Flock v Universal Furniture Products (1934) CA

Maple flock contracted to sell 100 tons of rag flock to be delivered in thrice weekly instalments, each of 1.5 tons. Out of 20 instalments which had been delivered, one was not up to the agreed standard and on this basis the buyers purported to cancel the rest of the contract. The issue for the court was whether this breach was severable from the whole contract.

Held s 31(2) provides that this question should be considered in light of the terms of the contract and the circumstances of the case. The court stated that the main tests should be the ratio quantitatively which the breach bears to the whole contract and the probability that the breach will be repeated. In this case the delivery complained of amounted to 1.5 tons out of a total of 100 tons. As only one delivery out of 20 had proved to be unsatisfactory, it could not be inferred that further breaches would occur. Thus the breach was severable and the contract as a whole stood.

Warinco v Samor (1977)

In a contract to supply rape seed oil in instalments, the buyers rejected the first instalment alleging that the oil was the wrong colour. The sellers disputed this and stated that the second instalment would be identical to the first. The buyers insisted that the oil should conform to the contract and the sellers treated this as a repudiation of the whole contract and declined to supply any more oil. It was later settled that the oil did conform to the contract and so the buyer's rejection of the first instalment was wrong. The issue for the court was whether the buyer had evinced an intention to repudiate the whole contract or merely reject the first instalment.

Held the test is in three parts: (i) the degree to which one instalment is linked to another; (ii) the proportion of the contract affected by the allegedly repudiatory breach; and (iii) the probability that that breach will be repeated. In the circumstances, the buyer had not repudiated the whole contract.

Note

This decision was reversed by the Court of Appeal because the law was *applied* incorrectly. However, the law *as stated* was accepted as correct.

Regent v Francesco of Jermyn Street (1981)

Francesco contracted to buy 62 high quality men's suits; they were delivered in five instalments. However, one of the instalments was short by one suit and Francesco purported to cancel the whole contract. There were two issues for the court: was this a severable contract? and if it was, did the breach entitle the buyer to repudiate the whole contract?

Held this was a severable contract and as the breach did not go to the root of the contract the buyers were not entitled to repudiate the whole contract.

13.2.3 Late payment and instalments

Withers v Reynolds (1831)
Under a contract to supply straw in instalments of three loads per fort-
night, payment was to be made upon each delivery. After several weeks
the buyer insisted that payment should be made one delivery in arrears.
The seller refused to supply any more straw.

Held the buyer's refusal to pay upon delivery and insistence on credit
amounted to a repudiation excusing the seller from further performance
under the contract.

Freeth v Burr (1874)
Under a contract for iron to be delivered by two instalments, a late delivery of the first instalment entitled the buyer to damages. The buyer then
withheld payment for the second instalment in the erroneous belief that he
had a set-off against the seller with regard to the damages. He did, though,
express his willingness to persist with the contract and eventually paid for
the first instalment.

Held the buyer's refusal to pay was based upon a genuine mistake of
law and so this did not amount to a repudiation of the contract.

Mersey Steel v Benzon (1884) HL
A bankruptcy petition was filed against the seller of 5,000 tons of steel to
be delivered by five instalments. Acting on erroneous advice, the buyer
refused to pay for two instalments (already delivered) without the leave of
the court; however, he did express his willingness to persist with the contract, and make payments if possible.

Held the buyer's refusal to pay was based upon a genuine mistake of
law and so this did not amount to a repudiation of the contract.

Booth v Bowson (1892)
There was a contract to supply two trucks of coal per week for 12 months,
cash on delivery. Between September and February, deliveries were paid
for between six and eight weeks late. The sellers constantly objected to this.

Held the buyer's behaviour evinced an intention to repudiate the whole
contract.

Decro-Wall International SA v Practitioners in Marketing Ltd (1971) CA
The defendants contracted to buy tiles from the French plaintiffs and create a market in Britain as sole concessionaire. The tiles were delivered as
required by instalments. However, 26 out of 27 payments were made late,
some as late as 20 days.

Held this was not a repudiation of the contract by the buyers as the breaches did not go to the root of the contract.

13.3 Acceptance and repudiatory breach

Braithwaite v Foreign Hardwood Co (1905) CA

Under a contract for 100 tons of rosewood to be delivered in two instalments the seller dispatched 63 tons by ship. The buyers (wrongfully) repudiated the contract because they regarded sales of wood by the seller to another as a breach of a collateral contract. The sellers insisted upon making delivery but the buyers still refused to accept it. Eventually, the sellers resold the rosewood elsewhere. Later, the buyers discovered that some of the rosewood in question did not conform to the contract description and in defence to an action for non-acceptance they claimed that the sellers could not have performed in any case. In other words, the buyers' repudiation was correct, even if initially for the wrong reason.

Held the sellers would succeed because, in reselling the rosewood, they (eventually) accepted the buyers' repudiation and so the contract, with the seller's duty to deliver conforming goods, was terminated. Consequently, the buyers could no longer rely on that defence.

British & Beningtons Ltd v Western Cachar Tea Co (1923) HL

The buyers contracted to purchase tea to be delivered in London; no time was set for delivery, so delivery was to be within a reasonable time (s 29(3) of the SGA). However, by an order of the Shipping Controller the ships carrying the tea were diverted to various ports around Britain. The buyers repudiated the contract on the basis that a reasonable time for delivery had passed. It was held that a reasonable time had not passed and on appeal the buyers argued that the sellers had to prove that they had the *capacity* (as well as the will) to deliver in time.

Held the buyers' repudiation was an anticipatory breach. The sellers were not bound to prove their capacity to perform the contract. The buyers were liable in damages for non-acceptance.

Gill & Duffas SA v Berger (1984) HL

The sellers had agreed to deliver 500 tons of beans in two loads (445 tons and 55 tons). The buyers rejected both loads insisting that they were unmerchantable. It was found as fact that the first load was merchantable and so wrongfully rejected. However, the second load was unmerchantable and so that rejection was good.

Held the rejection of the first load was a repudiation of the contract which had been accepted by the sellers who, accordingly, were discharged from further obligations to deliver.

Note ───

This case remains unaffected by s 3 of the SASGA 1994 which provides for the buyer's right to *partial* rejection.

Fercometal v Mediterranean Shipping Co (1988) HL

Under a charterparty ('hire' of ship) the shipowners had to deliver the ship on a day certain for loading. They informed the charterers that it was going to be late. The charterers responded by repudiating the charterparty, which they had no right to do at that time under its terms. So the charterers were in anticipatory breach. The owners refused to accept that repudiation and then falsely said that, after all, the ship would be ready on time. The ship was delivered late but the charterers still refused to continue. The owners sued for breach of the charterparty. The charterers stated that although their repudiation may have been wrongful, the shipowners never had the capacity to perform and so the repudiation was correct, even if the wrong reason for it was given.

Held an anticipatory breach must be accepted or refused. So the innocent party (here the shipowners) must either: accept it and destroy duties of both parties; or reject it and keep the contract alive. If the shipowners had accepted the repudiation they would have been discharged from their obligation to perform the contract and could have sued the charterers for breach. However, as they did not accept the repudiation they were obliged to perform the contract; as they failed to do this the charterers were not liable. The innocent party could not reject the repudiation, thus keeping the contract alive, and yet be free from any duty to perform the contract.

Vitol v Norelf, *The Santa Clara* (1996) HL

Under a CIF (cost, insurance, freight – see below, 20.1) contract for the sale of propane at $400 per tonne it was agreed that the bill of lading (see below, 18.1) would be forwarded immediately after loading (which was to take place during certain days in March 1991). It was also agreed that payment was due 30 days after the date of the bill of lading. When March came, the propane market was falling. Whilst the ship was loading, the buyers telexed the sellers repudiating the contract on the grounds that the ship would not be loaded on time. The sellers completed loading and informed the buyers of this. However, they failed to send a bill of lading or do anything else in performance of the contract. Instead, they sold the propane elsewhere at just $170 per tonne – which was the market price at the time. The sellers then sued the buyers for the difference between the contract price ($400 per tonne) and the resale (or market) price ($170 per tonne) under s 50(3) of the SGA (see below, 14.2). It was held that the buyers' telex amounted to an anticipatory breach. The main issue was whether an acceptance of a repudiatory breach had to be communicated to the guilty party (here, the buyers) and whether the sellers' mere failure to perform the contract amounted to such an acceptance.

Held on the facts the failure of the sellers to forward the bill of lading as agreed was enough to notify the buyers that the sellers had accepted the buyer's repudiation. Lord Steyn stated:

For present purposes I would accept as established law the following propositions: (1) where a party has repudiated a contract the aggrieved party has an election to accept the repudiation or to affirm the contract: *Ferconmetal v Mediterranean Shipping* [above]; (2) an act of acceptance of repudiation requires no particular form: a communication does not have to be couched in the language of acceptance. It is sufficient that the communication or conduct clearly and unequivocally conveys to the repudiating party that the aggrieved party is treating the contract as at an end; (3) ... the aggrieved party need not personally, or by an agent, notify the repudiating party of his election to treat the contract as at an end. It is sufficient that the fact of election comes to the repudiating party's attention, for example, notification by unauthorised broker or other intermediatory may be sufficient ...

Postulate the case where an employer at the end of the day tells the contractor that he need not return the next day. The contractor does not return the next day or at all. It seems to me that the contractor's failure to return may, in the absence of any other explanation, convey a decision to treat the contract as at an end. Another example may be an overseas sale providing for shipment on a named ship in a given month. The seller is obliged to obtain an export licence. The buyer repudiates the contract before loading starts. To the knowledge of the buyer, the seller does not apply for an export licence with the result that the transaction cannot proceed. In such circumstances it may well be that an ordinary businessman, circumstanced as the parties were, would conclude that the seller was treating the contract as at an end.

Note

In *State Trading Corporation of India v Golodetz* (1989) the Court of Appeal suggested that saying or doing nothing at all cannot constitute acceptance of a repudiation. That was applied by the Court of Appeal in *Vitol*. That decision was reversed by the House of Lords, who took the view that all that is needed is that the decision to accept the repudiation came to the attention of the repudiating party.

Yukong Line v Rendsburg Investment Corporation of Liberia (1996)

In June 1995, Yukong ('owners') chartered a ship to Rendsburg ('charterers'). Before delivery of the vessel, due 23 January 1996, the charterers informed the owners that they no longer wished to proceed. This was an anticipatory breach. The owners replied the next day, stating that they were:

... really upset to receive notice of non-performance from charterers. Charterers' cancellation of charterparty is totally unacceptable and charterers are strongly requested to honour their contractual obligation according to charterparty ... In case of non-performance all damages, loss and other costs incurred ... thereby to be charterers' responsibility and liability.

Look forward to receiving honourable confirmation from charterers.

No confirmation was received and, on 1 February, the owners informed the charterers that they were accepting the repudiation. They then sued for breach of contract. In their defence the charterers argued that the owners' reply of 24 January amounted to an affirmation of the contract, and so after that it was no longer open to the owners to accept the repudiation, as they had purported to do on 1 February.

Held a party who repudiates a contract before the time for performance is not in breach; but the other party has a choice. He may elect to accept the repudiation and terminate the contract. Alternatively, he may affirm the contract. In that case the contract persists as though the repudiation never occurred: the repudiation is 'writ in water' (*per* Asquith LJ, *Howard v Pickford Tool Co Ltd* (1951) When deciding whether or not the innocent party has affirmed the contract, the court should not take an unduly technical approach. It should not find affirmation without an unequivocal statement to that effect. The doctrine of estoppel will prevent any injustice done to the repudiating party relying on such a statement. In this case, the owners' reply of 24 January did no more than try to persuade the charterers to continue with the contract. It did not amount to an affirmation of the contract.

Notes

1 The issue in this case was the *rejection* of the other party's repudiation whereas in *Vitol v Norelf* (above) it was the *acceptance* of the other party's repudiation.

2 Although this was not a sale of goods case, the principles are the same.

Glencore Grain Rotterdam BV v Lebanese Organisation for International Commerce (1997) CA

The buyers agreed to purchase 25,000 tonnes of wheat. The standard FOB contract (free on board, see below, 19.1) provided that the buyers would provide a ship and pay by an irrevocable and confirmed letter of credit (see below, Chapter 22). However, the buyers' letter of credit stipulated that the sellers' bill of lading (see below, Chapter 18) should be marked 'prepaid freight'. In due course the ship was a day late and for this reason the sellers refused to load. The buyers accepted this as a repudiatory breach and sued for damages. It was later settled that the sellers had no right to refuse to perform by reason that the ship was late. However, the sellers then argued that as the buyers were in breach by issuing a letter of credit inconsistent with the FOB contract, they were, after all, entitled to refuse to load the ship. In other words, although they gave a bad reason for refusing to perform, there existed a valid one, which they now sought to rely on.

Held the buyers were in breach of contract by stipulating that the bill of lading be marked 'prepaid freight'. So far as the sellers giving the wrong reason to perform is concerned, the general rule is that a party giving a wrong reason to justify non-performance is not deprived of a good reason if it existed, whether he was aware of it or not (*Taylor v Oakes Roncoroni* (1922)). However, the rule was subject three qualifications: (i) if the point not taken could have been corrected (*Heisler v Anglo-Dal* (1954); (ii) waiver and estoppel; (iii) where the goods or documents to title have been accepted (s 35 of the SGA, and see *Panchaud Frères SA v Etablissements General Grain Co* (1970)). In the instant case none of the qualifications applied, and so the sellers were not in breach of contract by refusing to load the ship because the buyers were already in breach by insisting upon the bill of lading being marked 'prepaid freight'.

Notes

1 Evans LJ thought that cases of waiver or estoppel would be very rare, because normally the non-performing party gives no reason at the time. Thus it would be difficult to imply a representation (necessary for estoppel) from a party's silence.

2 In *Panchaud Frères* Winn LJ suggested that a separate doctrine of 'fair conduct' was emerging. However the Court of Appeal in the instant case stated that there was no such doctrine.

3 *Panchaud Frères* was a case where the buyer accepted the documents of title and then tried to get out of the contract; the converse of the instant case where a party initially refused to perform and later relied on a valid reason to do so.

4 On the issue of the letter of credit see, further, below, 19.4.

14 Seller's remedies

14.1 Price – s 49(1) of the Sale of Goods Act 1979

Stein, Forbes & Co v County Tailoring (1916)

Under a CIF (cost, insurance, freight – see 20.1) contract for the sale of sheepskins the price was stipulated to be payable against the documents (which entitled the buyer to the goods) upon arrival of the ship. However, when the documents were tendered the buyers refused to accept them. The sellers sued for price under s 49(1) of the Sale of Goods Act (which required that property must pass for an action in price) arguing that although the property had not passed, this was the fault of the buyer.

Held as the property in the goods had not passed no action could lie for price under s 49(1); the only remedy for the sellers was an action for damages under s 50 of the SGA.

Colley v Overseas Exporters Ltd (1921)

By a contract to sell leather belting the buyers were obliged to nominate a ship and the seller obliged to load the goods. It was stipulated that the price would be paid when the goods were delivered to the ship. Despite several attempts the buyer failed to nominate a ship. The seller claimed the price from the buyer, asserting that although the property in the goods had not passed (a requirement of s 49(1)), this was the fault of the buyer.

Held no action could succeed for the price until the property had passed, save in special cases under s 49(2), even if the property did not pass because of a wrongful act by the buyer. The seller's remedy was an action for damages (under s 50).

14.1.2 Payment on a day certain – s 49(2) of the SGA

Polenghi v Dried Milk Co Ltd (1904)

By a contract for 500 tons of dried milk, sold by sample, payment was to be made 'in cash in London on arrival of the powders against shipping or railway documents'. The first instalment arrived and the documents were tendered, but the buyer (wrongfully) refused to pay until he had examined the bulk of the consignment.

Held a declaration was made that the sellers were entitled to payment. Further, the buyers were ordered to pay for the first instalment, which appeared to be a judgment based on s 49(2) and implies that the court considered the terms of the contract to refer to a 'day certain' in accordance with s 49(2).

Workman Clark & Co v Lloyd Brazileno (1908) CA

The seller agreed to construct a ship for the buyer, payment being due in instalments, the dates of which were to be ascertained by reference to stages of completion of the ship. The seller maintained an action for price under s 49(2) which provided that an action for price could be made when payment was due on a day certain.

Held the action would succeed because s 49(2) applied to instalments and that these instalments, by reference to stages of completion of the ship, were due on a day certain.

Stein, Forbes & Co v County Tailoring (1916)

For the facts, see above, 14.1.

The sellers also claimed that as the price was payable against the documents upon the arrival of the ship, the price was payable 'on a day certain' and so an action may be made under s 49(2).

Held the price was not payable 'on a day certain'; no *date* of payment was specified, the price was payable expressly upon the arrival of the ship and delivery of the documents and s 49(2) did not apply. The only remedy for the sellers was an action for damages (under s 50).

Muller, Maclean & Co v Anderson (1921)

Under a contract for a consignment of padlocks to be sent to Bombay, payment was due against the tender of the documents (which entitled the buyer to the goods).

Held the price was not payable 'on a day certain'; no *date* of payment was specified, the price was payable expressly upon the delivery of the documents and s 49(2) did not apply.

Hyundai Heavy Industries v Papadopoulos (1980) HL

Hyundai contracted to build and deliver a ship. Payment was to be made in five instalments, the dates of which were to be ascertained by reference to stages in the construction of the ship. The second instalment fell due on 15 July, but remained unpaid and on 6 September Hyundai (rightfully) cancelled the contract in accordance with its terms. The issue for the House of Lords was whether the July instalment remained due.

Held (*Dubitante* Lords Russell and Keith) this was a contract for services and not a contract of sale. The point of the distinction is that from the moment the contract was made the ship builder was obliged to incur expense in preparation, for example, the cost of design. Thus Hyundai were entitled to payment of the July instalment.

Q What if the entire price had been due; could the shipbuilders have sued for it and yet not be bound to deliver? See Atiyah, *The Sale of Goods*, 9th edn, pp 432–36.

Notes

1 Two (from five) of the Law Lords were *dubitante*. This means that although they had doubts about the law as stated by the majority, they did not go as far as to state that it was incorrect.

2 The majority's decision was followed by a unanimous House of Lords decision in *Stocznia Gdanska SA v Latvian Shipping Co* (1998)

14.2 Damages for non-acceptance – s 50 of the Sale of Goods Act 1979

14.2.1 Available market – s 50(3) of the SGA

In re Vic Mill Ltd (1913) CA

Vic Mill ordered seven lots of goods from the engineers, Arundel & Co. Five of those lots were to be manufactured by Arundel and two bought in and resold. However, after just one of the lots had been made Vic Mill went into liquidation and could not accept any of the goods. Arundel made a claim from the liquidators for their loss of profit. However, the liquidator claimed that the damages should be assessed by reference to the available market.

Held as most of the items had yet to be made, and others were yet to be purchased (by Arundel), there was no available market. Arundel were entitled to be put in the position as if the contract were performed and so the damages should reflect their loss of profit.

Thompson v Robinson (1955)

Robinson agreed to buy a Vanguard car from Thompson, a car dealer, but then wrongfully refused to accept delivery. Thompson would have made a profit of £61 and he sued Robinson for that amount under s 50(2) of the SGA. At the time retail prices were fixed and the supply of Vanguard cars exceeded demand. Robinson argued that the dealer could have sold the car elsewhere, and so his loss came under s 50(3) and was nominal.

Held an available market is the situation where in a particular trade in a particular area the particular goods were freely sold *and* that market could absorb readily all the goods thrust upon it should the buyer default. In the circumstances, there was no available market and Thompson was entitled to £61 loss of profit. Even where there was an available market, s 50(3) provided only a *prima facie* rule which need not be applied where it would be unjust to do so.

Charter v Sullivan (1957) CA

The defendant refused to accept delivery of a Hilman Minx car which he had agreed to buy from the plaintiff car dealers. The dealers resold the car within 10 days and admitted that they could sell all the Hilman Minx cars that they could get. They sued the buyer for their loss of profit. At the time retail prices were fixed.

Held an available market is the situation where 'goods are available for sale in the market at the market price in the sense of the price, whatever it may be, fixed by reference to supply and demand as the price at which a purchaser for the goods in question can be found, be it greater or less than or equal to the contract price'. In this case there was no available market because the retail prices were fixed. Nonetheless, on ordinary principles (that is, s 50(2)) it was held that the dealer could recover nominal damages only, as this was a substituted, not an additional sale. In the circumstances of demand outstripping supply the dealer did not sell one car less because of the buyer's repudiation. Therefore, the dealer suffered no loss of profit.

Lazenbury Garages Ltd v Wright (1976) CA

Wright agreed to buy a second-hand BMW car for £1,670 from Lazenbury Garages, but later refused to accept delivery. Some two months later the garage resold the car for £1,770, £110 more than Wright was going to pay for it. Nevertheless the garage sued Wright for the loss of profit on the sale, namely £345. They argued that had Wright taken the car, they would have sold another car to the second customer. Therefore Wright's repudiation meant that they had sold one car less.

Held a second-hand car is a unique chattel, therefore there was no available market for the BMW. Lazenbury suffered no loss at all and would not be awarded any damages.

Shearson Lehman Hutton Inc v Maclaine Watson (No 2) (1990)

The seller and buyer concluded contracts for the sale of nearly 8,000 tonnes of tin for a total price of £70m, delivery 12 March. The buyers refused to accept the goods and the sellers sued for damages. It was agreed that the damages should be assessed by reference to the available market. However, the price obtainable on 12 March was disputed.

Held it would be unfair on the buyers to assess the price as if such a huge amount as 8,000 tonnes were put into the market on a single day (12 March), because the price would be artificially low. It would be fairer to assume that the contracts for the disposal of the tin were negotiated over several days. This was permissible under s 50(3) of the SGA, and even if not permissible, the words *'prima facie'* in that sub-section allowed the court to depart from the strict words of the statute.

14.2.2 No available market – s 50(2) of the SGA

Hadley v Baxendale (1854)

The plaintiffs owned a flour mill and delivered a broken shaft to a carrier to be sent to engineers as a pattern for a new one to be made. Without the shaft, the mill could not operate. The carrier delayed in transporting the shaft and the mill owners suffered loss of profits. They sued for the loss.

Held the mill owners were only entitled to damages for loss directly and naturally resulting from the carriers' breach (the 'first rule' – see now ss 50(2), 51(2) and 53(3) of the SGA). This did not include loss of profits, as any reasonable carrier would have assumed that the mill possessed another shaft or that the mill would be inoperative for other reasons. If the mill owners had informed the carrier of the special circumstances then they could have claimed for the loss of profits as special damages (the 'second rule' – see now s 54 of the SGA).

Harlow and Jones v Panex (1967)

Under a contract for the sale of 10,000 tons of steel blooms at $62.25 per ton, the buyers wrongfully refused to take delivery (see, further, below, 19.4). The sellers had ordered the steel from a Russian supplier and were left with the goods on their hands, as the market had fallen steeply. Eventually, the Russian suppliers took back 1,500 tons at cost and helped sell the remaining 8,500 tons at $56 per ton. The sellers claimed damages from the buyers.

Held there was no available market and so s 50(2) of the SGA applied: the loss directly and naturally arising in the ordinary course of events. In this case that was the difference between the contract price and the value of the goods at the date when the buyer ought to have accepted. As to the 1,500 tons, this meant the difference between the purchase price (the price charged by the Russians) and the contract price ($62.25). As to the 8,500 tons it meant the difference between the contract price ($62.25) and the price eventually obtained by the resale ($56).

14.3 Lien – ss 41, 42 and 43 of the Sale of Goods Act 1979

14.3.1 Right to withhold delivery – s 39(2) of the SGA

Ex parte Chalmers, Re Edwards (1873) CA

Under a contract of sale, goods were to be delivered by monthly instalments, with payment to be made 14 days after delivery. The penultimate instalment was delivered, but not paid for. So the seller withheld delivery of the final instalment until the price of these last two deliveries was paid. The property in the goods of the final instalment remained with the seller.

Held the seller was entitled to withhold delivery. This quasi-lien arose even though property had not passed.

14.3.2 When the lien arises

Spartali v Benecke (1850)

A contract for the sale of 30 bales of goats' wool allowed one month's credit. The sellers refused to deliver the bales until the price was paid.

Held the sellers enjoyed no lien over the goods during a period of credit. The buyers were entitled to immediate delivery.

Somes v British Empire Shipping Co (1860) HL

A shipwright took in a ship from Somes for repair. When it was finished, Somes asked for time to pay. The shipwright refused and enforced his (repairer's) lien for the cost of the repair plus £21 per day for keeping the ship in dock.

Held the lien was good against the repair cost, but could not be exercised in respect of storage charges arising from the exercise of the lien. Somes did not have to pay extra for the keeping of his ship in dock.

> Note
>
> The SGA twice states (s 39(1)(a) and s 41(1)) that the lien is for the *price*. See, generally, Atiyah, *The Sale of Goods*, 9th edn, 1995, p 404.

Great Eastern Railway v Lord's Trustee (1909) HL

The railway company regularly supplied coal to Lord, a coal merchant. Lord was allowed into the railway company's yard to stack and otherwise deal with the coal. When Lord fell into arrears the railway company exercised its lien over the coal and refused to deliver.

Held although Lord had a measure of control over the coal it remained under the general control of the railway company. Hence the lien was not lost and the railway company were entitled to withhold delivery against payment.

> Note
>
> Compare this case with *Cooper v Bill* (below, 14.3.3).

Poulton v Anglo-American Oil Co (1910) CA

Thames Paper Mills sold three boilers to Poultons. The boilers remained on the premises of Thames, who had physical possession; but for the purposes of a lien, possession was in Poultons. Poultons then sold the boilers to Harris on credit terms, and informed Thames of this. Harris resold the boilers to the defendants, Anglo-American Oil, and absconded without paying Poultons. By that time the credit period had expired. Poultons, being unpaid sellers, tried to set up a lien against the sub-buyers, Anglo-American Oil. They replied that the notice of the sub-sale to Thames transferred possession to Harris and so the lien had lapsed.

Held Poultons' lien against Anglo-American Oil was good. Poultons had no lien during the period of credit, but this was only a temporary waiver. It revived when the credit period expired (see s 41(1)(b) of the SGA). Poultons' lien was unaffected by the sub-sale, because they had not 'assented' to it (s 47(1) of the SGA); mere knowledge was not enough. Nor could that knowledge (of the sub-sale) be used as basis of estoppel against Poultons to defeat their lien. Poultons could exercise their lien even if they were in possession as bailees of the buyer (Harris). Finally, the notice of the sub-sale to Thames did not transfer possession to Harris. There had been no assent or attornment by Thames and so they did not hold the goods for Harris.

14.3.3 Loss of lien

Buyer (or his agent) obtains possession – s 43(1)(b) of the SGA

Wallace v Woodgate (1824)

A horse dealer, Woodgate, sold three horses to Wallace, but kept them in his stables pending payment. Woodgate allowed Wallace to ride the horses occasionally, but on one occasion Wallace abused this concession and took the horses away to his own stables and kept them there. Woodgate then repossessed the horses and claimed a lien against payment.

Held a lien existed originally. As the taking of the horses by Wallace was fraudulent, Woodgate was entitled to repossess them. Thus his lien revived.

Valpy v Gibson (1847)

Gibson sold goods on credit to Brown and sent them to shipping agents at Liverpool. The goods were loaded on to a ship. However, Brown then ordered that they be re-landed and sent back to Gibson for repacking. While Gibson had the goods for this purpose Brown became bankrupt. Gibson purported to exercise the unpaid sellers' right of a lien over the goods.

Held once the goods were delivered to the shipping agents, or at the latest, when Brown dealt with them as his own property by sending them for repacking, property passed to Brown; and this being a sale on credit the goods became Brown's absolutely. A lien could not be created if the seller obtained possession once more.

Cooper v Bill (1865)

Under a contract for the sale of timber, the sellers agreed to deliver the wood to canal boats. While the timber was lying in a wharf belonging to a canal company, the buyer measured, numbered and marked each tree; further, he incurred expense by 'squaring' it. The buyer became insolvent and the seller claimed a lien over the timber.

Held possession had passed to the buyers and the lien was lost.

Note ———
Compare with *Great Eastern Railway v Lord's Trustee*, above, 14.3.2.

Paton's Trustees v Finlayson (1923) Sc

Paton purchased a crop of potatoes growing on a farmer's land. Paton's employees handled the potatoes by lifting and storing them on the farmer's land. It was agreed that the farmer would transport the potatoes to the railway station. Paton went bankrupt and the farmer claimed an unpaid seller's lien against the trustees.

Held the property in the potatoes passed upon lifting. However, while they remained on the farmer's land he retained possession and so his lien was not lost.

Waiver – s 43(1)(c) of the SGA

Martindale v Smith (1841)

Under a contract for the sale of some stacks of oats, the buyer was given 12 weeks' credit. The oats remained on the seller's land at the buyer's convenience. At the end of the 12 weeks, the seller was unpaid. Some time later, the buyer offered payment but the seller refused to accept it. Later still, the seller resold the oats elsewhere. The buyer brought an action for conversion.

Held a lien was lost when the buyer paid for the goods or offered payment, even if that offer was refused. Therefore, as his lien was lost, the seller had no right to sell the goods elsewhere. The buyer would succeed.

Jones v Tarleton (1842)

A pig-dealer regularly shipped his pigs from Anglesey to Liverpool with the defendant shipowner. Following one shipment, the defendant withheld three pigs under a lien for the fare and an alleged debt resulting from a previous shipment. The pig-dealer denied the old debt but offered payment for the current fare. The defendant refused to accept anything but payment for both debts. It turned out that the old debt had never been due.

Held the defendant lost his lien by demanding a non-existent debt, which was an act inconsistent with the lien (for the current debt).

Chinery v Viall (1860)

By contract for the sale of sheep, the buyer was given credit and the seller retained possession at the buyer's convenience. Before payment was due, the seller resold the sheep to another. The buyer sued the seller for conversion and the seller argued that he had a lien on the sheep.

Held the seller was not entitled to resell the sheep. Therefore he was not entitled to a lien. Secondly, the measure of damages was not the price of the sheep, but the actual loss sustained by not having the sheep delivered at the agreed price.

14.4 Stoppage in transit – ss 44–46 of the Sale of Goods Act 1979

14.4.1 Duration of transit

The Constantia (1807)

By a contract for sale, 100 hogsheads of brandy were to be shipped to the buyer. While the goods were on board ship the seller erroneously anticipated that the buyer was about to become insolvent. He purported to exercise a right of stoppage and instructed the ship's master not to deliver the brandy to the buyer. The master complied.

Held the right of stoppage could only be exercised once the buyer became insolvent. The goods were the property of the buyer. As to the liability of the master, see *The Tigress* (1863) below, 14.4.2.

Bolton v Lancashire & Yorkshire Ry Co (1866)

Wolstencroft agreed to sell to Parsons 11 skips of cotton twist, which were lying at a railway station in Salford. The first three were dispatched via Brierfield station but Parsons was unhappy with the quality and he told Wolstencroft not to send any more. Nevertheless, Wolstencroft sent four more skips to Brierfield station. Parsons declined to collect these from the station. Then the final four skips were forwarded to Brierfield station and Parsons' driver collected them. When Parsons discovered this, he returned those four skips to Brierfield station and all eight skips were sent back to Salford. They remained with the railway company for several weeks until Parsons became bankrupt and Wolstencroft exercised his right of stoppage. The issue for the court was whether the eight skips were still in transit for the purpose of stoppage.

Held the goods were still in transit when the seller exercised the right of stoppage. As to the four skips collected by the driver, they were collected without Parsons' knowledge and against his will; it was as though they had been carried by a wrong-doer and this did not terminate the transit.

Taylor v Great Eastern Ry Co (1901)

Under a contract for the sale of barley the seller delivered the goods to a railway station. The railway company notified the sellers that the barley was being held to the buyer's order and that the buyer would be charged rent. The sellers did nothing until the buyers became insolvent. Then the sellers tried to exercise their right of stoppage.

Held by the time the sellers tried to exercise their right to stoppage the railway company had changed their role from carrier to warehousemen for the buyers. Assent by both parties was essential for the carrier to alter his role. The seller's assent could be inferred from his silence or delay; that was the case here. The right to stoppage was lost when the carrier became a warehouseman.

Reddall v Union Castle Mail SS Co (1914)

The buyer of goods in England instructed the seller to send them to South Africa via Southampton (transit in stages). The goods were sent to Southampton by rail to be loaded on a ship. However, the buyer then instructed the shipping company to hold the goods at Southampton. They did this (charging rent to the buyer) but then later delivered the goods to the seller – who was purporting to exercise his right of stoppage. The buyer sued the shipping company for conversion.

Held where the transit was in stages, transit continued until the goods reached their ultimate destination (in this case South Africa). However, where the journey was interrupted the test was whether the goods would be set in motion again without further orders from the buyers; if not, the transit ceased and the right to stop was lost. Therefore the purported stoppage by the sellers was ineffective; the goods were held on behalf of the buyers and judgment was given for them.

14.4.2 Exercise of the right to stoppage

The Tigress (1863)

Lucy & Son sold wheat to Bushe which was at sea on *The Tigress*. Then Bushe became insolvent without having paid for the wheat. So Lucy & Son instructed the ship's master to deliver the wheat to themselves. However, the master refused to do this without proof of the seller's ownership.

Held the seller took the risk that the stoppage was unjustified. Accordingly the master should have complied with the instructions of stoppage as soon as he was satisfied that it was the seller (not necessarily the owner) who was claiming the goods.

14.5   Right to resell – ss 47 and 48 of the Sale of Goods Act 1979

Mordaunt Bros v British Oil & Cake Mills (1910)

BOCM sold oil to Crichton who resold it to Mordaunt who paid Crichton for it. BOCM were sent delivery orders which they recorded in their books. However, BOCM retained possession and delivered instalments to Mordaunt as and when they were paid by Crichton. When Crichton fell into arrears, BOCM refused to deliver any more. Under s 47(1), the unpaid seller may lose his lien if he *assents* to a sub-sale by the buyer.

Held the acknowledgment of delivery orders did not constitute assent for s 47(1). BOCM had done no more than acknowledge that Mordaunt had a right to the goods subject to their lien.

Q Do you think that this case may have been decided differently if it concerned specific goods?

Commission Car Sales v Saul (1956) NZ

CCS sold a Plymouth car to Saul for £1,200. Payment was by a deposit of £300, the balance to be paid in a few days. Without paying the balance Saul returned the car and declined to continue with the sale. CCS then resold the Plymouth for £1,100. Saul claimed the return of his deposit.

Held CCS were entitled to keep the deposit and the proceeds from the resale. This was not a case of resale under the (New Zealand) SGA because here, the seller did not have continuing possession. So the common law applied. When Saul returned the Plymouth car he repudiated the contract and hence forfeited his deposit. CCS, in accepting the car, treated the contract as discharged. Thus property re-vested in them and they could resell the car as their own. It followed that they could keep the proceeds of the resale as well. This was in contrast to a resale under the SGA, where all the money received by the seller (deposit plus resale price) must be accounted for, and any surplus above the original contract price should be refunded.

Mount v Jay (1960)

Jays owned 500 cartons of tinned peaches laying in the wharf of Delta Storage. The market was falling when Merrick approached Jays stating that he had a sub-buyer for 250 cartons; he offered to buy them if he could make payment after the resale. Jays were keen to sell and agreed; they gave Merrick a delivery order which he sent to Delta. Merrick resold the goods to the sub-buyer and was paid. However, Jays remained unpaid and claimed a lien on the goods.

Held in the circumstances Jays had assented to the sub-sale within the meaning of s 47(1). Hence, the lien was lost.

Ward v Bignall (1967) CA

Wards sold two cars to Bignall for a total price of £850. Bignall paid a £25 deposit and Wards kept possession pending payment. A dispute arose over one of the cars and Bignall refused to accept delivery or to pay. Wards gave notice that if payment was not made within five days they would sell the cars (see s 48(3) of the SGA). No payment was made and Wards sold one car but could not sell the other. So they sued Bignall for price (the unsold car) and damages (loss of profit on the other car).

Held the price was not payable. The contract was rescinded irrespective of s 48(3). Bignall's failure to pay amounted to repudiation of the contract and Wards' resale of one of the cars was acceptance of this. Although s 48(3) did not provide for rescission (unlike s 48(4)) a repudiation and resale could rescind the contract. Wards could only recover damages for non-acceptance.

Notes

1 In this context (s 48(3)), the word *rescission* is used to mean *termination* as opposed to rescission *ab initio* used in misrepresentation when restoring the parties to their original positions.

2 If the seller has the property in the goods, he ought to be entitled to keep any profit from the resale. See *Commission Car Sales v Saul*, above.

15 Buyer's remedies

15.1 Right to reject

Lyons v May & Baker (1923)

The buyer of goods who had paid the price decided to reject them. He wished to retain the goods in order to have a lien for the return of the price.

Held The definition of 'seller' in s 38(2) of the SGA does not extend to the buyer. Thus, the buyer could not claim a lien against a refund from the seller.

Millar's Machinery v David Way & Son (1935) CA

Millar's made a 20-ton gravel-washing machine for Way, who paid £350 in advance. However, the machine failed to work and Way rejected it claiming a refund of the £350 and damages for having to go into the market and purchase another machine at a higher price.

Held a buyer who rightfully rejected goods was entitled to a refund of any money paid *and* damages for any consequential loss suffered, provided, of course, that loss was not too remote.

15.1.1 Acceptance by act inconsistent with ownership of seller – s 35(1)(b) of the SGA

Perkins v Bell (1893)

Under a contract for the sale of barley the seller (Perkins) delivered the goods to a railway station. At the station, the buyer (Bell) sent the barley on to a sub-buyer, who rejected it as 'quite unfit'. Bell then tried to reject the barley arguing that the first opportunity to examine it was at the sub-buyer's premises. But Perkins insisted that Bell could have examined it earlier at the place of delivery (that is, the railway station); once this opportunity had passed, Bell resold the barley and this act, inconsistent with the seller's ownership, amounted to acceptance. Thus Bell had lost his right to reject.

Held Bell could not reject the goods once they had been sent to a sub-buyer. Otherwise, the seller would have the risk of collecting them from wherever the sub-buyer(s) might be. The contract was silent on such a risk. Under this contract, the place of examination of the goods was the place of delivery to the buyer, that is, the railway station.

Molling v Dean (1901)

The sellers contracted to make and sell 40,000 books to the buyers, who in turn had agreed to sell them to an American sub-buyer. The contract between the sellers and the buyers stipulated that the consignment be sent direct to the sub-buyers with the books containing the sub-buyers' stamp. However, the sub-buyers rejected the books and the buyers brought them back from America at their own expense. Then they returned the books to the sellers, who argued that the goods had been accepted by the buyers because of an act inconsistent with the sellers' ownership – namely the sub-sale.

Held acceptance could not take place until there had been an opportunity to examine the goods. The proper place to examine the goods in this case was upon delivery to the sub-buyers. The buyers were entitled to reject the goods and could recover the cost of transportation.

Kwei Tek Chao v British Traders & Shippers Ltd (1954)

Sellers (in London) contracted to sell to the buyers in Hong Kong a chemical *Rongalite C*. Under the contract, property was to pass when the price was paid in exchange for the shipping documents. This happened and then the buyers pledged the documents to their bank. Later, however, they discovered that the documents had been forged to conceal the date of shipment, which actually fell outside of the contractual stipulation. This was held to be *prima facie* a breach allowing rejection. The problem was that the property had passed and the buyers, by pledging the documents, had acted inconsistently with the sellers' ownership.

Held the right to reject remained even though the property had passed: this was because only *conditional* property had passed. So the pledging of the documents by the buyer was a dealing with the *conditional* property. The sellers' 'ownership' was a reversionary interest in the goods which would be realised should they be rejected. Consequently, the pledging of documents was not an act inconsistent with the sellers' 'ownership'. The buyer could reject.

Hammer & Barrow v Coca-Cola (1962) NZ

Under a contract for the sale of 200,000 yo-yos, the seller was bound to deliver them directly to the sub-buyers. The sub-sale had been made before this contract and the sellers were fully aware of it. Upon delivery to the sub-buyers it was found that the goods were defective. The buyers tried to reject the goods but the sellers argued that the buyers, having resold the goods, had lost their right to reject.

Held the buyers had not acted inconsistently with the sellers' ownership because there had been no sub-sale *after* the contract had been made and the contract contemplated that the place of examination was the place of delivery, that is, the sub-buyers premises. Thus the buyers had not accepted the goods and had not lost their right to reject.

15.1.2 Lapse of reasonable time – s 35(4) of the SGA

Farnworth Finance v Attryde (1970) CA

Farnworth supplied a new Royal Enfield motor-cycle on hire-purchase to Attryde. Delivery was made in July. From the beginning the motor-cycle gave trouble and was returned to the dealers and manufacturers for repairs. These were only partially successful and the motor-cycle continued to give trouble until November, when Attryde rejected it. He had paid four instalments. The motor-cycle had covered 4,000 miles and given seven weeks' use since delivery four months earlier. Farnworth disputed the right to reject.

Held Attryde was entitled to reject. He had not affirmed the contract; in fact he made it plain that he would not affirm unless the defects were remedied.

Note

This was not a sale governed by the SGA, but a hire-purchase agreement, where the right to reject was governed by the common law.

Porter v General Guarantee Corporation (1982)

Porter took delivery of a car on hire-purchase at the end of January. On 4 March he tried to reject it. Attempts were made to repair the car but by 20 March Porter finally rejected it.

Held the rejection was not too late.

Note

This was not a sale governed by the SGA, but a hire-purchase agreement, where the right to reject was governed by the common law.

Lutton v Saville Tractors (Belfast) Ltd (1986)

A three year old Ford Escort XR3 car was sold by a dealer to a consumer with a three-month warranty. The car had or developed many minor faults and many attempts to remedy them had been made by the dealer. After seven weeks and having covered 3,000 to 4,000 miles, the buyer rejected the car claiming *inter alia* that it was not of merchantable quality.

Held the rejection was not too late. The buyer had not 'accepted' the goods under s 35 SGA by assenting to repairs beforehand. Further, he had not affirmed the contract for the purposes of rescission for misrepresentation by agreeing to repairs.

Note

This case also concerned implied terms, see above, 9.4.3.

Bernstein v Pamson Motors (1987)

Bernstein purchased a new Nissan car. After three weeks and 140 miles the car broke down because of a serious defect in the engine. Bernstein tried to reject the car arguing that a 'reasonable time' in s 35 meant time enough to discover any fault.

Held a 'reasonable time' in s 35 was not related to the opportunity to discover any particular defect. It related, in commercial terms, to the nature and function of the goods from the buyers' point of view and the desirability of the seller to close his ledger. The complexity of the function of the goods was important; more time would be given to nuclear submarine than a bicycle. In this case a reasonable time had elapsed and Bernstein could not reject the car.

Notes——
1 This case was settled before it reached the Court of Appeal.

2 Also note that the SSGA 1994 has added to s 35 of the SGA that a question determining whether a reasonable time has elapsed should include whether the buyer has had a reasonable opportunity to examine the goods.

15.2 Damages for non-delivery – s 51 of the Sale of Goods Act 1979

15.2.1 Available market – s 51(3) of the SGA

Williams v Reynolds (1865)
On 1 April the parties made a contract for 500 piculs of cotton at 16 3/4 d per lb, delivery to be made any time during August. The buyer in turn contracted to resell the cotton for 19 3/4 d per lb. At the end of August the seller had failed to deliver; the market price had then risen to 18 1/4 d per lb. The buyer sued for his loss of profit from the sub-sale.

Held the correct amount of damages should be assessed by reference to the market price at the end of August. If the seller failed to deliver, the buyer could buy from the market to fulfil the sub-sale. He would be entitled to compensation for this, which was the difference between the contract price and the market price. He was not entitled to damages for loss of profit where there was an available market.

Rodacanachi v Milburn (1887) CA
The plaintiff purchased cotton seed and chartered a ship to transport it to the UK. The plaintiff had resold the seed to buyers in the UK at a price lower than the market price prevailing at the time when the ship should have arrived. However, the cargo was lost because of the negligence of the shipowners. The plaintiff sued the shipowners, who claimed that the damages should be the difference between the contract price and the resale price, because that represented the plaintiff's loss.

Held the fact that the plaintiff had resold the goods was not relevant. The proper assessment is the difference between the contract price and the market price prevailing at the time when the ship should have arrived.

Williams v Agius (1914) HL

Agius contracted to sell coal at 16 s 3 d (81 p) per ton to Williams, who in turn contracted to sell the coal to a sub-buyer at 19 s (95 p) per ton. However, Agius failed to deliver. The market price on the delivery date had risen to 23 s 6 d (£1.18) per ton. Williams sued for non-delivery; Agius claimed that the market price should be assessed by reference to the resale price (19 s per ton) rather than the higher market price (23 s 6 d per ton).

Held the resale should be disregarded; the buyer has to buy in the market in order to fulfil his sub-sales. He was entitled to be put in the position as if the contract had been performed. Therefore, he should be compensated for having to buy the coal at the market rate (23 s 6 d).

Date of market price

Melachrino v Nickol and Knight (1920)

By a contract for the sale of cotton seed, delivery was expected between 10 January and 10 February 1917. However, the sellers repudiated the contract on 14 December 1916, when the market price was high. However, the market price fell below the contract price after 10 January 1917. The issue was at what date should the market price be assessed for damages. If it were the latter date, the buyer would receive nominal damages only, because he could buy elsewhere at no extra cost.

Held the market price was assessed by reference to the date of expected delivery, not the date of the sellers' repudiation. Consequently, the buyers were entitled to nominal damages only. *Obiter*, if the action came to trial before the contractual date of delivery, the court should assess the price as best it can.

Millet v Van Heeck & Co (1921) CA

Millet agreed to sell cotton to Van Heeck in Holland, to be delivered within a reasonable period after a wartime embargo. Before the embargo lapsed Millet announced their intention not to supply Van Heeck at all; so they were in anticipatory breach and Van Heeck were entitled to damages. The issue for the court was at what date should they refer to an available market to assess the damages. No date had been specified in the contract, only 'a reasonable period after the embargo'. The concluding words of s 51(3) of the SGA provide that if no date was fixed then it should be the date of the refusal to deliver.

Held the concluding words of s 51(3) cannot apply to a case of anticipatory breach. The *prima facie* rule was that damages should be assessed by reference to the available market at the date(s) of delivery to be decided by the court.

Tai Hing Cotton Mill Ltd v Kamsing Knitting Factory (1979) PC

Tai Hing contracted to sell to Kamsing 1,500 bales of cotton yarn. Delivery was to made as the buyers required it, provided they gave one month's notice. On 31 July, the Tai Hing repudiated the contract, with 424 bales undelivered. The buyers made repeated requests for delivery, but eventually issued a writ on 28 November, claiming damages for breach of contract.

Held the sellers' breach was accepted by the issue of the writ. It was then that the contract came to an end. The latest date on which the buyers could have requested a delivery was 28 November. Therefore the last date on which delivery could have been made was 28 December, which was the date by which the market price should be assessed.

15.2.2 No available market – s 51(2) of the SGA

Hammond v Bussey (1887) CA

The plaintiff purchased coal from the defendant and then resold it to a sub-buyer. The sub-buyer was unhappy with the quality of the coal and successfully sued the plaintiff and recovered damages. The plaintiff then sued the defendant.

Held the plaintiff had acted reasonably in defending the action against the sub-buyer. Thus he was entitled to damages to cover the compensation paid to the sub-buyer and the costs of defending that action.

Payzu v Saunders (1919) CA

Under a contract for the sale of silk to be delivered by instalments, the buyers were given a 2.5% discount for prompt payment on each delivery. The buyers failed to pay punctually for the first delivery; the sellers (erroneously) understood this to mean that the buyers were insolvent. So the sellers declined to deliver any more instalments unless they were paid for in advance and without the 2.5% discount. The buyers sued seeking damages assessed at the difference between the contract price and the market price (which had risen).

Held the buyers' failure to pay promptly for the first instalment did not amount to a repudiation and so they were entitled to damages. However, the buyers could have mitigated their loss by accepting the sellers' offer to take the goods at the contract price, without the discount, which was still lower than the prevailing market price. The measure of damages would be the difference between the contract price (with discount) and the contract price without the discount.

Re Hall and Pim's Arbitration (1928) HL

A contract for the sale of a specific cargo of corn on a specific ship, at 51s 9d (£2.59) per quarter, contemplated that the buyer might resell that cargo during the voyage. After the contract was made the buyers indeed resold the cargo, at 56 s 9 d (£2.80) per quarter. However, before delivery the sellers resold the cargo elsewhere. At the delivery date the market price had fallen to 53 s 9 d (£2 69). The seller offered the buyers the difference between the contract price and the market price as compensation. The buyers claimed the difference between the contract price and the (higher) resale price.

Held the resale was of the specific cargo was contemplated in the contract and so the buyers were entitled to compensation for their loss of profit, that is, the difference between the contract price and the resale price.

Note ———————————————————————————————

For a criticism of this case, see *Benjamin's Sale of Goods*, 5th edn, 1997, para 17-031.

Patrick v Russo-British Export Co (1927)
Patrick bought 2,000 tons of wheat from the defendants for the purpose of resale; the defendants were aware of this purpose. A few days later, but before delivery, Patrick resold the wheat to a sub-buyer. However, the defendant failed to deliver to Patrick, who sued for damages. On the date of delivery there was no available market for the wheat.

Held the measure of damages should be the difference between the contract price and the resale price.

Leavey v Hirst (1944)
The buyer agreed to purchase material which, to the sellers' knowledge, was to be used to make into raincoats. However, a general shortage led to the seller not being able to supply any material. The buyer sued for damages.

Held as there was a general shortage there was no 'available market'. Therefore the damages were assessed as if the contract had been performed. That is the profit that would have been made on each raincoat manufactured by the buyer.

Household Machines v Cosmos Exports Ltd (1947)
The defendants agreed to buy a large quantity of cutlery for the purpose of resale. The sellers were aware of that purpose. However, the sellers failed to deliver some of the cutlery. The buyer sought an indemnity in respect of any action brought against them by their sub-buyers and damages for a loss of profit which was represented by a 12% mark-up on the purchase price.

Held the buyer was entitled to a declaration of the indemnity but in the court's opinion the profit margin was too high and damages would be awarded in respect of a profit margin of 10%.

15.2.3 Late delivery

Victoria Laundry v Newman Industries (1949) CA
Newman agreed to sell a boiler to Victoria Laundry, who proposed to use it to fulfil some highly paid government contracts. This was not known, nor could it be reasonably contemplated, by Newman. The delivery of the

boiler was delayed and the laundry claimed damages for their loss of profits from the government contracts.

Held given that the reasonable man would not have foreseen that the extra loss of profits was a likely result of the breach, recovery for that loss was not possible.

The Solholt (1983) CA

By a contract to sell a ship for $5m, delivery was set at 31 August at the latest. The sellers did not deliver the ship until 3 September and the buyers (rightfully) refused to accept the ship. The market price had risen to $5.5 million and the buyers claimed the difference ($0.5 million).

Held the buyers' refusal to accept terminated the contract. This brought about their duty to mitigate. The reasonable action would have been to negotiate a settlement with the sellers and take late delivery of the ship. In the circumstances the buyers could recover no damages.

15.3 Specific performance – s 52 of the Sale of Goods Act 1979

Cohen v Roche (1927)

The plaintiff purchased eight genuine Hepplewhite chairs at an auction. However, the owner of the chairs felt that the price achieved was too low and refused to deliver them. The plaintiff brought an action for specific performance.

Held the goods were ordinary articles of commerce of no special value or interest. Thus, specific performance would not be granted; damages were the appropriate remedy.

Société des Industries Metallurgiques v Bronx Engineering (1975) CA

A contract was made for the sale of a machine to be manufactured by the sellers; it weighed 220 tons, cost £287,500 and could only be bought in the market at 9–12 months delivery. Problems with the ship which was to transport the machine to the buyers in Tunis led to a delay in delivery. Meanwhile the sellers found an interested Canadian third party and were prepared to deliver the machine to them. The buyers sought an injunction to prevent this happening. To succeed they had to show that if the sellers failed to deliver they would be entitled to specific performance.

Held the machine was one which was ordinarily obtained in the market in the ordinary course of placing an order. Therefore, damages were sufficient remedy. The injunction was refused.

CN Marine v Stena Line (1982)

In May 1976, Swedish owners agreed to let their ship to Canadian charterers for the summer season and for each of the six following summers; the ship reverted to the Swedish owners each winter. At the end of the five years, the Canadians had an option to purchase. In September 1981, the ship was delivered back to Swedish owners in accordance with the agreement. The Canadians looked forward to having the ship once again in 1982 to serve alongside her two sister ships. However, the Swedish owners then agreed to let the ship to Belgium charterers for two years with an option to purchase; the Belgiums took delivery in February 1982. Unaware of this, the Canadians then exercised their option to purchase. When they discovered the truth they claimed specific performance.

Held specific performance was denied. Damages were an adequate remedy.

Sky Petroleum Ltd v VIP Petroleum Ltd (1974)

The defendants supplied fuel to filling stations and the plaintiffs owned several filling stations. The parties agreed a contract for the sale of fuel to the entire needs of the plaintiffs at a fixed price. During an oil crisis the defendants purported to terminate the contract. No fuel was available from other sources. The plaintiffs sought an injunction to restrain the defendants from withholding supplies.

Held the injunction would be granted to enforce the contract to supply petrol. Otherwise the buyers would be forced out of business in the very special circumstances of this case.

15.4 Remedy for breach of warranty – s 53 of the Sale of Goods Act 1979

Bence Graphics v Fasson UK (1996) CA

Over a number of years the buyers purchased vinyl film to make into decals, which would be used to label cargo containers. The sellers were aware that the buyers would be selling the decals to other companies. It was a term of the contract that the film would survive in good condition for five years. The buyers used most of the film and sold the resultant decals. However, it turned out that the film supplied would not last five years, because of a latent defect: it contained insufficient stabiliser to protect it from the effects of ultra violet light. That would cause the final product (the decals) to fade in sunlight and become illegible. The buyers claimed damages for breach of warranty. The trial judge awarded damages based upon s 53(3) of the SGA, that is, the difference between the actual value of the goods at the time of delivery and their value if they were up to contract quality. And as the latent defect rendered the goods valueless, the damages amounted to a refund of the purchase price (£564,328). The buyer had received no complaints from their customers, and so they had suffered no loss; the damages were a windfall. The sellers appealed.

Held (2:1) the appeal was allowed. Section 53(3) provided a *prima facie* rule only. Section 53 codifies the common law ('1st') rule of *Hadley v Baxendale* (see above, 14.2.2) that the damages should be based upon the loss 'directly and naturally resulting, in the ordinary course of events, from the breach'. The loss could have been greater than the purchase price (for example, if sub-buyers had sued the buyers because their containers had gone missing) or nil, because the buyers had suffered no loss. In this case, the buyers were awarded damages only for the remainder of the film which they could not use. This amounted to £22,000. They were granted further an indemnity against any subsequent claims by their sub-buyers.

15.5   Special damage – s 54 of the SGA

Braude v Porter (1959)

Porter agreed to sell Braude 300 tons of scrap metal, knowing that Braude intended to resell the metal to a German sub-buyer and book freight space on a ship accordingly. In the event Porter only delivered 62 tons; consequently, Braude had to pay for 237 tons 'dead freight' (that is, the empty space on the ship) and go into the market and purchase scrap metal to satisfy the sub-contract.

Held Braude could recover the 'dead freight' cost and the costs of having to purchase in the market.

Note ──────────────────────────────────

See, also, the cases on loss of profit from resale, above, 15.2.2.

Part 4 Credit

16 Consumer credit agreements

16.1 Types of credit agreement

16.1.1 Conditional sale

Lee v Butler (1893), see above, 12.5.1.

16.1.2 Hire-purchase

Helby v Mathews (1895), see above, 12.5.1.

16.1.3 Credit cards

Re Charge Card Services (1988) CA
CCS Ltd (creditor) ran a charge card operation whereby various garages (retailers) would supply fuel to card holders (debtors) and receive payment from CCS. In turn, CCS would bill the card holders monthly. The garages had supplied fuel to the card holders when CCS became insolvent, leaving the garages unpaid. The question arose whether the garages could sue the card holders directly for their losses. They argued that payment by card was the same as payment by cheque: if a customer's cheque is dishonoured then the customer becomes liable; payment by cheque is conditional upon it being honoured. However, as some of the card holders *had* paid CCS, this argument would result in them paying twice for the fuel.

Held the card holders were not liable to the garages. Payment by a charge or credit card is *absolute* and not conditional. Those card holders who had not yet paid CCS for the fuel were still liable to do so (to the liquidator). The legal nature of the typical charge card or credit card arrangement was considered. There were three underlying contracts:

(i) an agreement between the creditor and the retailer whereby the retailer would accept the card as payment for supplying goods to the card holders and the creditor would pay the supplier, normally less a commission;

(ii) an agreement between the creditor and the card holder whereby the creditor gave credit and the card holder would pay it off;

(iii) as between the retailer and the card holder, there was a sale contract within the SGA 1979.

Note ───

The credit agreements in this case were not regulated because the debtors were actually registered companies (not 'individuals', s 8 of the Consumer Credit Act). What if the agreements were regulated? See Macleod, *Consumer Sales Law*, 1989, para 7.10, and Sayer (1986) 136 NLJ 1030. Generally, see Tiplady [1989] LMCLQ 22 and Jones [1988] JBL 457.

16.1.4 Total charge for credit

R v Baldwin's Garage (1988)

Baldwin's placed an advertisement in their local newspaper offering new Austin Rover cars at 20% discount cash, or on credit at 8.9% APR (Annual Percentage Rate). The credit terms were based on the retail price of the cars before any discount for cash. Baldwin's were charged under s 167(2) of the Consumer Credit Act 1974 for breach of the Consumer Credit (Advertisement) Regulations 1980 (now SI 1989/1125).

Held the advertisement mis-stated the cost of the credit because it was based upon the retail price and not the actual cash (or discounted) price. If the credit terms were based upon the discounted price the APR would be 46.8%. Hence, Baldwin's were guilty.

Note ───

This case is a reminder that when calculating the total charge for credit one must take account of any discount given to cash customers.

Humberclyde Finance v Thompson (1996) CA

Humberclyde loaned £14,982 to Mrs Thompson so that she could buy a car, which Humberclyde supplied. The agreement included an insurance waiver policy option, which Mrs Thompson exercised for £796. (The policy would cancel the debt should Mrs Thompson die.) Mrs Thompson fell into arrears and Humberclyde repossessed the car. Mrs Thompson argued that the agreement was a 'regulated agreement' under the Consumer Credit Act 1974 and so the repossession was unlawful because the car was a 'protected good' under s 90 of the Consumer Credit Act (see below, 17.4.2). Humberclyde argued that the agreement was not regulated because the loan (for the car and insurance) exceeded £15,000. At the time s 8 of the Consumer Credit Act provided that an agreement could not be a regulated agreement if the credit exceeded £15,000.

Held under s 9 of the Consumer Credit Act, 'credit' and 'charges for credit' were to be distinguished. Under Pt 2 of the Consumer Credit (Total

Charge for Credit) Regulations 1980 SI 1980/51 reg 4 defines charges for credit as '... (b) other charges at any time payable under the transaction by or on behalf of the debtor or a relative ...'. The insurance premium was a charge for credit, even though that charge attracted interest. Thus, the 'credit' in this case amounted to no more than the loan for the car, which was less than £15,000. It followed that this was a regulated agreement and the car was a protected good.

Notes

1 The limit for a regulated agreement has been raised from £15,000 to £25,000 with effect from 1 May 1998. See Consumer Credit (Increase of Monetary Limits) (Amendment) Order 1998 SI 1998/996 (made under s 181 of the Consumer Credit Act).

2 Aldous LJ also relied on this extract from *The Consumer Credit Legislation* by Professor Goode, which states (para 1131):

'*Payable* [from reg 4(b)]. Does this word denote charges which the debtor is legally committed to pay, or does it signify all charges that are payable on the assumption that the debtor chooses to avail himself of the options, services or facilities to which they relate? It is thought that the latter is the correct interpretation of the regulations ... More generally, all charges for which the transaction provides, even if relating to services or facilities that are purely optional, fall within reg 4 and thus form part of the total charge for credit unless excluded by reg 5.'

16.1.5 Cancellable agreements

Bayerische Hypotheken-Und Wechselbank AG v Dietzinger (1998) ECJ

The 'doorstep selling' European Directive 85/577 – implemented in the UK by the Consumer Protection (Cancellation of Contracts Concluded away from Business Premises) Regulations 1987 SI 1987/2117 – provides consumers with a right of cancellation (a 'cooling off period') of contracts made at home following an unsolicited visit by the seller.

The facts of this case occurred in Germany. Dietzinger (D) guaranteed a loan to his father by the bank. The guarantee was executed at D's parents' home. Subsequently, the bank tried to enforce the guarantee. D argued that it was unenforceable because it was covered by the Directive and the bank had not informed him of his cancellation rights, which is a requirement under the Directive.

Held (i) guarantees could be covered by the Directive; (ii) the Directive only applies to the supply of goods and services to consumers. Although D entered into the guarantee as a consumer (that is, not in the course of his trade or profession), the principal contract (for a loan between the bank and D's father) was made by D's father in the course of his profession. Thus, as the principal contract (not being a consumer contract) did not fall within the Directive, neither did the derivative one for the guarantee.

Note ———

The Consumer Credit Act (ss 67–73) and the Regulations both provide a cooling off period to protect consumers from the pressure of doorstep selling. Both are drafted wider than necessary (for example, 'away from business premises'). However, the Consumer Credit Act, having its roots in credit legislation, covers only regulated *credit* agreements, whereas the Regulations extend to all sales. Also, the cooling off periods vary slightly, depending on the circumstances

16.2 Obligations of the parties

16.2.1 Title – common law

Karflex Ltd v Poole (1933)
Karflex (creditor) let a 'Riley Nine' car to Poole (debtor) on hire-purchase terms. Under the agreement an initial payment of £95 was made. Then Poole failed to pay the instalments and Karflex repossessed the car and sued for the balance owing. However, before the trial Poole discovered that the car had been stolen before it came into Karflex's hands. Consequently Karflex (who were innocent) had no title to pass to Poole should he exercise the option to purchase within the hire-purchase agreement. Poole counter-claimed that Karflex were in breach of an implied condition that they had title when the agreement was made.

Held at common law there was an implied condition that the creditor (Karflex) under a hire-purchase agreement had title to the goods when the debtor (Poole) took possession.

Note ———

Section 8 of the SG(IT)A 1973 implies a condition that the creditor has title to the goods at the time *property is to pass* (that is, only when the debtor exercises his option to purchase).

Mercantile Union v Wheatley (1937)
Dunns (supplier) supplied a Commer lorry to Wheatley (debtor) using a hire-purchase arrangement. As is usual with these arrangements, Dunns were to sell the lorry to the creditors, Mercantile Guarantee, who would then let it to Wheatley, the debtor, under a hire-purchase agreement. The hire-purchase agreement was signed on 7 February, although the creditor did not purchase the lorry from Dunns until 11 February. It was delivered to Wheatley on 8 March. Wheatley subsequently went into arrears and the

creditor repossessed the lorry and sued for the balance owing. Wheatley claimed that the creditors were in breach of the implied condition that the creditor had title at the time the agreement was made, that is, 7 February.

Held the material date when the creditor should have title to the goods in question was not necessarily when the agreement was signed, but when it came into operation, that is, the date of delivery. Therefore the creditors were not in breach and were entitled to judgment.

Warman v Southern Counties Finance (1949)

Warman, the debtor, hired a Hillman car under a hire-purchase agreement from Southern Counties, the creditor. After the agreement was made, Warman discovered that Southern Counties never had title to the car. However, Warman continued using the car and kept up the payments until the true owner issued a writ for its return. Warman had the car for seven months before giving it up to its true owner. Warman then claimed from Southern Counties the return of all sums paid under the hire-purchase agreement, stating that Southern Counties were in breach of a contractual condition that they had title upon delivery. Southern Counties counter-claimed for a reasonable sum accounting for the seven months' use of the car by Warman.

Held judgment for Warman. The condition (of good title) applied upon delivery and so the discovery of the defective title after that was irrelevant: there was a total failure of consideration by the creditor. The counter-claim would fail because the debtor entered into the hire-purchase agreement with a view to eventually buying the goods. That was the whole basis of such an agreement.

Butterworth v Kingsway Motors (1954)

A Jowett Javelin car was acquired by A on hire-purchase terms. Before completing the payments A sold the car to B (mistakenly believing that she had a right to sell, as long as she kept up the payments). B, who of course had no title, sold to C, who sold to Kingsway Motors. They sold the car to Butterworth, who used the car for 11 months before discovering the defect in title. Thereupon he wrote to Kingsway repudiating the contract. One week later, A completed her hire-purchase payments (including the option to purchase) and so the hire-purchase company no longer had a claim to the car. Butterworth sued Kingsway for breach of the implied condition that the seller had good title, claiming a refund of the purchase price. A, B, and C were joined to the action and each party claimed up the line similarly for breach of contract.

Held Butterworth was entitled to a refund, despite enjoying 11 months use of the car. However, the other parties were only entitled to damages for breach of warranty. This is because when A completed her payments, title passed to her from the hire-purchase company; this title was 'fed down the line' to B, C and Kingsway. It never came to Butterworth, though, because he repudiated before A acquired the title. Thus, the others all received title, albeit belatedly.

This case was decided before the enactment of Pt III of the Hire Purchase Act 1964, which provides a *nemo dat* exception (see above, 12.7): a *private* purchaser acting in good faith and without notice can claim good title to a motor vehicle subject to a hire purchase or conditional sale agreement. Under the Hire Purchase Act the result would have been different for Butterworth *if* either B or C were private purchasers acting in good faith and without notice. In that case, Kingsway would have acquired good title from C before the agreement was made with Butterworth. On the other hand, if Butterworth was the first private purchaser (acting in good faith and without notice), then the result would have been the same; see *Barber v NWS Bank* below.

Kelly v Lombard Banking Ltd (1958)

A hire-purchase agreement was made between Lombards (creditor) and Kelly (debtor) in December 1954 in respect of a Jaguar car. Kelly had to make an initial payment of £186 and then pay the remainder over 21 months. Once the instalments were paid Kelly had an option, for £1, to purchase the car. The total hire-purchase price was £534. Kelly paid the initial fee and the instalments until February 1956, when an entirely separate matter allowed Lombards to terminate the agreement and repossess the car. By then Kelly had paid £419 in total. Kelly sued for the return of his initial payment, arguing that there had been a total failure of consideration as he had never received the benefit of the option to purchase.

Held he could not recover the initial payment because the option to purchase existed from the beginning of the agreement. Although he had to meet certain conditions (for example, payment of all the instalments) in order to exercise the option, it still was an existing right.

Barber v NWS Nank plc (1996) CA

In October 1989, Barber agreed with a dealer to buy a Honda Accord car on credit. As is usual in these transactions, the dealer sold the car to the creditor (NWS) who then sold it to Barber under a conditional sale (that is, property passing when all the instalments were paid). Naturally, the agreement contained an express term that property remained with NWS until full payment. In May 1991 (18 months later), Barber discovered that the car was subject to a prior finance agreement; this meant that NWS had no title. Barber rescinded the agreement and claimed a refund of all payments made under it.

Held judgment for Barber: (i) the term in the contract (that property remained with NWS until full payment) amounted to an express term that NWS had title at the time the agreement was made; (ii) that term was a condition; (iii) thus Barber was entitled to rescind the contract and was entitled to a full refund of any moneys paid. This was despite the fact that he had had 18 months' use of the car; (iv) Pt III of the Hire Purchase Act

1964 (see above, 12.7) did not undermine Barber's case: although that Act can give a private buyer (in this case Barber) good title to a motor vehicle which is subject to a prior finance agreement, s 27(6) made it clear that this did not exonerate a trade purchaser, such as NWS, from civil (or criminal) liability.

Note ───────────────────────────────────────

Barber could not rely on s 12 of the SGA (above, 9.2), because that only implies a condition that the seller has title *at the time* property is to pass, in this case when Barber had paid all the instalments.

16.2.2 Description – common law

Karsales v Wallis (1956) CA

The debtor, Wallis, inspected an American Buick car, which was in very good condition, belonging to Stinton. He agreed to buy it through a hire-purchase agreement if Stinton could make the arrangements. The credit was arranged and one night, about a month after Wallis had inspected the car, it was towed to his house. It was in a substantially poorer condition: the new tyres had been changed for old ones; the radio had been removed; chrome strips were missing; the engines' cylinder head was removed; engine valves were burnt out; and two pistons broken. The car was incapable of self-propulsion. Wallis refused to accept the car and the creditor sued for payments.

Held Wallis was entitled to reject because the car delivered was not the thing contracted for. *Per* Denning LJ, it was an implied term of the agreement that, pending delivery, the car will be kept in suitable order and repair.

16.2.3 Quality – common law

Drury v Victor Buckland (1941) CA

Bucklands supplied an ice-cream maker to Drury on hire-purchase terms. The creditor was Equipment Trust Ltd. So Bucklands sold the machine to Equipment Trust who let it on hire-purchase terms to Drury. However, the machine proved defective and Drury sued Bucklands for breach of a warranty implied by s 14 of the SGA 1893.

Held this was not a contract of sale between Bucklands and Drury, but a hire-purchase agreement between Equipment Trust and Drury. Thus Bucklands were not liable as they had no contract with Drury. Drury should have sued Equipment Trust under the hire-purchase agreement.

Note ───────────────────────────────────────

For regulated agreements see s 75 of the Consumer Credit Act, where both supplier and creditor can be liable.

Andrews v Hopkinson (1956)

Hopkinson, car dealers, supplied a Standard car to Andrews on hire-purchase terms, after the salesman had told Andrews: 'It's a good little bus. I'd stake my life on it. You will have no trouble with it.' As is usual with hire-purchase, Hopkinson sold the car to the creditor, who then let it to Andrews on hire-purchase terms. Subsequently, while driving the car, Andrews was seriously injured following a collision with a lorry. The accident was caused by the car's defective steering mechanism, which any reasonable car dealer ought to have detected. Andrews sued Hopkinson.

Held although there was no contract between Andrews and Hopkinson, there was a warranty by Hopkinson that the car was in good condition and safe to use. The warranty was brought about by the salesman's statement about the car's condition and Andrews' reliance upon it (by entering into the finance agreement with the creditor). Therefore, Hopkinson would be liable to Andrews. Secondly, as the fault in the steering was detectable by the reasonable dealer, Hopkinson were liable in negligence to Andrews for not detecting the fault.

16.2.4 Quality – Consumer Credit Act 1974

United Dominions Trust v Taylor (1980) Sc

UDT made a loan to Taylor in order that he may purchase a car from Parkway Cars. However, Parkway misrepresented the condition of the car and Taylor rescinded the contract with them and at the same time ceased to make any payments to UDT, who sued for repayment of the loan. Taylor relied upon s 75 of the Consumer Credit Act which provides that a debtor (Taylor) under a DCS agreement falling within s 12 (b) or (c) who has a claim against the supplier (Parkway) has a *like claim* against the creditor (UDT).

Held where the debtor had a right to rescind the supply agreement he also had a right to rescind the loan agreement.

Notes————————————————————————————————————

1 Section 75 of the Consumer Credit Act provides that a debtor (under a DCS agreement within s 12(b) or (c)) who has a claim against the supplier for misrepresentation or breach of contract will enjoy a like claim against the creditor. Section 75 does not apply to non-commercial agreements (see s 189(1)) or where the claim relates to any one item costing less than £101 or more than £30,000.

2 See Dobson [1981] JBL 179, p 185, and Davidson (1980) 96 LQR 343.

16.2.5 Formalities

Lombard Tricity Finance v Paton (1989) CA

Lombards loaned Paton £218 for the purpose of purchasing an Amstrad computer. The loan agreement, which was regulated, contained a statement that the interest rate on the loan was 'subject to variation by creditor from time to time on notification as required by law'. The interest rate was increased from 2.3% to 2.45% and, after Paton fell into arrears, it rose again to 2.95%. Lombards sued, claiming arrears. Paton argued that the notice of variation of interest rates did not comply with the Consumer Credit (Agreements) Regulations 1983 (Sched 1, para 19) which require that to be effective such a statement must indicate 'the circumstances in which any variation ... may occur'. Hence, this was not a properly executed agreement and so unenforceable.

Held the statement was effective, enabling the creditor to increase the interest rate. It conveyed to the average reader that Lombard were entitled to raise the interest rate should they wish.

R v Modupe (1991) CA

Modupe gave false information, including a false address, to a finance company in order to obtain a loan for a Mercedes car. In all, £50,000 was outstanding. He was charged with evading liability by deception under the Theft Act 1978. Section 61(1) of the Consumer Credit Act provided that a regulated agreement was not properly executed unless it contained the details set out in the regulations made under the Act (SI 1983 No 1553). In this case the creditor had omitted to enter the total amount payable on the agreement contrary to Sched 1, para 11 of the regulations. Section 65 of the Consumer Credit Act provided that an improperly executed agreement was not enforceable without a court order. In his defence, Modupe claimed that as the agreement was not enforceable (there being no such court order) there was no liability to evade; hence he was not guilty.

Held the fact that the agreement was not enforceable without a court order did not mean that there was no existing liability. Section 65 of the Consumer Credit Act restricted the remedies of the creditor, not the liability of the debtor.

16.2.6 Delivery and acceptance

National Cash Register Co Ltd v Stanley (1921)

Stanley signed a hire-purchase agreement with NCR in respect of a cash register. Stanley postponed delivery for two weeks and eventually wrote to NCR cancelling the contract, stating that he had bought a register elsewhere. NCR brought an action under the agreement for instalments due up until the date of the summons.

Held no debt had been incurred by Stanley as the agreement did not commence until the debtor (Stanley) took delivery. NCR were entitled only to damages for non-acceptance.

Bentworth Finance v Lubert (1967) CA

Lubert agreed to take an Austin car on hire-purchase from Bentworth. The car was delivered, but without a log book. Lubert told Bentworth that she could not tax nor use the car without the log book and, until they supplied one, she would not pay any instalments. Bentworth never supplied a log book and after six months deadlock they repossessed the car, which had been damaged. Bentworth sued Lubert for £50 under the agreement which provided that the debtor (Lubert) was liable for any damage to the goods.

Held the claim would fail. It was an implied term of the agreement that the creditor (Bentworth) would supply a log book with the car. Until this was done, the agreement did not come into existence. Consequently, Lubert was not obliged to pay any instalments and nor was she liable for the damage because there was no agreement.

16.2.7 Right to reject

Farnworth Finance v Attryde (1970), see above, 15.1.2.

Porter v General Guarantee Corp (1982), see above, 15.1.2.

UCB Leasing v Holtom (1987) CA

In October 1980, Holtom agreed to lease (or hire) an Alfa Romeo car from UCB for a 37 month period. Between August and October the car suffered three complete electrical failures and other serious problems. Holtom ceased to pay any instalments after November, but continued to use the car occasionally until the end of December. He finally returned the car in March the following year. In April UCB treated the agreement as terminated and sued Holtom for all the payments under the agreement. Holtom argued, *inter alia*, that in hire agreements (unlike sale of goods) the supplier had a *continuing* obligation that the goods were fit for their purpose. Hence he was entitled to reject the goods at any time during the hire period.

Held the right to reject goods was the same for hire as it was for sale contracts. It was a question of fact in each case. Here, by using the car until the end of December and keeping it until March, Holtom had affirmed the contract and lost his right to reject.

16.2.8 Duty to take care of the goods

Brady v St Margaret's Trust Ltd (1963) CA

A Ford Zephyr car was let to Brady on hire-purchase terms. The agreement included a clause that the debtor (Brady) should keep the car in good order, repair and condition. Brady defaulted and the creditor terminated the agreement and repossessed the car. The creditor claimed, *inter alia*, damages for Brady's failure to keep the car in good order.

Held the creditor was entitled to damages for breach of the agreement to keep the car in good order. The amount was to be assessed by reference to the condition of the car at the time the agreement was made and by how much Brady had failed to keep the car in good order.

Q Do you think there is a common law duty to take reasonable care of the goods irrespective of the requirements of the agreement? For a statutory duty to take care of goods when a regulated agreement has been cancelled, see s 72(3) of the Consumer Credit Act 1974.

16.3 Sale by debtor

See, also, above, Chapter 12.

Wickham Holdings Ltd v Brooke House Motors Ltd (1967) CA

Wickham (creditor) let a Rover car to Pattinson (debtor) under a hire-purchase agreement. However, Pattinson sold the car to Brooke House, while still owing Wickham £274.10 s. Wickham terminated the agreement and sued Brooke House in conversion for the return of the car or its value (£365), assessed at the time of the conversion.

Held Wickham were only entitled to recover damages representing their loss caused by the wrongful sale of the debtor, Pattinson. Thus, they were entitled to just £274.19 s.

Union Transport Finance v British Car Auctions (1978) CA

UTF (creditor) let an Audi car to Smith (debtor) on hire-purchase terms. The agreement stipulated that the debtor should not alter any identifying marks on the car and nor should he sell it. It also provided that if the debtor committed any breach of the agreement, the creditor could terminate it by serving a default notice and then repossess the car. Smith changed the registration number of the car and sold it through British Car Auctions. UTF sued BCA for conversion. BCA defended by arguing that as UTF had not served a default notice they did not have a right to immediate possession of the car.

Held UTF had a right at common law to terminate the agreement without notice if the debtor acted in a way repugnant to the agreement. The term allowing termination on breach after the service of a default notice was an *addition* to the creditor's rights at common law. Hence UTF succeeded.

Q This case was decided on the law before the passing of the Consumer Credit Act 1974. That Act (by s 87 of the Consumer Credit Act) requires the creditor to serve a notice before termination. Do you think that this statutory requirement would be held to be an 'addition' to the creditors' common law rights?

Chubb Cash v John Crilley (1983) CA

Chubb supplied a cash register to the debtor on hire-purchase terms; Chubb was also the creditor. Subsequently, bailiffs acting for a third party seized the register – but not before being assured by the debtor that it was his property. This was untrue: the debtor still owed Chubb £1,200. The bailiffs sold the register at auction for £178.25. Chubb then sued the bailiffs in conversion and claimed £1,200 representing the sum owed by the defaulting debtor. The defendants claimed that the damages should be the value of the goods at the time of the conversion.

Held the damages for conversion of goods subject to a hire-purchase agreement is the value of the goods or the amount still owing on the agreement, whichever is the lower. Chubb's claim for the amount of the debt owed by their debtor would have the effect of making the innocent convertors (here the bailiffs) guarantors of the debt for the benefit of Chubb. *Wickham Holdings v Brooke House Motors* (above) was distinguished.

16.4   Lien

Albemarle Supply v Hind (1927) CA

Albemarle let three taxi cabs to Botfield on hire-purchase terms. The agreement required Botfield to keep the cabs in good repair and prohibited him from creating a repairer's lien in favour of anyone who might be entrusted with maintenance or repairs of the vehicles. Botfield kept the cabs at Hind's garage, where they were maintained and repaired as necessary. Subsequently, Botfield fell into arrears with the hire-purchase payments and Albemarle terminated the agreement and demanded the possession of the cabs from Hind. As Hind was also owed money by Botfield he refused to give the cabs up, claiming a repairer's lien.

Held the common law repairer's lien was good against the creditor even if the repairer was aware that the goods were subject to a hire-purchase agreement. The hirer (Botfield) had implied authority to grant the lien notwithstanding the private restriction in the hire-purchase agreement. Thus Albemarle would have to pay Botfield's debt with Hind to obtain the release of the cabs.

Note

Diplock LJ in *Tappenden v Artus* (below) explained this case as one of estoppel: Albemarle represented to Hind that Botfield had authority to grant the lien.

Q Would the decision have been the same if Hind knew of the restriction in the hire-purchase agreement?

Bowmaker v Wycombe Motors (1946)

In August 1945 Bowmakers let a car on hire-purchase to Payne. The agreement required Payne to keep the car in good repair and prohibited him from creating a repairer's lien in favour of anyone who might be entrusted with maintenance or repairs. On 12 December, Bowmakers terminated the agreement because Payne was in arrears. Payne disregarded the termination and on 27 December he had an accident and put the car into Wycombe Motors for repair. Bowmakers sought to recover the car but Wycombe Motors claimed a lien in respect of the repairs, which had not been paid for.

Held the authority of Payne to create a lien in favour of a repairer (see *Albemarle v Hind* (above)) ceased with the termination of the agreement. Thus when Payne put the car into the garage after Bowmakers had terminated the agreement, he did so without any authority and no lien was created.

Tappenden v Artus and Rayleigh Garage (1963) CA

Tappenden, a car dealer, agreed to let Artus have the use of his Bedford Dormobile motor van if Artus would tax and insure it. So this was a contract of bailment for reward. While Artus was using the van, it broke down and he then put it into Rayleigh Garage for repairs. However, he refused to pay Rayleighs. Then Tappenden revoked the bailment and demanded possession of the van from Rayleighs. Rayleighs refused to give up the van, claiming a lien against Tappenden.

Held Rayleighs were entitled to their lien. Diplock LJ reviewed the cases and produced the following summary:

(i) bailment *per se* did not give the bailee the right to give possession of the goods to another;

(ii) where there was bailment for reward and the bailee was entitled to use the goods (for example, hire-purchase and hire) he was entitled to have the goods repaired so that he could continue to use them;

(iii) in that case the bailee was entitled to deliver the goods to an expert repairer;

(iv) delivery of possession to a repairer created a lien in favour of the repairer against the creditor and any clause in the hire contract (between debtor and creditor) would not affect this lien unless the repairer knew of it (*Albemarle v Hind*, above, explained as estoppel);

(v) if the bailment was terminated before the repairer gets possession there can be no lien. This was because the debtor no longer had the right of use and so no longer had the right to have the goods repaired (see *Bowmaker v Wycombe Motors*, above).

16.5   Dealer as agent

Campbell Discount v Gall (1961) CA

A car dealer, Windsor Autos, agreed to supply a Vauxhall car to Gall and arrange hire-purchase terms with the creditor, Campbells. The price was agreed at £265 and Gall signed a proposal form leaving the dealer to fill in details, including the price. The dealer fraudulently entered the price as £325 and Campbells accepted this offer, paid the dealer and let the car to Gall. When the truth was discovered, Gall refused to pay any instalments and Campbells sued him. Gall argued that: (i) the dealer was the agent of the creditor and so Campbells were bound by the dealer's fraudulent act; and (ii) there was a mistake as to the price of the goods and so the contract was void and unenforceable by Campbells.

Held: (i) in the absence of express words there is no presumption that the dealer was an agent of the creditor; (ii) the contract was void for mistake and so unenforceable.

Financings Ltd v Stimson (1962) CA

Stimson inspected an Austin car at the premises of Stanmore Motor Co and agreed to buy it on hire-purchase terms. Stanmore asked Stimson to sign a proposal form of the creditor, Financings. He did this and on 18 March he was given possession of the car. However, Stimson did not like the car and, on 20 March, he returned it to Stanmore. Neither party informed Financings of this. Four days later, the car was stolen from the dealer's premises and recovered in a damaged condition. On 25 March, Financings counter-signed the proposal form. Subsequently they sold the car and sued Stimson for breach of the hire-purchase agreement. Stimson claimed that there was no agreement. When a proposal form is signed and sent to the creditor (Financings) an offer is made by the debtor (Stimson). Only when the creditor countersigns the proposal form is that offer accepted and thus only then does a hire-purchase agreement come into existence. Thus when Stimson returned the car he revoked his offer before it was accepted. In reply, Financings stated that revocation must be communicated to the offeree (Financings) and that the dealer has no authority to accept revocation on their behalf.

Held (2:1) for the purposes of revocation only, the dealer (Stanmore) was the agent of the creditor and so communication of revocation to the dealer was effective as against the creditor. Thus, there was no hire-purchase agreement between the parties; judgment for Stimson.

> Note
>
> This rule is now reinforced by s 57 of the Consumer Credit Act. Where s 57 applies the debtor also enjoys a lien over the goods to compel repayment of, for example, a deposit (s 70(2) of the Consumer Credit Act).

Branwhite v Worcester Works Finance (1969) HL

A car dealer, the Raven Motor Co, enjoyed an ongoing relationship with the creditor (Worcester Works) and kept a stock of the creditor's proposal forms on their premises. Ravens agreed to supply a Rapier car to Branwhite on hire-purchase terms. The price agreed was £430. Branwhite paid Ravens a deposit of £130 and signed one of the creditor's proposal forms, leaving Ravens to fill in the details, including the price. In fact Ravens entered £649 as the price on the proposal form; the creditor accepted this offer, paid Ravens £519 (£649 less the deposit of £130) and let the car to Branwhite. When the truth was discovered, Branwhite refused to pay any instalments and the creditor repossessed the car. Branwhite then sued the creditor for the return of his deposit. Branwhite argued that: (i) there was a mistake as to the price of the goods and so the contract was void; and (ii) that the dealer was the agent of the creditor and so the creditor was bound by the dealer's fraudulent act.

Held on point (i), the contract was void for mistake and so Branwhite was entitled to a refund. On point (ii) (3:2), in the absence of express words, there is no presumption that the dealer is an agent of the creditor.

Note ──

On point (ii) this common law position was reversed by s 56 of the Consumer Credit Act which provides that the supplier (of goods financed by a DCS agreement within s 12(b) or (c) of the Consumer Credit Act) negotiates with the debtor as an agent for the creditor.

United Dominion Trust v Western (1976) CA

Romanay Car Sales agreed to supply Western a Ford Corsair car on hire-purchase terms. The price agreed was £550. The dealer asked Western to sign a form for the hire-purchase arrangement. Western signed the form without reading it. In fact it was not a form for hire-purchase, but a proposal form for a loan from the plaintiffs, UDT. The dealer entered a figure of £730 instead of £550, and sent it to UDT. The finance was agreed and Western took delivery of the car. However, Western was unhappy with the car and hardly used it. Eventually, it was stolen. He also failed to repay any of the loan to UDT, who sued. In his defence, Western argued that, as the figures in the loan form were inconsistent with the agreed price of the car, the agreement was void for mistake and so unenforceable.

Held Western was under a duty of care to UDT to ensure that the form he signed truly represented his contractual intention. Thus it was for him to show that he acted carefully. In signing a form in blank and not reading it, he did not act carefully and UDT could recover under the agreement.

Moorgate Mercantile Leasing v Gell and Ugolini Dispensers (1988)

Mrs Gell ran a newsagent and confectioner shop. She was approached by Ugolini who interested her in an ice-shake machine for her shop. Consequently, she entered into a leasing agreement with Moorgate (who had bought the machine from Ugolini) for 36 months, at a total cost of £1,825. The agreement gave Mrs Gell no right to terminate. After making two payments Mrs Gell found the machine not to be profitable and she returned it to Moorgate, who sued her for damages for breach of the agreement. In her defence, Mrs Gell alleged certain misrepresentations by Ugolini and that by s 56 of the Consumer Credit Act, Ugolini (the 'suppliers') were agents for Moorgate (the 'creditor'). Thus, Moorgate were liable for the misrepresentations of Ugolini.

Held s 56 was not applicable here as the agreement was a 'hire agreement' falling within s 15 of the Consumer Credit Act (which is not covered by s 56) and not a credit agreement falling within s 12 of the Consumer Credit Act (which *is* covered by s 56). Although 'credit' was broadly defined by s 9 of the Consumer Credit Act, the agreement afforded no credit whatsoever and could not, therefore, fall within s 12. Thus, Ugolini was not an agent for Moorgate who could not be held liable for any misrepresentations made by Ugolini. Mrs Gell was liable to Moorgate for damages for breach.

Note ————————————————————————————————

This case was followed in *Lloyds Bowmaker v MacDonald* (1993).

Lease Management Services Limited v Purnell Secretarial Services Limited (1994) CA

Canon (South West) Ltd supplied photocopiers in the south west of England. They employed a typical triangular arrangement whereby they would sell machines to Lease Management Services (LMS) who in turn would hire or lease them to Canon's customers. A salesman of Canon visited Purnell with a demonstration model of a new photocopy machine. Purnell were concerned that the machine could produce photo plates or 'paper plates'. The demonstration model did this and so Purnell ordered one from the salesman. Purnell signed an agreement which was headed 'Canon (South West) Finance'. Beside the word 'Supplier' appeared 'Canon (South West) Limited'. The words 'Canon (South West) Limited' were printed in red in large type. The word 'Canon' was printed in the distinctive form of that company's logo. These words were eye catching and were the most prominent feature on the page. Further down, much more tightly typed, were the words 'Lessor – Owner: Lease Management Services trading as Canon (South West) Finance'. Quite reasonably, Purnell thought that they had signed an agreement with the salesman's company Canon (South West) Ltd. In fact, the agreement was with LMS trading as Canon (South West) *Finance*. The photocopier that was delivered did not produce paper plates, as the demonstration model had. Purnell tried to reject the machine for breach of a collateral warranty (given by the salesman's demonstration). However, LMS claimed that the collateral warranty had been made by Canon and not them. Further, neither Canon nor the salesman were agents of LMS. LMS tried to enforce the agreement against Purnell.

Held the use of the forms, and especially the use of the trading name Canon (South West) *Finance*, was bound to lead customers into believing that they were dealing with Canon (South West) Ltd and not LMS. Accordingly, LMS were estopped from denying that Canon and their salesman were agents for them. Accordingly, LMS were liable for the collateral warranty that the photocopier would produce paper plates.

Note

This was not a regulated agreement under the Consumer Credit Act. But even if it was, it would have been a 'consumer hire agreement' within s 15 of the Consumer Credit Act and accordingly s 56 of the Consumer Credit Act would not have applied. See *Moorgate Mercantile Leasing v Gell and Ugolini Dispensers* (above).

Williams Leasing v McCauley (1994) CA

A company called Channel 9 used a typical triangular arrangement to supply video and projection equipment to clubs. Salespersons from Channel 9 approached clubs with the idea that the clubs hire or lease the equipment. If a club agreed to this, Channel 9 *sold* the equipment to Williams, who in turn leased the goods to the club. Channel 9 and Williams had a close working relationship: they had made some 200 agreements over two and a half years; and Channel 9 had even had Williams' forms printed for their own use. In the instant case Mr Stevens – a salesman for Channel 9 – had made a typical deal with the defendant club. However, when doing so he had fraudulently misrepresented that *Channel 9* were the leasing company involved. In due course, the club fell behind with the payments and Williams Leasing sued them. In their defence the club argued that it could be inferred from the 'close working relationship' of Channel 9 and Williams that Channel 9 and Mr Stevens were the agents of Williams. It followed that the agreement between Williams and the club was unenforceable because of the fraud perpetuated by Mr Stevens.

Held applying *Branwhite v Worcester Works* (above) there was nothing to suggest that Channel 9 had been authorised by Williams to act as agents. This was so despite the 'close working relationship'. Judgment for Williams.

Woodchester Equipment (Leasing) Ltd v British Association of Canned and Preserved Foods Importers and Distributors Ltd (1995) CA

Two suppliers of office equipment, Magnum and Business Products Ltd, operated typical triangular arrangements to supply and sell office equipment. They employed salespersons to approach and secure deals from customers. Once that was done, the suppliers would sell the equipment to a finance company, who in turn would hire or lease it to the customer. The suppliers would install the equipment. Magnum used Woodchester Equipment (Leasing) Ltd as the finance company and Business Products used Total Office Service Products (TOSP). Late in 1989, Mr Black, a salesman for Magnum, approached the defendants with a view to supplying them with a fax machine. In January 1990, he returned and closed the deal, procuring a signature from the defendants. However, by this time Mr Black was working for another supplier, Business Products, and the leasing agreement that the defendants had signed was with TOSP. Mr Black did not disclose his change of job and so the defendants thought that they were signing an agreement with Woodchester. Then in February Mr Marco, a salesman for Magnum, approached the defendants and fraudulently told them that the agreement which they had signed was ineffective, and they would have to sign another. The defendants did this. This (second) agreement was, of course, between the defendants and Woodchester. The truth began to surface when two fax machines had been delivered to the defendants. They tried to rescind the agreement (induced by Mr Marco) with Woodchester, who sued for payment. The defendants argued that Magnum and Mr Marco were agents for Woodchester and accordingly Mr Marco's fraud could be attributed to Woodchester. Thus the defendants were entitled to rescind the agreement.

Held applying *Branwhite v Worcester Works* and *Williams Leasing v McCauley* (above) there was nothing to suggest that Magnum and Mr Marco had been authorised by Woodchester to act as their agents. Thus the agreement between Woodchester and the defendants was not infected by the fraud of Mr Marco and Woodchester could recover money owed under the agreement.

PB Leasing v Patel and Patel (t/a Plankhouse Stores) (1995)

A dealer in retail video products used a typical triangular arrangement to supply and sell goods. They employed salespersons to approach and secure deals from customers. Once that was done, the suppliers would sell the equipment to a finance company, who in turn would hire or lease it to the customer. In this case the finance company was PB. A salesman of the dealer approached the Patels and told them (falsely) that the agreements could be terminated at any time without penalty. The Patels agreed to hire video cassettes, racking and an electronic cash register. They signed the agreement, believing it to be with the dealer, and left the salesman to fill in the details later. The goods were delivered the following day but the Patels tried to cancel the agreement. No second copy of the agreement was sent to the Patels. Eventually, the dealer took back the goods before going into liquidation. PB looked to the Patels for recompense. They claimed from them: (i) payment under the leasing agreement; or (ii) damages for misrepresentation. This second claim was based upon the contention that the dealer (and his salesman) was an agent for the *Patels*. In turn the Patels claimed that the dealer (and his salesman) were agents for PB and as principal PB were liable for the misrepresentation by the salesman.

Held the dealer (and his sales staff) were agents for neither PB nor the Patels: *Branwhite v Worcester Works* applied. However, the agreement was not enforced against the Patels for two reasons: (i) as the agreement was signed before the details were filled in it was improperly executed (s 61(1)(a)) and unenforceable (s 127(3)); (ii) as no copy was provided, contrary to s 62(1), the court would not enforce the agreement because it would be unjust to do so (s 127(1)).

Note

Although this was a regulated agreement, s 56 of the Consumer Credit Act (dealer is agent) did not apply because this was a 'consumer hire agreement' within s 15, which is not covered by s 56. See *Moorgate Mercantile Leasing v Gell and Ugolini Dispensers* (above).

Forthright Finance Ltd v Ingate (Carlyle Finance Ltd, third party) (1997)

Mrs Ingate wanted to buy a Fiat Panda car for £2,995 from a dealer. Her existing car, an Austin Metro, was the subject of a conditional sale agreement, on which she owed £1,992 to Forthright. In what could only be termed loosely as a part exchange, the dealer agreed to take Mrs Ingate's Metro off her hands and settle her debt with Forthright. This, of course, raised no money for Mrs Ingate; it simply discharged her debt to Forthright. At the same time, Mrs Ingate put a £1,000 deposit on the Fiat and funded the balance with a conditional sale – arranged by the dealer – with another finance company, Carlyle Ltd. However, the dealer failed to pay off the Metro debt to Forthright and then went into liquidation. Subsequently, Forthright sued Mrs Ingate, the debtor on the Metro agreement, for their money. Mrs Ingate argued that *Carlyle* were liable, as the dealer was acting as their agent when he agreed with Mrs Ingate to settle her debt with Forthright. Section 56 of the Consumer Credit Act provides that the dealer is deemed to be the agent of the creditor in respect of 'antecedent negotiations' conducted 'in relation to goods sold or proposed to be sold'. Section 56(1)(b) of the Consumer Credot Act provides that the dealer (as 'credit broker') is deemed to be the agent of the creditor in respect of 'antecedent negotiations' conducted 'in relation to goods sold or proposed to be sold'. So the issue for the Court of Appeal was whether the dealer's representation (that he would pay off the Metro debt) was a statement 'in relation to' the sale of the Fiat.

Held Carlyle were liable for the debt. The dealer was acting as their agent when they agreed to pay the debt on behalf of Mrs Ingate. Thus, the dealer's failure to do so was attributable to Carlyle, as principal. The decision was influenced by two main factors. First, the Metro transaction was 'related' to the Fiat one because it was clear on the facts that although this was not a conventional part exchange, Mrs Ingate would not have agreed to buy the Fiat had the dealer not offered to settle the Metro debt. Secondly, (*per* Henry LJ), s 56(4) of the Consumer Credit Act provided that the term 'antecedent negotiations' should be given a wide construction.

Notes

1 Section 56(4) provides that 'antecedent negotiations shall be taken to begin when the negotiator and the debtor ... first enter into communication (including communication by advertisement), and to include any representations made by the negotiator to the debtor ... and any other dealings between them'.

2 This decision should settle a debate illustrated by two conflicting cases in lower courts. Each case involved a (conventional) part exchange deal where the dealer had reneged on an agreement to settle the debt owing on the traded in car. In *Powell v Lloyds Bowmaker* (1996), the representation in relation to the traded in car was held not to be made 'in relation to' (NB s 56) the main transaction; the Sheriff's Court refusing to follow *UDT v Whitfield* (1986) where, upon identical facts, an English county court came to the opposite decision. Of course, such cases, involving a conventional part exchange, would come well within the Court of Appeal ruling *Forthright v Ingate*.

3 See Dobson, 'Agency of car dealers' (1997) 18(1) Bus LR 5–7.

16.6 Early payment

16.6.1 Common law and equity

Lancashire Wagon Co v Nuttall (1879) CA

Nuttall hired from LWC 24 wagons. The agreement was for three years at £249 per year. Property was to pass when the payments were completed, so this was a conditional sale. After two years, Nuttall sent payment to cover the whole of the remaining third year and claimed that, consequently, the property in the wagons had passed to him. LWC claimed that Nuttall was not entitled to decide when the property passed by pre-payment.

Held the property passed to Nuttall upon payment of the three years' rent. The credit given was for the benefit of the purchaser (Nuttall) and so he was entitled to make early payment and have the property in the goods transferred. *Obiter*, had Nuttall demanded a discount (or 'rebate') the matter would have been different.

Stamford Finance v Gandy (1957)

Gandy, who had taken a car on hire-purchase from Stamford Finance, asked for an (early) settlement figure. He was told that the sum required was £78. In fact there had been a clerical error; the sum was actually £145. However, Gandy paid the £78 and title to the car was passed to him. When the mistake was discovered, Stamford sued Gandy for the balance.

Held the agreement to purchase the vehicle was void for mistake because Gandy knew, or ought to have known, that Stamford made a mistake when requesting just £78. Secondly, the doctrine of unjust enrichment would not allow Gandy to escape liability. Thus, he had to pay the balance of £67.

Lombard North Central v Stobart (1990) CA

Stobart entered a conditional sale agreement with Lombards in respect of a VW 'Kamper' van. The total price was £11,000. After he had paid 23 of the 60 instalments Stobart asked for a settlement figure, as he wished to sell the van in order to pay for a holiday. The figure given by Lombards was £993 if paid within 10 days. Stobart failed to make that payment but inquired again of a settlement figure. He was told £1,003 if paid immediately. This was confirmed in writing and again on the telephone to Stobart's son, who then sold the van for £5,100. Lombards then realised that they had made a mistake; the true settlement figure was nearly £6,000.

Held as Stobart honestly believed the quoted figure, and relied upon it, it was equitable to prevent Lombards relying on their strict legal right. Stobart need only pay £1,003.

16.6.2 Consumer Credit Act 1974

Home Insulation Ltd v Wadsley (1987)

Mr Mossess entered into a credit agreement with HIL to finance the purchase of some double-glazing units. The agreement provided for a rebate in the event of Mr Mossess making an early settlement. After he had paid one instalment Mr Mossess wished to pay off the loan and so he telephoned HIL and requested an early settlement statement. The statement sent indicated a rebate in accordance with the Consumer Credit (Rebate on Early Settlement) Regulations 1983. However, this was £68.42 less than the rebate stated in the (more generous) agreement. Three weeks later Mr Mossess made a written request for an early settlement statement. The statement which followed was the same as the first. The Trading Standards Officer brought a prosecution, *inter alia*, in relation to the second statement, under s 97(3) of the Consumer Credit Act (and the regulations thereunder) for failing to provide a statement indicating the amount required to discharge the debt. In their defence HIL argued:

(i)   s 97 stipulated that the statement must contain the 'amount required' to discharge the debt. This, they maintained, meant the amount required under the Regulation of 1983 and not under the agreement and accordingly the statement was correct; alternatively

(ii) that by s 97(2) the creditor was not obliged to provide a statement within one month of complying with a previous request and although that previous request was made over the telephone and not in writing (as required by s 97(1)), the need for a written request had been waived in the circumstances. Thus, the prosecution must fail because the second statement, being the subject of the prosecution, was not a statement made under s 97.

Held: (i) the 'amount required' in s 97 meant the 'amount *legally* required' to discharge the debt. This meant the amount given by the Regulations of 1983 (which set out a *minimum* rebate) or the amount allowed in the agreement, whichever favoured the debtor. Here Mr Mossess was entitled to a rebate in accordance with the more generous rate stated in the agreement and so the settlement statement was false and misleading. (ii) A request for an early settlement statement must be made in writing and cannot be waived. Therefore the second statement was the one made under s 97. Hence the prosecution succeeded.

17 Enforcement and remedies

17.1 Damages for breach

Brady v St Margaret's Trust (1963), above, 16.2.8.

Interoffice Telephones v Freeman (1957) CA
Interoffice installed a telephone system in Freeman's premises and hired it to them for a fixed period. When the agreement still had six years to run Freeman wrongfully repudiated and Interoffice sued for breach. At the time, the supply of telephone installations exceeded the demand.

Held the damages should be assessed in the same way for a hire contract as they are for a sale contract. In this case there is no available market to absorb the service and so Interoffice were entitled to damages for the loss of six years' rental, less their maintenance costs and a deduction for accelerated receipt of the rental. The sale of goods case, *Thompson v Robinson* (1955) (see above, 14.2.1) was applied.

Yeoman Credit v Waragowski (1961) CA
Yeoman let a Ford Thames van to Waragowski on hire-purchase terms. The hire-purchase price was £434. Waragowski paid a £72 deposit but failed to pay any instalments. After six months Yeoman treated the agreement as repudiated by Waragowski, repossessed the van and sued for damages for wrongful repudiation. Upon repossession the van was worth £205.

Held the measure of damages for repudiation of a hire-purchase agreement was any arrears (here £60) plus the difference between the hire-purchase price less a £1 option to buy fee (£433) and the deposit plus the value of the goods recovered (£72+£205=£377). Thus, £433 less £377 is £96. After adding the arrears the total sum awarded was £156.

Overstone v Shipway (1962) CA
Overstone let a car on hire-purchase to the Shipway. The hire-purchase was price £452, to be paid with a £73 deposit and 36 monthly instalments. Shipway paid the deposit, obtained possession but failed to pay any instalments. Four months later Overstone repossessed the car and, in a separate action for debt, were awarded the four instalments due. In the instant case Overstone sued Shipway for damages for wrongful repudiation. The damages calculated on the *Waragowski* basis (above) came to £48.

Held if the agreement were carried out Overstone would have received the payments over a three year period. However, the debtor's repudiation means that, on the *Waragowski* basis, Overstone would receive accelerated payment. Thus it is right to discount the award to account for this. The court should not act as mathematicians, but endeavour to ascertain the loss to the creditor so far as money can compensate. The award was reduced to £25.

Financings Ltd v Baldock (1963) CA

Financings let a Bedford truck to Baldock on hire-purchase terms, which provided for 24 monthly payments. Baldock failed to pay the first two instalments but told Financings that he hoped to pay off the arrears. Financings terminated the agreement, repossessed the car and claimed damages assessed on the *Waragowski* (above) basis, that is, (i) the arrears plus (ii) a sum calculated on future rentals.

Held the arrears were recoverable but sum (ii) was not. This was deemed to be a penalty and so unenforceable (see below, 17.2.1). *Waragowski* was distinguished on the ground that in the instant case the debtor's breach did not amount to repudiation of the agreement. Here, it was the creditor who repudiated and in that case he cannot claim for loss of future payments.

Lombard North Central v Butterworth (1987) CA

A leasing agreement in respect of a computer stipulated that prompt payment of instalments was of the essence. When a number of instalments were overdue, the lessor terminated the agreement, repossessed the computer and claimed damages on the *Waragowski* (above) basis.

Held the lessor was entitled to damages on the *Waragowski* basis. *Financings v Baldock* (above) was distinguished because in this case prompt payment was a *condition* of the agreement. Hence, as soon as one payment became overdue the lessee (or debtor) was in repudiatory breach, whereas in *Baldock* it was the creditor who repudiated.

Note ⸺

A simple change by the draftsmen of credit agreements appears to have rendered *Baldock* obsolete. See Treitel [1987] LMCLQ 143. This was not a regulated agreement; s 89 of the Consumer Credit Act states that the debtor must be given an opportunity to bring his payments up to date.

17.2 Minimum payment clauses

United Dominions Trust v Ennis (1967) CA

UDT let a Jaguar car on hire-purchase terms to Ennis. The agreement gave Ennis a right to terminate at any time. In that case he should return the car and pay UDT a sum in addition to his previous payments to make up two thirds of the hire-purchase price, this being compensation for depreciation of the goods. Ennis worked in the Port of London and soon after he made the agreement there was a dockers' strike which severely affected his wages. He wrote to UDT stating that as he could no longer pay the instalments he wished to terminate. UDT sued Ennis under the agreement for the sum to make up two-thirds of the hire-purchase price.

Held Ennis did not terminate the agreement, he merely intimated that he could not pay. Hence, UDT terminated the agreement and the minimum payment clause was void as a penalty for the debtor's default.

Q If the debtor defaults, a minimum payment clause may be void as a penalty (*Bridge v Campbell Discount* (1962), below, 17.2.1). However, if the debtor exercises a contractual right to terminate, the minimum payment clause is enforceable (*Associated Distributers v Hall* (1938), below, 17.2.1).

Do you think that this explains the reluctance of the Court of Appeal to find that Ennis had terminated the agreement?

Wadham Stringer v Meaney (1980)

Meaney (debtor) entered into a conditional sale agreement with Wadhams in order to finance the purchase of a Triumph car. Payment was by a deposit and 36 monthly instalments. The agreement was regulated by provisions similar to the Consumer Credit Act 1974 in the Hire-Purchase Act 1965. Under its terms, the creditor (Wadhams) had the right to call for accelerated payment of the whole amount upon default, in which case property in the car would pass to Meaney upon payment. Meaney paid the deposit but failed to pay any instalments. Wadhams issued a default notice (see now s 87 of the Consumer Credit Act) giving 10 days for payment of the accelerated payment. Meaney failed to pay within the 10 days and Wadhams sued for the amount. Meaney argued that the accelerated payment clause infringed her statutory right to terminate 'at any time before the final payment' (now s 99 of the Consumer Credit Act) because final payment did not fall due until the last of the 36 instalments.

Held the accelerated payment would be the final payment for the purposes of s 99 of the Consumer Credit Act and so the clause was not inconsistent with the debtor's statutory right to terminate.

17.2.1 Penalties

Associated Distributers v Hall (1938) CA

The plaintiffs (creditor) let under a hire-purchase agreement a tandem bicycle to Hall (debtor). The agreement provided that Hall had a right to terminate at any time. Further, if he exercised this right he would return the goods to the plaintiffs and pay them a sum in addition to his previous payments to make up half of the hire-purchase price. This was stated to be compensation for depreciation of the goods. Hall exercised his right to terminate the agreement and the plaintiffs sued for their compensation under the agreement. Hall disputed this, arguing that the 'compensation' was a penalty and so unenforceable.

Held where the *hirer* (here Hall) exercised a contractual right to terminate, the doctrine of penalties did not apply and the plaintiffs could recover whatever the contractual terms provided for.

Q Is the hirer better off defaulting?

Bridge v Campbell Discount (1962) HL

Bridge entered into a hire-purchase agreement with Campbells in respect of a Bedford Dormobile motor caravan. Clause 6 of the agreement provided Bridge with the right to terminate at any time; in that event clause 9 would apply. Clause 9 provided that in the event of termination the hirer would return the goods and pay Campbells a sum in addition to his previous payments to make up two thirds of the hire-purchase price, this being compensation for depreciation of the goods. After making one payment Bridge wrote to Campbells stating that his personal circumstances had changed and he could no longer afford to pay the instalments. Subsequently, he returned the goods and Campbells sued him for the amount prescribed by clause 9.

Held (4:1) this was not a case where the hirer (Bridge) had exercised his right under clause 6 of the agreement to terminate. He merely declared his inability to persist with the agreement and Campbells, having got possession of the goods, asserted their rights under clause 9. In that case the operation of clause 9 amounted to a penalty, not being a genuine pre-estimate of the depreciation or loss to Campbells. Campbells were entitled only to damages for their actual loss suffered. As the termination was not by the hirer *Associated Distributers v Hall* (above) did not apply.

Note ──

Associated Distributers v Hall was approved by Viscount Simonds and Lord Morton; but disapproved by Lords Denning and Devlin. Lord Radcliffe left the question open.

Anglo Auto Finance v James (1963) CA

In April 1960, James entered into a hire-purchase agreement with Anglo Auto in respect of a Vauxhall car. The hire-purchase price was £652 payable by 48 monthly instalments. The agreement required prompt payment of the instalments and in the event of default Anglo Auto were entitled to terminate the agreement. In that event, James would pay an amount by which the hire-purchase price exceeded all payments already made together with the value of goods when repossessed. In other words, Anglo Auto would recover in effect the total hire-purchase price. In November 1961 Anglo Auto terminated the agreement because James had fallen into arrears. They repossessed the car and sold it for £130. They then claimed £236 from James under the agreement.

Held the term in the agreement amounted to a penalty clause and so was unenforceable. In effect, it provided for recovery of the total hire-purchase price whether the termination was at the beginning or the end of the hire period. Damages, representing Anglo Auto's loss, of £25 only were recoverable.

17.3 Extortionate credit bargains

A Ketley Ltd v Scott (1981)

Scott, a businessman, needed a loan urgently in order to purchase a house on the day that the notice to complete expired. He applied for a loan from Ketley but failed to disclose: that his bank had a charge on the property (which if registered first would take priority); that he had given a guarantee of £5,000 to some of his companies; and that he had an overdraft of £2,000. He also told Ketley that the property was worth £30,000 when in fact it had been valued at £24,000. Ketley advanced £20,500 to Scott that day without making inquires as to his financial standing. The rate of interest was 48% per annum. Scott later defaulted and Ketley sought payment and repossession. Scott argued that the agreement was extortionate under s 138 of the Consumer Credit Act 1974.

Held the extortionate credit bargain provisions of the Consumer Credit Act apply to non-regulated agreements as long as the debtor was an individual within s 8(1). Having regard to the prevailing interest rates when the bargain was made, the fact that the loan was for 82% of the property's value (so repossession and a resale would be unlikely to cover the creditor's loss), that Ketley had no chance to make inquires into Scott's financial circumstances and that Scott was a businessman, the bargain was not extortionate under the Consumer Credit Act. Even if it was extortionate s 139 allows intervention 'if the court thinks just'. Scott's failure to disclose material facts to Ketley in any event meant that the bargain would not be reopened.

Coldunell Ltd v Gallon (1986) CA

Gallon needed to raise £20,000 and used deceit to induce his father, an 86 year old pensioner, to put up his bungalow as security against a loan from Coldunell. Gallon made only four payments and Coldunell brought an action seeking arrears or possession of the property. The defence argued that the agreement was brought about by undue influence and second, that because of this it was an extortionate credit bargain within the Consumer Credit Act 1974.

Held as the person exerting the undue influence (Gallon) was not an agent of the creditor, there could be no equitable relief on that basis. The burden of showing that the bargain was not extortionate (which was on the creditor) was discharged once it was shown that there was no undue influence by Coldunell. They had acted properly at all times and their charge on the bungalow was good. (In the event, the taking of possession was unnecessary.)

17.4 Repossession

17.4.1 Common Law

Bowmakers v Barnet Instruments (1945) CA

Bowmakers let on hire-purchase to Barnet some machine tools. Barnet made only occasional payments and then wrongfully sold the tools. Bowmakers sued Barnet for conversion. Barnet argued that the hire-purchase agreement was an illegal contract (for unconnected reasons) and consequently it could not be enforced by the courts.

Held Bowmakers had the property in the goods at the time of the sale by Barnet. Hence they had a right to their property and this right is independent of any contractual claims. So, even if the contract was illegal, this did not affect Bowmakers' claim to their own property and they would succeed.

17.4.2 Protected Goods

Section 90 of the Consumer Credit Act 1974:

(1) At any time when:

(a) the debtor is in breach of a regulated hire-purchase or a regulated conditional sale agreement relating to goods; and

(b) the debtor has paid to the creditor one third or more of the total price of the goods; and

(c) the property in the goods remains with the creditor,

the creditor is not entitled to recover possession of the goods from the debtor except on an order of the court.

Bentinck v Cromwell Engineering (1971) CA

Bentinck (creditors) let an MG car to Faulkner (debtor) on hire-purchase terms in May 1967. In October, the car was badly damaged in an accident and Faulkner left the car at a garage but gave no instructions. Three months later Bentinck contacted him about arrears. Faulkner did not pay the arrears, gave a false telephone number and disappeared without trace. After another six months, Bentinck traced the car to the garage and repossessed it. However, Faulkner had paid over a third of the price and the car was a 'protected good' under the Hire Purchase Act 1965 and could not be recovered without consent unless with a court order (see now ss 90, 91(b) of the Consumer Credit Act).

Held where the debtor had in law abandoned his rights to the (protected) goods, the recovery of those goods by the creditor was not in breach of the statute and the agreement was still enforceable (in this case against a guarantor).

Carr v James Broderick & Co (1942)

Broderick let furniture to Carr on hire-purchase terms. After he had paid over a third of the price (and the furniture became 'protected goods') Carr fell into arrears. Broderick repossessed the furniture in contravention of s 11 of the Hire Purchase Act 1938 (now s 90 of the Consumer Credit Act) which provided that the creditor could not repossess protected goods without consent unless he had a court order. Carr sued Broderick for conversion.

Held an action in conversion failed because property in the goods subject to hire-purchase (or conditional sale) agreements belonged to the creditor (Broderick). The proper course of action was to sue the creditor for a full refund of any money paid under the agreement (now s 91 of the Consumer Credit Act).

Capital Finance v Bray (1964) CA

Bray took an Austin car on hire-purchase terms from Capital. After Bray had paid over a third of the price, he fell two months in arrears. Capital repossessed the car without a court order in the middle of the night. The next morning Bray threatened legal action and Capital returned the car to outside Bray's house. Bray continued to use the car but failed to make any payments. Eventually Capital sued Bray for arrears. Bray counter-claimed that by s 11 of the Hire Purchase Act 1938 (now ss 90, 91 of the Consumer Credit Act) the repossession of protected goods (that is, where over a third of the total price was paid) without consent or a court order terminated the agreement and entitled him to a refund of all the money paid. Capital claimed that the original agreement subsisted because Bray had continued to use the car after the repossession.

Held the wrongful repossession terminated the agreement and so Bray was not liable for any arrears – he was actually entitled to a full refund.

Mercantile Credit v Cross (1965) CA

The creditor (Mercantile Credit) let an Ariel motor-cycle to Cross on hire-purchase terms. In accordance with s 2(2) of the Hire Purchase Act 1938 (now s 90 of the Consumer Credit Act) the agreement contained a notice stating that once a third of the price had been paid the goods could not be repossessed without Cross' consent unless with a court order. After he had paid over a third of the total price, Cross fell into arrears. The creditor sent a notice demanding the return of the motor-cycle and Cross complied. However, he discovered two months later (after taking legal advice) that he need not have given up the machine. He claimed that as he did not consent to the repossession the creditor had wrongfully enforced the agreement and accordingly he was entitled by s 11 of the Hire Purchase Act 1938 (see now ss 90, 91(b) of the Consumer Credit Act) to the return of all the money paid under the agreement.

Held the creditors had not contravened the statute and so Cross was not entitled to a refund. Although he did not want to give up possession Cross had consented to it freely; he had at the time a copy of the agreement containing a statement of his rights.

Chartered Trust v Pitcher (1987) CA

Pitcher entered into a hire-purchase agreement with Chartered Trust for a Ford Granada car. The agreement was governed, in part, by the Hire-Purchase Act 1965. Some time later Pitcher was made redundant. He informed Chartered Trust of this and asked if he could keep the car and reschedule the payments. Chartered Trust told Pitcher that the only option was for him to terminate the agreement: allowing Chartered Trust to repossess the car, sell it and recover a sum from Pitcher in accordance with a formula in the agreement. They did not inform Pitcher that the court had the power to re-schedule his payments. So Chartered Trust repossessed the car with Pitcher's permission and then sued him for the sum under the agreement. It was held that the car was a 'protected good' (under the Hire Purchase Act) and could not be recovered without Pitcher's consent. A further issue was whether Pitcher had actually 'consented' to the repossession.

Held Pitcher had not 'consented' to the repossession and consequently he was entitled to a full refund of all payments made under the agreement. 'Consent' under the statute meant 'informed consent'. When he permitted Chartered Trust to repossess the car, Pitcher was unaware of the court's power to reschedule his payments. Therefore, his consent to repossession was not 'informed consent'; it was clear that he wanted to keep the car and reschedule his payments. (*Mercantile Credit v Cross* (above) was distinguished on the ground that in *Cross* the debtor had been given a notice of his rights.)

Julian Hodge Bank v Hall (1997) CA

Hodge supplied a Ford Sierra car to Hall under a conditional sale. The total price was £8,335. Under the agreement, Hall was obliged to pay interest on late payments and £1 for every letter sent by Hodge following default by Hall. In due course, Hall fell into arrears incurring extra charges for interest and letters of £26. Hodge repossessed the car without a court order and informed Hall that he had paid, in total, £2,780. This was just over one-third (£2,778) of the total price and so Hall claimed that the repossession was wrongful because the car was a protected good. However, once in court, Hodge argued that £26 of Hall's payments had been allocated to the extra charges. Therefore, Hall had paid just £2,754 towards the total price, just under one third. Consequently, Hodge argued, the car was not a protected good and the repossession was lawful.

Held (i) a creditor was free to allocate payments either towards the total price or to other outstanding debts. However, the creditor must communicate the allocation to the debtor. Once communicated, the allocation becomes irrevocable; (ii) in this case Hodge (creditor) initially informed

Hall that all his payments had gone towards the total payment. They could not go back on this at a later time. Thus the car was a protected good when repossessed.

> **Note**
>
> Although the debtor in this case prevailed, the decision means that creditors can allocate payments to other debts in order to postpone the date when goods become protected goods. Of course, most debtors, receiving notice of the allocation, will not realise this consequence.

17.4.3 Time orders

Section 129 of the Consumer Credit Act provides:
(1) If it appears to the court just to do so:

(c) ... in an action brought by a creditor or owner to enforce a regulated agreement or any security, or recover possession of any goods or land to which a regulated agreement relates, the court may make an order under this section (a 'time order').

(2) A time order shall provide for one or both of the following, as the court considers just:

(a) the payment by the debtor or hirer or any surety of any sum owed under a regulated agreement or a security by such instalments, payable at such times, as the court, having regard to the means of the debtor or hirer and any surety, considers reasonable;

(b) the remedying by the debtor or hirer of any breach of a regulated agreement (other than non-payment of money) within such a period as the court may specify.

Section 136 of the Consumer Credit Act provides:

The court may in an order made by it under this Act include such provision as it considers just for amending any agreement or security in consequence of a term of the [time] order.

First National Bank v Syad (1991) CA
Under a regulated agreement the plaintiff bank loaned a sum of money to the defendants, who put up their house as security. After a long period of unemployment, the defendants were in serious arrears and the bank sought possession of the house. There were no immediate prospects of the defendants finding work and paying the outstanding sums and future instalments. Under s 129 of the Consumer Credit Act the court may make a time order (that is, reschedule the payments) 'if it appears just to do so'.

Held consideration of what was just was not limited to the position of the debtors; the court had to consider the position of the creditor as well. In this case there was no reasonable prospect of the defendants being able to afford to meet the accruing interest on the arrears, let alone the actual debt and future payments. Hence it would not be just to force the bank to accept payments which the defendants could afford, which would be so small so as not to begin to pay off the debt. An order for possession was granted.

Southern and District Finance plc v Barnes (1996) CA

Mr and Mrs Barnes borrowed £12,000 from the plaintiffs, Southern and District Finance (SDF), repayable over 10 years by 120 instalments of £260 per month. The Barnes put their house up as security on the loan. This was a regulated agreement. Ten months later they had fallen into arrears of £1,300. SDF sought possession of the Barnes' house. The Barnes applied for a time order under s 129 of the Consumer Credit Act for the whole of the loan. SDF argued (i) that the words 'any sum owed' in s 129(2)(a) (above) meant that a time order could only be made in respect of the £1,300 outstanding; it did not relate to future payments not yet due; (ii) that s 136 (above) did not empower a court to vary the rate of interest in relation to a time order. That would leave s 137 (which allows a court to vary extortionate credit bargains, see above, 17.3) otiose.

Held (i) ordinarily, a time order may only be made in respect of outstanding debts and not in respect of future payments. However, in cases where land is put up as a security, the position is different. An application for an order of possession is an exercise by the creditor of the right to realise the total indebtedness secured by the charge (security) on the property. As a matter of law as well as of common sense, when a creditor brings a possession action he demands payment of the whole of the sum outstanding under the charge. Thus when SDF brought proceedings for possession, they effectively called in the whole loan, which then became 'any sum owed' within s 129. Accordingly, a court could make a time order rescheduling the repayments of the whole loan; (ii) s 136 empowers a court to vary an agreement 'in consequence of a term of the [time] order'. Accordingly, a court may vary the interest of the rescheduled payments under a time order. Section 137 would not be otiose, because unlike s 136: (a) it also applies to unregulated agreements; and (b) it also applies whether or not the debtor is in arrears. As a matter of guidance when varying the interest, courts should consider, on the one hand, the contractual monthly interest accruing on the deficiency of payments under the time order, that is, the difference between the contractual payments and the lesser 'time order' payments. On the other hand, the creditor should be entitled to a greater sum to compensate them for a slower rate of repayment.

In the instant case, an order for possession should be suspended, so long as the rescheduled payments are made. In order to mitigate the impact of the interest charged on the unpaid instalments, the interest should be reduced from a monthly rate of 1% to 1.952% during the period of suspension of the possession order.

Part 5 International trade and finance

18 Bills of lading

18.1 General

Hansson v Hamel & Horley (1922) HL

Under a contract on CIF (see 20.1) terms for the sale of cod guano, the sellers, Hansson, agreed to ship the goods from Norway to Japan, shipment March/April. In fact Hansson shipped the goods from Norway to Germany, and then transferred them to a Japanese ship sailing direct to Japan. A 'through' bill of lading, which explained the transhipment arrangement, was signed by the owners of the Japanese ship. Later, when the bill of lading was presented, the buyers rejected it. Hansson sued them for price.

Held the buyers were entitled to reject. That bill of lading did not provide continuous documentary cover. The bill related to the Japanese carrier only, who took no responsibility for the prior voyage. Hence, this was not a through bill.

Note ───

For a commentary on this case, see *Benjamin's Sale of Goods*, 5th edn, 1997, para 19-026.

18.2 Bill as a contract of carriage – Bills of Lading Act 1855

Brandt v Liverpool, Brazil & River Plate Steam Navigation Co (1924)

Vogal shipped a number of bags of zinc ash from Buenos Aires to Liverpool. He obtained a bill of lading from the carrier and then endorsed it to Brandt as security for a loan. So Brandt took the bill as pledgee and the whole of the property in the goods did not pass to them. The ship arrived in Liverpool three months late. Brandt presented the bill to the carriers and, after paying freight costs, took possession of the goods. The market in zinc ash had fallen and Brandt sued the carriers *in contract* for late delivery. Under s 1 of the Bills of Lading Act when the property in the goods passed 'upon or by reason of' indorsement of the bill of lading, the rights and lia-bilities under the contract of carriage also passed from the seller to the indorsee.

Held Brandt would succeed. Although s 1 of the BLA did not apply because property had not passed 'upon or by reason of' the endorsement of the bill of lading, a contract between the carrier and Brandt was inferred from the circumstances: Brandt obtained possession of the goods after pre-senting the bill and paying for freight costs.

Note ───
See, generally, *Benjamin's Sale of Goods*, 5th edn, 1997, paras 18-103–08.

Ardennes (SS) (Owner of cargo) v Ardennes (SS) (Owner) (1950)

An oral contract of carriage was made for the shipping of mandarin oranges to London. It was agreed that the ship should go directly to London in order to avoid an expected rise in import tax. However, the bill of lading subse-quently issued allowed for deviation from the agreed route. In the event, the ship went via Antwerp and arrived in London after the tax increase. The shippers had to pay the higher duty and sued the carriers for compensation. The carriers relied on the terms contained in the bill of lading.

Held for the shippers. As between shipper and carrier, a bill of lading was a receipt for the goods which stated the terms on which they were being transported; hence it was excellent evidence of those terms but it was not a contract. The carriers were bound by the oral contract made.

Leigh & Sillavan v Aliakmon Shipping, *The Aliakmon* (1986) HL

L & S contracted to buy on C & F (see below, 20.1) terms steel coils to be shipped from Korea to Humberside, England. As is usual in C & F and CIF contracts the sellers contracted with the carriers and risk passed to the buy-ers on shipment. However, while the goods were on their way, a planned sub-sale by L & S fell through and they were unable to pay. A variation of the contract was negotiated whereby the sellers indorsed the bill of lading to L & S, enabling L & S to take possession of the goods on arrival at Humberside and store them as agents for the sellers. The sellers reserved property in the goods until they were paid for. When the steel coils were unloaded at Humberside they were damaged; this had been caused by the negligence of the carriers. All the same, L & S subsequently paid for the goods. Under s 1 of the Bills of Lading Act, when the property in the goods passed 'upon or by reason of' indorsement of the bill of lading, the rights and liabilities under the contract of carriage also passed from the seller to the indorsee (here the buyer, L & S). So L & S sued the carriers for breach of contract. They also sued them for negligence.

Held for the carriers. In CIF and C & F contracts the property passes when the buyer takes up and pays for the documents. Further, it was agreed in the variation of the contract that property would not pass until payment. Thus, s 1 of the Bills of Lading Act did not apply because property did not pass 'upon or by reason of' the indorsement of the bill of lading; it passed upon payment, which occurred later. Thus, L & S had no contractual claim against the carriers. The negligence claim would also fail because L & S had no legal or possessory right to the goods when the damage occurred. Lord Brandon commented that the cause of the problem was the 'extremely unusual' contract created by the variation. L & S should have either:

(i)   made it a term that the sellers sue the carriers on their account; or

(ii) had the rights to sue the carrier assigned to them.

Notes
1 See, generally, Bradgate, *Commercial Law*, 2nd edn, 1995, p 633; Reynolds (1986) LMCLQ 97 and Schmitthoff, *The Law and Practice of International Trade*, 9th edn, 1990, p 44.

2 The Bills of Lading Act 1855 has now been repealed by the Carriage of Goods by Sea Act 1992. The stipulation that property should pass with the transfer has been removed. Section 2(1) of the 1992 Act now provides that the person who becomes the lawful holder of a bill of lading shall 'have transferred to and vested in him all rights of suit under the contract of carriage as if he had been party to that contract'. Section 3 severs the link between the transfer of rights with that of liabilities under the contract of carriage so that now, in general, a transferee of a bill of lading cannot be held liable on the contract of carriage unless he claims the benefit of that contract. See, generally, *Benjamin's Sale of Goods*, 5th edn, 1997, paras 18-058 (transfer generally), 18-059 (transfer of rights) and 18-087 (transfer of liabilities).

Mitsui v Novorossiysk Shipping Co, *The Gudermes* (1992) CA
In December 1986, Mitsui agreed to buy some 30,000 tonnes of oil, ex Aden, from SNE. Property was to pass at the time of loading. SNE had made a contract of carriage (to Italy) with the defendants. In January 1987 the oil was loaded into the tanker, which headed for Italy. However, at the Italian port, the oil was rejected because the tanker did not have heating facilities; thus the oil was too cold (and so too thick) to discharge into port because there was a risk of blocking the terminal pipeline. The shipowners agreed with Mitsui to transship the oil into another tanker, which did have heating facilities. This second tanker would then discharge in Italy. The shipowners had expressly refused to bear the expense of the operation, which was $500,000. Meanwhile, the bills of lading were indorsed to Mitsui. Mitsui sued the shipowner, *inter alia*, for breach of contract, in that the tanker was not seaworthy. However, s 1 of the BLA did not operate to transfer the rights of the contract of carriage to Mitsui because the property in the oil passed before the indorsement of the bills of lading; so Mitsui alleged that there was a *Brandt* contract (see *Brandt v Liverpool, Brazil and River Plate Steam Navigation Co* (above)).

Held for a *Brandt* contract to be implied, the parties' actions 'must be consistent only with there being a new contract implied, and inconsistent with there being no such contract'. The alleged contract was a hybrid. On the one hand, Mitsui were relying on terms in the original contract of carriage ('seaworthiness') and on the other, terms of transshipment. On the facts, the shipowners merely co-operated with Mitsui to solve a problem. At the time they expressly refused to bear any expense of the transshipment. There was no contract between the parties.

Q The court stated *obiter* that the shipowners were in breach of the contract of carriage: it incorporated the Hague-Visby Rules, Art III, r 1 of which provides that shipowners were obliged to use due diligence to make the ship seaworthy, which includes 'cargoworthy'. Of course, as it was held that Mitsui had no rights under that contract, they could not sue on it. Do you think that the Court of Appeal's approach was unduly technical, given that the shipowners used a tanker clearly unsuitable for the task?

Notes————————————————————————————————

1   The Court of Appeal also held that the shipowners were not liable to Mitsui in negligence or bailment.

2   This case was governed by the (now superseded) Bills of Lading Act: the (new) Carriage of Goods by Sea Act 1992 not applying to bills of lading issued before 16 September 1992. The 1992 Act overcomes the 'property problem' of the Bills of Lading Act and so if the case were decided under the 1992 Act Mitsui could have enjoyed the rights of the contract of carriage.

Effort Shipping v Linden Management SA, *The Giannis* NK (1998) HL
The shippers sent a cargo of groundnuts on Effort's ship. Subsequently, it was discovered that the groundnuts were infested with Khapra beetles. In consequence the ship had to dump all its cargo at sea and then be fumigated. The ship was two and a half months late for its next charter. Meanwhile, the property in the groundnuts had been transferred by the indorsement of the bill of lading. Effort sued the shippers under the bill of lading for the cost of fumigation and the delay. The bill of lading incorporated the Hague Rules. Article IV, r 6, provided: 'Goods of an inflammable, explosive or dangerous nature to the shipment' may be destroyed by the carrier (Effort), who may claim damages for all expenses so arising. It was held that 'dangerous' in r 6 should be given a broad meaning to extend beyond 'physically dangerous to the ship' to 'legally' dangerous in that it may cause delay. Thus there was liability under r 6. The issue then became: had the shipper transferred his liability with the bill of lading? Under s 1 of the Bills of Lading Act 'every indorsee of a bill of lading ... shall have transferred to and vested in him all rights of suit, and be subject to the

same liabilities in respect of such goods as if the contract [of carriage] contained in the bill of lading had been made with himself'.

Held although s 1 states rights shall be 'transferred and vested in' the indorsee, it then states merely that he shall be 'subject to the same liabilities' as the original party to the contract. Thus, the shippers remain liable: the indorsee's liability is an *addition*, not a substitution.

Note _____

Lord Lloyd noted that although the Bills of Lading Act 1855 has been replaced by the Carriage of Goods by Sea Act 1992 (see Note 2 to *Leigh and Sillavan v Aliakmon Shipping* (above)) there were a number of outstanding cases still governed by the 1855 Act.

18.3 Document of title

Lickbarrow v Mason (1787) HL

Turing had sold and shipped a cargo of corn to Freeman. He obtained the bills of lading from the ship's master, indorsed them in blank and sent them to Freeman. While the ship was at sea, Freeman sold the goods to the plaintiffs, who paid for them. Freeman transferred the bill to the plaintiffs. Then Freeman became bankrupt without having paid Turing, so Turing purported to sell the goods to the defendants, who obtained possession when the ship arrived. The plaintiffs claimed that they had title to the goods.

Held for the plaintiffs. The unpaid seller (Turing) had a right to stop the goods in transit if the buyer (Freeman) became insolvent (see above, 14.4). But if the bill of lading was delivered to the buyer and he had indorsed it for valuable consideration to a third party (the plaintiffs) who acted in good faith, the property in the goods passed to that third party and the unpaid seller's right was divested. Hence, the property was transferred with the documents to the plaintiffs and Turing had no title to transfer to the defendants.

Wait v Baker (1848)

Lethbridge sold barley to the defendant on FOB (see below, 19.1) terms. The goods were shipped under bills of lading to the sellers' order. However, Lethbridge then refused (wrongfully) the defendant's offer to pay against the bills of lading. Instead, he transferred them to the plaintiff third party. When the ship arrived, the defendant managed to obtain some of the barley in question and the plaintiff sued claiming that the property was his.

Held by taking the bills of lading to his own order the sellers reserved the right of disposal and so the property in the goods never passed to the defendant.

Note ──────────────────────
Section 19(2) of the SGA codifies this case: the seller is *prima facie* taken to have reserved the right of disposal where the goods shipped are, by the bill of lading, deliverable to the sellers' order.
──────────────────────

18.4 Bill as a receipt

Golodetz v Czarnikow-Rionda, *The Galatia* (1980) CA
A contract was made for the sale of sugar C & F (see below, 20.1) Iran. After loading a fire broke out on the ship and the sugar was damaged by fire and/or water. These events were recorded on the bill of lading. Upon presentation for payment the buyers rejected the bill of lading, claiming that it was not 'clean'.

Held the bill of lading was clean; it did not cast doubt on the condition of the goods *at the time* of shipment.

18.5 Delivery order as a bill of lading

Comptoir D'achat v Luis de Ridder, *The Julia* (1949) HL
A cargo of rye was sold 'CIF Antwerp' (see below, 20.1). The contract made the sellers liable for the condition of the goods upon arrival and provided for payment against presentation of a delivery order. The sellers' agent presented the documents to the buyer, who paid upon them. In the event the rye was never delivered because of the German occupation of Belgium; the ship was diverted to Lisbon and the goods were sold there. The buyer claimed a refund of the price. The sellers claimed that under a CIF contract property passed upon payment against the documents and so they had performed the contract.

Held the buyers were entitled to a refund. This was not a CIF contract in substance. The documents gave the buyer no property rights in the goods entitling him to deal with them while afloat. Also the fact that the seller undertook liability for the condition of the goods until delivery indicated that this was an 'ex-ship' contract. Hence, the sellers had not performed and a refund was ordered.

Note ──────────────────────
Compare *The Julia* with *Law & Bonar v BAT* (1916), below, 20.5.
──────────────────────

18.6 Quality and condition – common law

Silver v Ocean Steamship Co Ltd (1929) CA

Cans of frozen eggs were shipped under a bill of lading which stated that the goods were loaded 'in apparent good order and condition'. However, when the ship arrived at port to unload, the cans were found to be damaged: some were gashed or punctured while others had pinhole perforations. The owner of the goods (indorsees of the bills of lading) claimed damages from the shipowners.

Held the shipowner was estopped as against an indorsee of the bill of lading. The shipowner who gave a clean bill did not promise to deliver the goods 'in apparent good order and condition' to the consignee, and may prove that the damage was caused by peril of the sea. However, he would be estopped from denying that he received the goods in apparent good order. In this case it was held that the estoppel applied to the major damage (the gashes and punctures) but not to the minor damage (the pinholes) because this was not reasonably apparent to the shipowners when loading.

18.7 Quantity – common law

Grant v Norway (1851)

The plaintiffs took a bill of lading as security against a debt of £1,684. The bill covered 12 bales of silk and stated that the goods had been shipped on the *Belle*; it was signed by the master of the ship. However, the debt was never paid and in fact the goods under the bill were never shipped. The plaintiffs sued the shipowners to recover their loss (£1,684), claiming that they were bound by the act of the master.

Held the shipowners were not liable for the act of the ship's master. He had no express authority to sign for goods which had not been shipped and, further, he had no such apparent authority since it was well known that a master did not have such authority. (See, generally, Reynolds (1967) 83 LQR 189.)

19 FOB (Free on Board) contracts

19.1 General

Pyrene Co Ltd v Scindia Navigation Co Ltd (1954)

Pyrene sold FOB a fire tender to the Indian Government. The buyers made the contract of carriage with Scindia. During loading, the crane broke and the tender crashed on to the quay and was damaged. Pyrene sued Scindia in negligence for the cost of repairs – £966. However, Scindia relied on a clause, incorporated into the carriage contract by the Hague Rules (now Hague-Visby), which limited the liability of the carrier to £200. The issue then was whether Pyrene could be bound by a contract to which they were not directly a party.

Held Devlin J described three types of FOB contract:

(i) the 'strict' or 'classic' type: the buyer nominated the ship and the seller put the goods on board (for account of the buyer) procuring a bill of lading. The seller was directly party to the carriage contract;

(ii) 'FOB with additional duties', a variant on the first; the seller arranged for the ship to come on the berth. Again the seller was a direct party to the carriage contract;

(iii) 'buyer contracts with carrier', which involved the buyer making the carriage contract in advance; the bill of lading going directly to the buyer. Here the buyer was a party to carriage contract from the beginning.

In the instant case, the contract was of this third type: Pyrene were not directly party to the carriage contract. However, they participated in the carriage contract sufficiently to be bound by the Hague Rules. Alternatively, there was a collateral contract between Pyrene and Scindia into which the Hague Rules would be incorporated by custom. Hence Pyrene could recover just £200.

19.2 Export licences

Brandt & Co v Morris & Co (1917) CA

A contract was made where an American buyer, through English agents, purchased goods from an English seller, FOB Manchester. However, before delivery an export-licensing scheme was introduced (because of the outbreak of the First World War). A dispute arose about who's duty it was to obtain the licence.

Held as the licence was required when the ship carrying the goods left the country, the duty fell on the buyer.

Note ──

Schmitthoff, *The Law and Practice of International Trade*, 9th edn, 1990, p 31, argues that this decision was wrong and the normal rule was that the seller was obliged to obtain the licence under FOB contracts.

Pound v Hardy (1956) HL

Pound sold goods FAS (free alongside) lying in Portugal, to Hardy. Pound were aware at the time that the probable destination of the goods was East Germany, in which case an export licence was necessary. The goods could not be put alongside nor through customs without one. Further, a licence could only be obtained by Pound's Portuguese suppliers, who were undisclosed to Hardy. In the event a licence was refused. Meanwhile, the sellers had nominated a ship which was ready to load at Portugal. The buyers refused to name another destination and so the goods were not loaded. Both parties blamed each other for the failure to obtain an export licence.

Held the FAS contract was subject to the same rules as an FOB contract. There was no general rule in these cases as to which party was obliged to procure an export licence. In the circumstances of this case, the obligation was on the sellers (Pound) to obtain an export licence. This was because the sellers knew that the buyers wished to export to Germany and only the sellers knew of their Portuguese suppliers, who were the only party able to obtain a licence. As Pound had done all that was reasonable to obtain one and failed, the contract was frustrated and the parties' obligations discharged.

19.3   Duties of the buyer

Forrestt v Aramayo (1900) CA

The sellers agreed to build a steam launch and deliver it FOB London by 7 January 1899 (the launch was to be transported to its destination by ship). However, on 12 December 1898 the buyers wrote to the sellers asking for delivery to be at a different place and date. The sellers (rightfully) refused and the buyers replied that there was no further opportunity for shipment until April 1899. The launch was not completed until April and, on 17 April, it was loaded aboard the ship eventually nominated by the buyers. The buyers claimed damages for late delivery.

Held the claim would fail because the buyers did not give shipping instructions in accordance with the contract.

Note
For a commentary on this case, see *Benjamin's Sale of Goods*, 5th edn, 1997, para 20-047. Compare this with *Turnball v Mundas* (1954) (below).

Cunningham v Munro (1922)
A cargo of bran was sold FOB Rotterdam, shipment during October. The seller delivered the goods to the port on 14 October, but the buyer did not nominate a ship until 28 October. By that time the bran had deteriorated and the buyer sought to reject it.

Held the buyer's duty was to do no more than nominate a vessel so as to enable the seller to load the goods within the shipment period; thus the buyer's nomination was not late.

Turnball v Mundas (1954) Aus
A term of a contract for the sale of 250 tons of oats FOB Sydney stipulated that the buyer should nominate a ship and give the seller 14 days' notice. During the shipment period the sellers informed the buyers that oats were not available at Sydney and requested that they send their ship to Melbourne. The buyers agreed but it was not possible to load the ship at Melbourne. Eventually, the buyers sued for non-delivery. The sellers defended by stating that as the buyers had not complied with the term to give 14 days' notice, they (the sellers) were not liable.

Held (3:1) the buyers would succeed. The sellers, by their conduct, discharged the sellers from their strict contractual duty to give notice. The sellers were unable to supply oats at Sydney and induced the buyers not to insist upon delivery at Sydney.

Agricultores Federados Argentinos v Ampro SA (1965)
Under an FOB contract for the sale of maize, shipment was to be made from 20–29 September. The buyer, in accordance with the contract, nominated a ship which was expected at the port on 26 September. But by 29 September at 4 pm it became clear that it would not reach the port in time; so the buyer nominated a second ship, which was at the port. The sellers declined to load even though they could have loaded the second ship before midnight of the 29 September at no extra trouble. The buyers claimed damages.

Held the sellers were liable for damages for failing to load. The sellers had adequate notice to load and suffered no disadvantage by the substitution of the second ship. The goods were not perishable and the sellers had not acted in reliance on the first nomination. Widgery J said that the general law applying to an FOB contract is that 'the buyers shall provide a vessel which is capable of loading within the stipulated time, and if, as a matter of courtesy or convenience, the buyers inform the sellers that they propose to provide vessel A, I can see no reason in principle why they should not change their mind and provide vessel B at a later stage, always assuming that vessel B is provided within such a time as to make it possible for her to fulfil the buyers' obligations under the contract'.

Bunge & Co v Tradax England (1975)

A contract was made for the sale of 1,000 tons of barley. The buyer nominated a ship which was not ready to load until two hours before the end of the last working day of the shipment period. The sellers managed to load 110 tons in the time remaining, but loaded no more after the shipment period. The buyer claimed that the seller had waived his right to treat the shipping period at an end by partially loading the goods.

Held the seller was not obliged to load beyond the shipment period and he had not waived his right to cease loading at the end of the shipping period by partially loading the goods.

Napier v Dexters (1962) CA

Napier sold on FOB terms to Dexters 20 tons of London sweet fat, 'delivery in the month of October FOB London steamer'. Dexters nominated a ship on 27 October but Napier (reasonably) could only load 17 tons in the time left. When the ship arrived Dexters rejected the goods for short delivery under s 30(1) of the Sale of Goods Act.

Held in the circumstances Dexters were not entitled to reject. The goods were loaded according to Dexters' instructions which came too late for the whole consignment to have been put on board.

Cargill v Continental (1989) CA

An FOB contract called for the giving of provisional and final notice by the buyer so that the seller could have the goods ready for loading. The buyer nominated a ship and gave the requisite notice. However, he then nominated a substitute vessel and there was no time in which to give notice to the seller. The seller refused to load the substitute ship and cancelled the contract.

Held the seller was entitled to cancel as the buyer was in breach of contract.

Phibro Energy AG v Nissho Iwai Corp, *The Honam Jade* (1991) CA

Phibro agreed to sell to Nissho 50,000 barrels of crude oil FOB Fatah, shipment in January. As is usual under FOB terms, the buyer had to nominate a ship for the seller to load. The Fatah marine terminal was small and so the operators ran a strict routine in order to allow constant and orderly progress. Oil tankers were only allowed into port for a three day slot for loading and it was stipulated that the seller in an FOB contract should either accept or reject the buyer's nomination within five days. In this case the buyer nominated a ship on 19 December and requested loading to be 15–20 January. The seller failed to acknowledge within five days but eventually offered a slot near the end of January. This was unacceptable to the buyer, who terminated the contract. However, the seller claimed that the buyer had repudiated the contract by not accepting the date offered.

Held it was the *seller* who had repudiated the contract. The sale contract had to be read incorporating the terminal operator's conditions. Hence when the seller failed to acknowledge the buyer's nomination within five days they were in breach and this amounted to repudiation of the contract.

19.4 Duties of the seller

Bowes v Shand (1877) HL

Under a contract for the sale of 600 (8,200 bags) tons of Madras rice the goods were 'to be shipped during the months of March and/or April 1874'. The bulk of the rice (8,150 bags) was put on board the ship in February. Four bills of lading were issued; three were dated in February and the other in March. The buyers rejected the goods.

Held the buyers were entitled to reject. Sections 12–15 of the SGA 1979 apply to overseas sales. The expression 'shipped' *prima facie* means put on board; and goods are shipped if bills of lading have been issued. Thus the bulk of the rice was shipped in February. The time of loading was part of the contractual description of the goods. Thus a breach of the implied *condition* that goods will correspond with the description (s 13 of the SGA) entitled the buyer to reject the goods. Lord Cairns LC said: 'Merchants are not in the habit of placing upon their contracts stipulations to which they do not attach some value.'

Note

Compare this case with *Arcos v Ronaasen* (1933) and *Re Moore and Landauer* (1921), see above, 9.3.2.

Harlow and Jones v Panex (1967)

Under an FOB contract for the sale of 10,000 tons of steel blooms to be delivered in two instalments, shipment was agreed to be August/September at the suppliers' option. The sellers notified the buyers that 5,000 tons would be ready at the port at the beginning of August. The buyers failed to make the necessary shipping arrangements but later informed the sellers that a ship would be ready for loading in the middle of August. However, the seller failed to confirm this. The buyers then demanded the whole 10,000 tons be ready for shipment in 20–27 August. The sellers refused to guarantee this and the buyers treated this as repudiation and cancelled the contract.

Held the buyers were in breach of contract. This is not a classic FOB contract (see *Pyrene v Scindia Navigation*, above, 19.1) in that the time of shipment in this case was at the *sellers'* (rather than the buyers') option. Hence, once the buyers were informed of the time of shipment it was for them to nominate the ship for that period specified by the sellers.

Note

For the calculation of damages in this case, see above, 14.2.2.

Glencore Grain Rotterdam BV v Lebanese Organisation for International Commerce (1997) CA

The buyers agreed to purchase 25,000 tonnes of wheat. The standard FOB contract provided that the buyers would provide a ship and pay by an irrevocable and confirmed letter of credit, (see below, Chapter 22). However, the buyers' letter of credit stipulated that the sellers' bill of lading (see above, Chapter 18) should be marked 'prepaid freight', although the buyers gave an undertaking to pay the freight.

Held the buyers were in breach of contract by stipulating that the bill of lading be marked 'prepaid freight'. Under an FOB contract, special terms apart, the sellers are under no obligation to pay the freight. FOB is the antithesis of C & F – cost and freight. The buyers' undertaking to pay the freight did not alter this. The letter of credit mechanism ensures that the bank guarantees payment. The security that this gives to the seller would be destroyed if separate undertakings were recognised.

19.4.1 Delivery by sea transit – s 32(3) of the SGA

Wimble v Rosenburg (1913), see above, 13.1.2.

Law & Bonar v BAT (1916), see below, 20.5.

Mash & Murrell v Emmanuel (1961), see above, 11.1.6.

19.5 Passing of property

See, generally, Chapter 10 and, in particular, *Carlos Federspiel v Twigg* (1957), above, 10.3.1. Also, *Wait v Baker* (1848), above, 18.3.

Browne v Hare (1859) Ex Ch (CA)

Under an FOB contract for the sale of 10 tons of refined rape oil, payment was to made upon delivery of the bill of lading. The oil was shipped and the bill of lading, which was in the name of the sellers, was indorsed by them to the buyer and sent to the broker who had negotiated the contract. However, the ship was lost and when the broker presented the bill of lading to the buyer, he refused to pay. The sellers sued for price, claiming that property had passed.

Held the sellers would succeed as the property passed upon shipment. The sellers showed their intention by immediately indorsing the bill in the name of the buyer.

Note ———————————————————————

For an analysis of this case, see *Benjamin's Sale of Goods*, 5th edn, 1997, para 20-065.

———————————————————————

The Kronprinsessan Margereta (1921) PC

A Brazilian firm sold and shipped coffee on FOB terms to several European buyers. The sellers obtained bills of lading to the buyers' order but retained them until payment was arranged. The issue arose as to whether the property passed to the buyers when the bills of lading were taken out to their order.

Held the property did not pass at that time. The passing of property depends upon the intention of the parties. The sellers, by taking out the bills in the buyers' names, could not demand possession without the buyers' indorsement. Equally, though, the buyers could not obtain possession until they received the bills. Clearly the intention was that the sellers would keep the bills until payment was arranged. Thus although the bills were taken out to the order of the buyers, this did not necessarily evince an intention to pass property at that time.

Mitsui v Flota Mercante Grandcolumbiana SA, *The Ciudad de Neiva* (1989) CA
Cartons of prawns were sold on FOB terms and shipped under bills of lading to the sellers' order. By the terms of the sale contract 80% of the price was paid in advance. Before the balance was paid, the prawns were damaged. The issue was whether the property had passed to the buyer.

Held the property had not passed to the buyer. By s 19(2) of the SGA, the seller was *prima facie* taken to have reserved the right of disposal where the goods shipped are, by the bill of lading, deliverable to the sellers' order. Thus the property could not pass until the condition (to pay the balance) imposed by the sellers was satisfied. As the balance had not been paid the property remained with the sellers.

19.6   Risk

Inglis v Stock (1885), see above, 11.1.2.

Wimble v Rosenburg (1913), see above, 13.1.2.

Mash & Murrell v Emmanuel (1961), see above, 11.1.6.

Cunningham v Munro (1922)
For the facts, see above, 19.3.

Held normally the risk passes to the buyer when the goods cross the ship's rail. As the goods had not been loaded the risk remained with the seller.

Pyrene Co Ltd v Scindia Navigation Co Ltd (1954)
For the facts, see above, 19.1.

Held normally the risk passes to the buyer when the goods cross the ship's rail. Here, as the tender was dropped before it had crossed the rail, the risk was still with the seller.

Colley v Overseas Exporters Ltd (1921)

For the facts, see above, 14.1.

Held in the absence of a special agreement, property and risk did not pass until the goods were put on board.

20 CIF (Cost, Insurance, Freight) contracts

20.1 General

Clemens Horst v Biddell Bros (1911) HL

A contract for the sale of hops provided 'CIF to London, Liverpool or Hull. Terms net cash'; but it contained no term expressly calling for payment against the shipping documents. The goods were shipped and the bill of lading was presented to the buyer. But he refused to pay until he had inspected the goods.

Held under a CIF contract the buyer must pay the price against the tender of the shipping documents. At first instance, Hamilton J stated the duties of the parties under a typical CIF contract:

> A seller under a [CIF] contract ... has
>
> – first, to ship at the port of shipment goods of the description contained in the contract;
> – secondly, to procure a contract of affreightment, under which the goods will be delivered to the destination contemplated in the contract;
> – thirdly, to arrange for an insurance upon the terms current in the trade which will be available for the benefit of the buyer;
> – fourthly, to make out an invoice ...; and
> – finally, to tender these documents to the buyer so that he may know what freight he has to pay and obtain delivery of the goods if they arrive, or recover for their loss if they are lost on the voyage.
>
> It follows that against tender of these documents, the bill of lading, the invoice, and policy of insurance ... the buyer must be ready and willing to pay the price.

Smyth v Bailey (1940) HL

The facts are irrelevant.

Lord Wright described the main features of CIF contracts and how they are financed:

> The seller has to ship or acquire after that shipment the contract goods, as to which, if unascertained, he is generally required to give notice of appropriation. On or after shipment, he has to obtain proper bills of lading and proper policies

of insurance. He fulfils his contract by transferring the bills of lading and the policies to the buyer. As a general rule he does so only against payment of the price, less the freight, which the buyer has to pay. In the invoice which accompanies the tender of the documents on the 'prompt' – that is, the date fixed for payment – the freight is deducted, for this reason.

In this course of business the general property remains in the seller until he transfers the bill of lading ... The property which the seller retains while he or his agent, or the banker to whom he has pledged the documents, retains the bills of lading is the general property, and not a special property by way of security.

In general however the importance of the retention of the property is not only to secure payment from the buyer but for purposes of finance. The general course of international commerce involves the practice of raising money on the documents so as to bridge the period between shipment and the time of obtaining payment against documents ... By mercantile law, the bills of lading are symbols of the goods. The general property in the goods must be in the seller if he is to be able to pledge them.

20.2 Duties of the seller

Karberg v Blythe (1916) CA

Under a contract for the sale of Chinese horse beans, the goods were shipped aboard the German ship *Gernis*. Shortly afterwards, war was declared on Germany and so the contract of carriage within the bill of lading became void for illegality. The buyer refused to take up the documents.

Held the buyer was entitled to do so. The documents must be valid at the time tendered.

Diamond Alkali v Bourgeois (1921)

Under a contract on CIF terms for the sale of soda ash, the seller tendered the documents, which included a *certificate* of insurance, but not an insurance policy. Normally, a certificate states that the goods are covered by a *policy* and refers to that policy, but it does not contain any terms of the policy. The buyers rejected the documents.

Held the buyer was entitled to reject the documents on the grounds that no proper policy of insurance was tendered. Unless otherwise agreed, the seller must tender the insurance *policy*.

Note ───

The reason for this is that the person in receipt of the certificate shall not be able to determine what the terms are. It seems that modern English practice is to tender a certificate entitling the holder to demand the issue of a formal policy, unless the contract expressly stipulates otherwise. Compare with *Donald H Scott v Barclays Bank* (1923) (below). See, generally, Schmitthoff, *The Law and Practice of International Trade*, 9th edn, 1990, pp 39–40.

Donald H Scott v Barclays Bank (1923) CA

Under a contract for the sale of 100 tons of steel plates, payment was agreed to be by documentary credit. By the terms of the letter of credit the bank agreed to pay the sellers on presentation of documents accompanied by an insurance *policy* covering the shipment of goods. The sellers tendered an American certificate of insurance, which differs from the English: it is *not* a document issued by a broker stating that the goods are covered by a policy; it is tendered in lieu of an insurance policy and good tender in the United States (see *Uniform Commercial Code*, s 2-320(2)(c) and comment). The bank refused to pay.

Held the bank were entitled to refuse payment. The document did not contain the terms of the insurance. There was no means of asserting these terms except by reference to another document which was not in convenient reach for reference. See *Diamond Alkali v Bourgeois* (1921) above.

Kwei Tek Chao v British Traders & Shippers Ltd (1954)

For the facts, see above, 15.1.1.

Held the buyer has two rights to reject. *Per* Devlin J:

> ... the right to reject the documents arises when the documents are tendered, and the right to reject the goods arises when they are landed and when after examination they are not found to be in conformity with the contract.

20.3 Duties of the buyer

Law & Bonar v BAT (1916), see below, 20.5.

Groom v Barber (1915)

A contract for the sale of Hessian cloth CIF Calcutta was made on 8 June. One of the terms stated 'war risks for buyer's account'. The goods were insured but war risks were not covered. The goods were shipped on 5 July and war broke out on 4 August. The ship was sunk by a German cruiser. The buyer rejected the documents and refused to pay, claiming that the sellers should have taken out war risks insurance.

Held the contract was made in peacetime when it was not the custom of the trade to insure against war risks. Therefore, in the absence of a contrary intention the sellers were not bound to insure against war risks. The phrase 'war risks for buyer's account' cannot be said to mean that in times of peace, war risk insurance must be taken out by the seller.

Gill & Duffas SA v Berger (1983) HL

The sellers had agreed to sell on CIF terms 500 tons beans in two loads (445 tons and 55 tons). The first load was delivered but the buyers' wrongly considered it to be unmerchantable. The documents, which were in order, were then tendered and the buyers rejected them.

Held the rejection of documents which were in order amounted to a repudiation of the contract. Thus the sellers were released from their obligation to deliver the second load and the buyers were liable for non-acceptance of the whole 500 tons.

Note

See this case also in 13.3.

20.4   Passing of property

Leigh & Sillavan v Aliakmon Shipping, *The Aliakmon* (1986) HL.
See above, 18.2.

Cheetham v Thornham Spinning (1964)
One hundred bales of cotton were sold on CIF terms; it was agreed that payment in cash must be made upon tender of the shipping documents. The ship discharged the goods but upon presentation of the documents the buyers asked for credit; this was refused. However, the sellers were worried about incurring quay charges so it was agreed that the goods should be sent to the buyer's warehouse. The sellers retained the shipping documents. The buyers used or resold the cotton and then went into liquidation. The sellers claimed the proceeds of the resales, contending that the property did not pass to the buyers when the goods were delivered to their warehouse.

Held the property had not passed to the buyers. Although the buyers took possession of the goods they did so to avoid the quay charges; the sellers retained the documents. It was clear from the circumstances that the parties did not intend that property pass.

Ginzberg v Barrow Haematite Steel Co Ltd (1966)
Under a sale of manganese ore on CIF terms, it was agreed that payment must be made upon tender of the shipping documents. The goods arrived before the documents and to assist the buyers, who were anxious to obtain possession, the sellers sent a delivery note. This enabled the buyers to take possession. Subsequently, the buyers went into receivership without having paid. The receiver argued that the variation agreed changed this contract to 'ex-ship' and so payment was no longer a condition of property passing. Hence the property had vested in the buyers. The sellers sued for conversion.

Held the property had not passed and the sellers would be entitled to the return of their goods or their value. The sellers did not intend to depart from the CIF terms, they merely intended to expedite delivery.

20.5   CIF and risk

Groom v Barber (1915), see above, 20.3.

Law & Bonar v British American Tobacco (1916)
In May 1914, a contract was made for the sale of a quantity of Hessian cloth CIF Smyrna, to be shipped from Calcutta to arrive in Smyrna by September. A term in the contract stipulated that the risk would be with the seller until actual delivery. The seller took out insurance which was on the usual terms of the trade at that time – it did not cover war risks. The goods were shipped in July, but it was not until 21 August that the seller informed the buyer of the shipping details which would enable the buyer to take out any extra insurance. It was too late: on the same day the loss of the ship was reported in London. It was sunk by a German cruiser following the outbreak of the First World War on 4 August. The buyers refused to pay for the goods claiming that (i) the sellers failed in their duty (imposed by s 32(3) of the Sale of Goods Act) to give notice enabling the buyers to insure (against war risks); and (ii) in any case by the contract the goods were at the seller's risk.

Held for the seller. First, s 32(3) did not apply to CIF contracts in times when no one contemplated war. This was because CIF contracts cater for all the insurance usually needed or contemplated. On the evidence the parties and trade in general did not contemplate war at the time the contract was made. Secondly, the contract term retaining risk with the seller was repugnant to a CIF contract because the buyer was paying for insurance against all contemplated risks. Therefore, the term was inapplicable.

Manbre Saccharine v Corn Products (1919)
Corn Products sold quantities of starch and syrup to the plaintiffs. Subsequently, the ship carrying the goods was lost. Two days later Corn Products tendered the documents for payment; the plaintiffs refused to take up the documents or pay.

Held the plaintiff buyers were bound to take up the documents and pay the price. Risk normally passed to the buyer upon shipment. A CIF contract is a contract for the sale of goods performed by the delivery of the documents. The transfer of the documents transfers to the buyer the right to the goods or, in the case where goods are lost or damaged, rights to compensation from the shipper or insurer.

21 Bills of exchange

Note the Deregulation (Bills of Exchange) Order 1996 SI 1996/2993, which amends the Bills of Exchange Act 1882, and concerns, *inter alia*, the presentation of cheques and duties of holders of bills.

21.1 Definition of a bill of exchange – Bills of Exchange Act 1882

Orbit Mining v Westminster Bank (1962) CA

A cheque form was made out to 'pay cash or order'. The issue arose whether that was a cheque within the Bills of Exchange Act. Section 73 states: 'A cheque is a bill of exchange drawn on a banker payable on demand.' Section 3(1) provides that under a bill of exchange a sum must be payable 'to the order of a specified person, or the bearer'. Finally, s 7(3) provides that: 'Where the payee is a fictitious or non-existing person the bill may be treated as payable to the bearer.'

Held the document was not a cheque within the Bills of Exchange Act. The words 'cash or order' do not refer to a 'specified person' or 'the bearer'. Further, 'cash' could not be said to be a fictitious or non-existent person.

Williamson v Rider (1962) CA

A promissory note was marked payable 'on or before 31 December 1956'. Section 83(1) of the Bills of Exchange Act stipulates that a promissory note, like a bill of exchange, must be payable 'on demand or at a fixed or determinable future date'.

Held (2:1) that instrument was not a promissory note. The introduction of the date 31 December limited the time in which payment should be made but it did not fix the date of payment, to bring it within the s 83(1) of the Bills of Exchange Act. *Per* Ormerod LJ (dissenting), although there was an option to pay earlier, the obligation to pay arose on a date certain.

> Note
>
> See *Hudson*, (1962) 25 MLR 593, pp 595–96. The Court of Appeal in *Claydon v Bradley* (1987) ('by' a certain date) felt bound to follow the majority. However, the dissenting judgment was followed in Canada in *Burrows v Subsurface Surveys* (1968) and in Ireland in *Creative Press Ltd v Harman* (1973).

Korea Exchange Bank v Debenhans (Central Buying) Ltd (1979) CA

A bill was payable '90 days D/A [documents against acceptance] of this first bill of exchange'. One issue was whether that instrument was a bill of exchange. Section 2(1) states that a bill of exchange must be payable 'on demand or at a fixed or determinable future date'.

Held the instrument was not a bill of exchange because it was not payable on a date certain. The words could mean payable 90 days after presentation, or after acceptance or after its date.

21.2　Transfer of bill of exchange

Bank of England v Vagliano Bros (1891) HL

A clerk employed by Vagliano forged the drawer's signature to a series of bills and made them payable to 'C Petridi & Co', which was the name of a real company doing business with Vagliano. In ignorance of the forgeries Vagliano accepted the bills payable at the Bank of England. The clerk then forged the indorsement of C Petridi & Co as payee and presented them to the Bank of England, who paid him £71,500 on them. The clerk never intended that Petridi should be paid. At issue was whether the bank was entitled to pay the bearer of the bills and consequently debit the amount from Vagliano's account. Section 7(3) of the Bills of Exchange Act provides that 'Where the payee is a fictitious or non-existing person the bill may be treated as payable to the bearer.' However, Vagliano argued that as the name of the payee was the name of a real company it was not 'fictitious'; to be fictitious the name must be nothing but one of the imagination.

Held (6:2) the bank were entitled to pay the bearer and debit Vagliano's account accordingly. This was because (5:3) the proper meaning of 'fictitious' is 'feigned' or 'counterfeit' and not 'imaginary' and so it does not matter whether the name is of a real person or not. Also (4:4), the bank was misled by the conduct of Vagliano.

Vinden v Hughes (1905)

A clerk was employed by Vinden to fill out cheques with the names of various customers, obtain the signatures of his employers and then post the cheques to the respective customers. Over a three year period the clerk made out 27 cheques to the order of various customers, obtained his employer's signatures, forged customers' indorsements and sold them to Hughes, who took in good faith. Hughes was paid on the cheques by Vinden's bank. Vinden sued Hughes for the return of the money. Hughes relied on s 7(3) of the Bills of Exchange Act which provided: 'Where the payee is a fictitious or non-existing person the bill may be treated as payable to the bearer.'

Held when Vinden drew these cheques they did not use the names as a pretence; consequently, the payees were not 'fictitious' within the meaning of s 7(3). Vinden were entitled to recover the money.

North and South Wales Bank v Macbeth (1908) HL

Macbeth was fraudulently induced by White to draw a cheque in favour of Kerr, a real person. White then forged Kerr's endorsement on the cheque and paid it into his own account at his bank, who received the money from Macbeth's bank. Macbeth sued White's bank for the recovery of the money. The bank claimed it was protected by s 7(3) of the Bills of Exchange Act, which provided that: 'Where the payee is a fictitious or non-existing person the bill may be treated as payable to the bearer.'

Held although misled, Macbeth intended that Kerr receive the proceeds of the cheque. Thus the payee (Kerr) was not a 'fictitious person' within s 7(3). Thus Macbeth could recover from the bank.

Hibernian Bank v Gysin and Hanson (1939) CA

A bill of exchange was drawn by the Irish Casing Co payable three months after date 'to the order of the Irish Casing Co Ltd only the sum of £500' and crossed 'not negotiable'. The bill was accepted by the defendants, indorsed by the Irish Casing Co and then transferred to the Hibernian Bank for value. When the bank presented it to the defendants it was dishonoured.

Held a bill crossed 'not negotiable' was not transferable and judgment would be entered for the defendants.

21.3   Holder for value

Oliver v Davis and Another (1949) CA

Davis owed Oliver £350 and gave him a post-dated cheque for £400. However, when it fell due Davis was unable to honour it and so discharge the debt. So he asked his fiancée's sister, Miss Woodcock, to give Oliver a cheque for £400, in order to discharge his debt to Oliver. This she did. Oliver did not present the cheque at once and meanwhile Miss Woodcock, discovering that Davis never intended to marry her sister, stopped the cheque. Oliver sued Miss Woodcock on the cheque and she argued that there was no consideration for it. The only consideration was the discharge of a debt of a third party, namely Davis. Section 27(1) of the Bills of Exchange Act provides that 'valuable consideration for a bill may be constituted by ... (b) an antecedent debt or liability'.

Held the antecedent debt must be due from the maker or negotiator of the instrument and not from a third party. As the debt was Davis' and not Woodcock's, Oliver's claim would fail.

Diamond v Graham (1968) CA

Graham wished to induce Diamond to lend a sum of money to Herman. So he drew a cheque in favour of Diamond. In response, Diamond made the loan to Herman. Finally, Herman drew a cheque in favour of Graham. However, Graham's cheque was dishonoured and Diamond sued him upon it. Graham argued that as no value had passed between himself and Diamond, Diamond was not a holder for value, and therefore could not sue on the cheque. Section 27(2) of the Bills of Exchange Act states that where value has been given for a bill, the holder is deemed the holder for value.

Held Diamond was a holder for value. Section 27(2) required that value was given by the holder (Diamond); it was enough that value was given. Here there were two transactions which gave value for the bill. Diamond made a loan to Herman and Herman gave a cheque to Graham. See Thornley [1968] CLJ 196.

21.4 Holder in due course

Jones Ltd v Waring and Gillow Ltd (1926) HL

A rogue owed Warings £5,000. So he fraudulently induced Jones Ltd to give him a cheque for £5,000 payable to the order of Waring and Gillow Ltd. The cheque was paid and later, when the fraud was discovered, Jones claimed for repayment of the proceeds because of mistake. One defence argued by Warings (who had acted in good faith) was that they were 'holders in due course' within s 21(2) of the BEA and so entitled to keep the proceeds.

Held that defence would fail because a 'holder in due course' did not include the original payee of a cheque. Judgment (3:2) was given to Jones on the principle of *Kelly v Solari* (1841), that money honestly paid by a mistake of fact was recoverable.

Arab Bank Ltd v Ross (1952) CA

Ross made a promissory note payable on demand to 'Fathi and Faysal Nabulsy Company or order'. One of the partners of that firm indorsed the note 'Fathi and Faysal Nabulsy' omitting the word 'company' and discounted it to the Arab Bank. The Arab Bank claimed against Ross arguing, *inter alia*, that they were 'holders in due course'. Section 29(1) of the Bills of Exchange Act states that a holder in due course must take the bill 'complete and regular' on the face.

Held the Arab Bank were not holders in due course. The omission of the word 'company' raised a reasonable doubt whether the payees and the indorsers were the same. (The bank succeeded on its other claim as holders for value.)

Jade International v Nicholas (1978) CA

Jade sold 2,000 tonnes of steel to Nicholas and drew a bill of exchange on them for the price. The bill was discounted by a German bank (who become holders in due course), who in turn discounted it to a second German bank who discounted it to the Midland Bank; Midland presented it to Nicholas for payment. However, because of a dispute over the quality of the steel, Nicholas dishonoured the bill. The Midland Bank exercised its right of recourse and the bill was passed back down the line until it reached Jade. Jade sued Nicholas on the bill, claiming to be a holder deriving his title through a holder in due course. Section 29(3) provides: 'A holder (whether for value or not), who derives his title to a bill through a holder in due course ... has all the rights of that holder in due course.'

Held Jade would succeed. Although they were not holders in due course (because they had notice of the dishonour) they derived their title from the discounting bank.

Note ────────────────────────────────
For criticism of this decision, see Thornley [1978] CLJ 236, pp 237–38.

21.5 Liability on the bill

Durham Fancy Goods v Michael Jackson (Fancy Goods) Ltd (1968), see above, 7.3.2

Bondina Ltd v Rollaway Shower Blinds Ltd (1986) CA

Ward, a director of Rollaway, signed his name on a company cheque under the pre-printed words 'Rollaway Shower Blinds Ltd'. Section 26(1) of the BEA provides that where a person signs a bill indicating that it is on behalf of a principal he is not personally liable. Ward denied that he was personally liable on the cheque.

Held Ward was not liable. When he signed the cheque he adopted all the writing on it, including the name of the company and its account number. This showed that the cheque was drawn on the company's account and no other.

21.6 Payment and discharge of a bill

Glasscock v Balls (1889) CA

Balls owed Wayman £289 and gave him a promissory note payable on demand to Wayman's order, as security on the debt. However, Balls' debt increased to £641 and so he executed a mortgage in favour of Wayman to cover the total debt. Wayman assigned the mortgage to Hall for £700, and then indorsed the promissory note to Glasscock. Glasscock, who took the note without notice of the previous transactions, sued Balls on it.

Held Glasscock could recover. The discharge of the underlying contract (the first debt between Balls and Wayman) by supplying fresh security did not discharge the note.

Eaglehill Ltd v Needham Builders Ltd (1972) HL

Needhams drew a bill of exchange on Fir View Furniture Ltd payable at Lloyd's Bank on 31 December. They then discounted it to Eaglehill (who become 'holder'). Shortly afterwards, Fir View Furniture went in liquidation and both Needhams and Eaglehill were aware that the bill would be dishonoured upon presentation for payment. Section 49 Bills of Exchange Act provides that the holder of a bill which has been dishonoured may hold the drawer or indorsers liable, but only if he gives a 'notice of dishonour' *after* the bill's dishonour to those parties. Eaglehill prepared a notice of dishonour dated 1 January but by mistake posted it on 30 December. In the first post of the morning of 31 December, Needhams received the notice and the bank received the bill. Eaglehill sued Needhams on the bill. Needhams argued that as the notice was given before the bill had been dishonoured they were discharged from liability.

Held Needhams were liable. First, the notice is 'given' within s 49 when received, and not when posted. Secondly, where the notice was given on the same day that the bill was dishonoured and it is impossible to prove which preceded the other, the court would assume that events took place in the order that they ought to have done. Therefore the House of Lords regarded the notice as having been given after the bill was dishonoured.

Barclays Bank v Simms (1980)

A Housing Association sent a cheque for £24,000 to Simms, a firm of builders, in respect of building work completed. The cheque was drawn on Barclays Bank. The following day Simms went into receivership and the Housing Association instructed Barclays not to pay the cheque. However the cheque was paid by mistake. Barclays sued the receivers for the return of the money.

Held Barclays could recover. If a person pays money under a mistake of fact he is *prima facie* entitled to recover that money. However, the claim may fail if: (i) the payer intended that the payee have the money in all events, be there a mistake or not; or (ii) consideration is given for the payment, especially the discharge of a debt; or (iii) the payee alters his position in good faith. First, clearly the bank did intend to pay in any event. Secondly, there was no consideration because the bank was acting without mandate and so the payment was not effective to discharge the drawer's (the Housing Association's) obligation on the cheque. Thirdly, there was no evidence of alteration of position by Simms or their receivers.

21.7 Documentary bills

Cahn & Mayer v Pockett's Bristol Channel Steam Packet Co Ltd (1899) CA

A Liverpool firm sold on CIF (see above, 20.1) terms a quantity of copper. The buyers resold it to sub-buyers. The sellers shipped the copper and forwarded the bill of lading and the bill of exchange (known collectively as a 'documentary bill') but the buyer refused to accept the bill of exchange; however he sent the bill of lading to his sub-buyer.

Held if a buyer fails to accept the bill of exchange he is bound to return the bill of lading to the seller. If he wrongfully retains the bill of lading, the property in the goods does not pass to him (s 19(3) of the SGA). However, this method of payment (documentary bill) does not prevent a buyer who has dishonoured the bill of exchange from passing good title to a third party under s 25 of the SGA (s 9 of the Factors Act) or other *nemo dat* exceptions.

22 Documentary credits

22.1 Revocable and irrevocable credits

Cape Asbestos Co v Lloyds Bank (1921)
Cape agreed to sell 30 tons of asbestos to a buyer in Poland, who, through their bank, instructed Lloyds to open a revocable credit in favour of the sellers. Lloyds informed Cape of this, adding that the credit was unconfirmed. Cape dispatched the first shipment of 17 tons and were paid for this through the credit. However, then the credit was revoked and although it was their practice to do so, Lloyds (by mistake) failed to inform Cape of the revocation. Cape dispatched the second shipment but Lloyds refused to pay. Cape sued Lloyds for the balance of the credit.

Held although it was the practice of the bank to give notice when a credit had been revoked, they were under no legal duty to do so. The sellers should have confirmed the credit before dispatching the goods.

22.2 Confirmed credits

Wahbe Tamari v 'Colprogeca'-Sociedada Geral de Fibras (1969)
A contract for the sale of 1,000 tonnes of coffee required payment by an irrevocable credit confirmed by a Lisbon bank – Ilbank. The bank confirmed the credit on terms (not in the contract) that: (i) the sellers would remain liable on any draft negotiated by Ilbank under the credit; and (ii) the sellers paid the confirmation charges. The sellers treated the contract as repudiated by the buyers because, *inter alia*, the credit did not conform with the contract, that is, it was not irrevocable.

Held the sellers were entitled to treat the contract as repudiated by the buyers. If the confirming bank reserved a right of recourse against the seller, its undertaking did not constitute a confirmation. See Schmitthoff [1957] JBL 17, pp 17, 18.

22.3 Straight and negotiation credits

European Asian Bank v Punjab and Sind Bank (No 2) (1983) CA
The defendant bank (PSB) was instructed by Indian importers to issue a credit in favour of exporters in Singapore. PSB asked their correspondent,

the ABN bank, to both advise and confirm the credit through the plaintiff (EAB) bank. The letter of credit contained two apparently conflicting provisions. Clause 6 stated that the credit was 'divisible and unrestricted for negotiation'. Clause 9 stipulated that negotiations were restricted to the ABN bank. EAB negotiated the credit with the sellers and paid them, but then the buyer, discovering that the seller had been fraudulent, instructed the PSB not to make payment under the credit. EAB then sued PSB for reimbursement, claiming that they were entitled to have negotiated the credit by clause 6 (a 'negotiation' credit). PSB argued that under clause 9 of the credit only ABN were entitled to negotiate it (a 'straight' credit).

Held this was a 'straight' credit. The two clauses were reconcilable. Clause 6 permitted unrestricted negotiation for the purposes of transfer of the letter of credit by the *beneficiary*. Clause 9 restricted negotiation by the banks.

Note ───

See *Benjamin's Sale of Goods*, 5th edn, 1997, para 23-045; Ellinger [1984] JBL 379.

22.4 The status of the UCP (Uniform Customs and Practice for Documentary Credits)

Forestal Mimosa Ltd v Oriental Credit Ltd (1986) CA

A marginal note in a documentary credit stated that the UCP was incorporated 'except so far as otherwise expressly stated'.

Held first, a marginal note was sufficient to incorporate the UCP. Secondly, where the UCP is not expressly excluded, the express terms of the credit should be interpreted so to avoid conflict with the UCP.

Royal Bank of Scotland v Cassa (1992) CA

Under a contract for the sale of pears the Italian buyer was to pay by irrevocable letter of credit in US dollars. The Royal Bank of Scotland (RBS) was the accepting bank and was to be reimbursed by MHT of New York, agents for the issuing (Italian) banks. RBS paid the seller upon presentation of the documents. The buyer then alleged fraud and, following instructions from the Italian banks, MHT refused to reimburse RBS. RBS sued the Italian banks for reimbursement. The case turned on the terms of the contract: the express terms stated that the place of reimbursement was New York, and so English courts had no jurisdiction. However, Art 16(a) of the UCP, which was incorporated into the contract, provided that the accepting bank *shall* be reimbursed by the issuing (Italian) bank.

Held the express terms of the contract prevail over the UCP and so the place for repayment was New York. The UCP is not a statutory code. It is a formulation of customs and practices. Thus, if there is a conflict between the express terms and the UCP, the express terms will prevail. If the contract is silent on an issue, then recourse to the UCP will be appropriate.

22.5 Autonomy of the credit

Urquhart, Lindsay & Co v Eastern Bank (1922)

The sellers agreed to supply some machinery to buyers in India, to be delivered by instalments. It was a term of the contract that additional charges could be made to reflect any increases in the costs of wages and materials, but these would be settled by later adjustments and not be charged on the invoices. The buyers opened a confirmed irrevocable credit with the defendant bank, who promised to pay the sellers upon production of the shipping documents and invoices. Two instalments of the machinery were shipped and the bank paid under the credit. Then the buyers discovered that the sellers had included in the invoices additional charges related to a rise in costs. The bank was instructed by the buyers not to pay the sellers. The sellers sued the bank for breach of contract.

Held the sellers would succeed. The bank was not concerned with the terms of the sale contract. Where a bank has issued an irrevocable credit and the seller has tendered the correct documents, the bank must pay.

Malas (Hamzeh) & Sons v British Imex Industries (1958) CA

A contract was made to sell steel rods to buyers in Jordan. They were to be delivered by two instalments and each one was to be paid for by a confirmed letter of credit. The first instalment was delivered and the bank paid. However, the buyers were unhappy with the quality of the goods and sought an injunction to prevent the bank paying on the second letter of credit.

Held a confirmed letter of credit is a contract between the bank and the seller which imposes upon the bank an absolute duty to pay, irrespective of any dispute between the buyer and seller. The injunction was refused and bank were ordered to pay the sellers. *Per* Sellers LJ *obiter* the court may interfere where there is a fraudulent transaction.

22.6 Strict compliance with the documents

Equitable Trust Co of New York v Dawson Partners (1927) HL

Under a contract to sell vanilla beans, payment was to be made by confirmed letter of credit. This called for payment against certain documents including 'a certificate of quality issued by experts who are sworn brokers'. The seller tendered a certificate issued by a single expert and was paid by the bank, who in turn demanded payment from the buyers. In fact there was a fraudulent sale and the buyers received mainly rubbish; they refused to reimburse the bank.

Held (4:1) as the certificate did not comply with the credit the bank paid at their risk. The buyer did not have to reimburse the bank.

Rayner & Co v Hambros Bank (1942) CA

Buyers of groundnuts instructed their bank to pay the sellers by documentary credit against a bill of lading covering 'Coromandel groundnuts'. The sellers presented bills of lading which referred to 'machine shelled groundnut kernals' which, according to the trade, were the same as Coromandel groundnuts. The bank refused to pay the sellers.

Held the bank were entitled to refuse payment. There was a discrepancy of the documents; it matters not that the two descriptions refer to the same produce, the bank were under no duty to know the custom of the trade.

Bank Melli Iran v Barclays Bank DCO (1951)

An irrevocable credit was opened by Bank Melli and confirmed by their agents, Barclays. The credit called for the tender of documents which confirmed shipment of '60 new Chevrolet trucks'. The documents presented by the seller included a certificate describing the goods as 'new, good, Chevrolet trucks', an invoice, describing them as 'in new condition' and a delivery order describing them as 'new-good'. Barclays accepted these documents and paid the sellers. Bank Melli claimed that Barclays were wrong to accept the documents.

Held the bank was wrong to accept the documents because they were inconsistent with each other. However, Barclays were entitled to reimbursement on different grounds: Bank Melli had ratified the act of their agent, Barclays, and so were bound by it.

Soprama SpA v Marine & Animal By-Products Corporation (1966)

Under a contract for the sale of 'Chilean fish full meal' the buyers opened a credit, instructing the bank to accept documents including bills of lading marked 'freight prepaid' and a certificate stating that the goods had a protein content of at least 70%. The credit was subject to the UCP. The bill of lading was marked 'freight collect'. Also, it described the goods only as 'fishmeal', although the invoice gave a full description. The buyers rejected the documents.

Held the buyers were right to reject the documents. Under what is now Art 41(c) of the UCP, if the invoice described the goods fully it was sufficient for the bill of lading to offer a general description. However, the omission of the mark 'freight prepaid' and the insufficient protein content entitled the buyer to reject the documents.

Seaconsar Far East Ltd v Bank Markazi Jomhouri Islami Iran (1993) CA

A confirmed letter of credit stipulated that each document called for against payment must bear the letter of credit number and the buyer's name. In the event, just one of the documents presented by the seller failed to meet this stipulation and the bank refused to pay. The sellers claimed that the omission was trivial and in any event could be cured by reference to the other (correct) documents.

Held (2:1) the bank were correct to refuse payment. The credit expressly demanded certain particulars.

Note ———————————————————————————————
The decision was reversed by the House of Lords on other grounds.

Seaconsar Far East Ltd v Bank Markazi Jomhouri Islami Iran (1996)

Article 16(d) of the UCP-400 stated that an issuing bank which has decided to reject documents, 'must give notice to that effect without delay by telecommunication or, if that is not possible, by other expeditious means'. Article 16(c) provided that the issuing bank shall have a 'reasonable time' in which to examine and decide whether or not to reject the documents. This case involved two presentations. The underlying contract was one for arms between Seaconsar and the Iranian Government. The paying bank was Melli, in London. The first presentation was made on 1 October 1987, under a covering letter giving the sales manager's telex number in Italy. Seaconsar's sales manager visited Melli on 5 October and was told that the documents were being rejected because of discrepancies. The second presentation was made on 3 December under a covering letter giving a telex number in Hong Kong. Again Melli found discrepancies. On the following Tuesday, 8 December, Melli sent a telex to the Hong Kong number informing Seaconsar of this rejection. On 9 December, Melli discovered that Seaconsar's telex number had changed. On 10 December, Seaconsar's sales manager visited Melli and was told of the rejection. It was contended by Seaconsar that: (i) the first rejection was invalid because it had not been made by 'telecommunication' (Art 16(d)); and that (ii) the second rejection was invalid because it was made too late under Art 16(c) and (d).

Held (i) the rejection of the first presentation was good. Although it was possible to communicate the rejection by telex to Italy, this was not 'expeditious' (Art 16(d)) as the sales manager was in London at the time. It was 'expeditious' to make the oral rejection; (ii) the second rejection was made on 8 December; it was the fault of Seaconsar that the wrong telex number was used. The rejection was made four working days after the presentation. That was a reasonable time.

Note ———————————————————————————————
1 See, also, *Bankers Trust v State Bank of India*, below, 22.9.

2 UCP-400 has been largely superseded by UCP-500 (in effect from 1 January 1994). The provisions for rejection have been preserved with the qualification to Art 16(d) that documents should be rejected 'no later than the close of the seventh banking day following the day of the receipt of the documents'.

22.6.1 Fraud

Guarantee Trust of New York v Hannay (1918) CA

Hannay, in England, purchased cotton from dealers in the US, who drew a bill of exchange on Hannay's bank. The plaintiffs purchased the bill (with the bill of lading attached) in good faith and sent it to Hannay's bank. Hannay paid the plaintiffs through their bank. However, Hannay then discovered that no cotton had been shipped and the bill of lading was a forgery. Hannay claimed a refund arguing that in presenting the bill with the bill of lading to their bank, the plaintiffs warranted that the bill of lading was genuine.

Held both the bank and the plaintiffs thought the bill to be genuine. The plaintiffs had not warranted that the bill was genuine. Judgment was given for the plaintiffs.

Singh (Gian) & Co v Banque de l'Indochine (1974) PC

The defendant bank was instructed by Gian Singh to open an irrevocable documentary credit. The credit required the tender of a certificate certifying the quality of the goods, signed by Balwant Singh, holder of Malaysian Passport E-13276. In the event, the passport and the signature were forgeries; however, the bank accepted the documents, paid the beneficiary and debited the account of Gian Singh, who claimed that the bank should return of the money.

Held the duty of the bank was to examine the documents tendered to ascertain if they appeared on their face to be in accordance with the credit (see Art 13(a) of the UCP). This case differed from the ordinary in that the credit required that the certificate was signed by the holder of a particular passport. This placed an additional duty on the bank to take reasonable care to see that the two signatures corresponded. The burden of showing lack of reasonable care was on the plaintiffs, Gian Singh. As they had not proved that the bank acted negligently, their claim would fail.

Discount Records v Barclays Bank (1975)

A contract was made for the sale of 94 boxes of records. Upon delivery 87 boxes contained tapes, five contained rubbish and two were empty. The buyer sought an injunction against the accepting bank to prevent payment being made to the seller.

Held the injunction was refused. The fraud was not proved and the court did not have the opportunity to hear the case of the seller. A better course of action would be to seek an injunction against the seller, then the court could hear the other side's case.

United City Merchants (Investments) Ltd v Royal Bank of Canada, *The American Accord* (1983) HL

A contract (and the related credit documents) for the sale of manufacturing equipment to Peruvian buyers provided that the goods would be shipped by 15 December. In fact, they were shipped on 16 December and the carrier's agent fraudulently issued a bill of lading showing shipment to have been on 15 December. The sellers knew nothing of the fraud and presented the documents to the bank for payment. The bank refused to pay because it suspected that the date of shipment stated was false. The sellers sued the bank.

Held in favour of the sellers. The documents were good on their face and conformed to the credit documents. The bank could only refuse payment if the beneficiary (here the sellers) were a party to the fraud.

22.6.2 'Clean' bills of lading

British Imex Industries v Midland Bank Ltd (1958)
In pursuance of a contract for the sale of steel bars the Midland Bank issued an irrevocable credit to the sellers, payment being on the production of documents including bills of lading representing the goods. On the reverse of the bills of lading was a clause which stated that the shipowners were not answerable for correct delivery unless every bar was marked with oil paint. However, there was no acknowledgment that the bars had been so marked and so the bank refused to pay, claiming that the bills of lading were not 'clean'.

Held when a credit calls for bills of lading, it means clean bills of lading. A clean bill of lading is one which does not contain any reservation as to the condition of the goods or packing. In this case there was no such reservation and the bills of lading were clean; the bank should have accepted them.

22.6.3 Security for credit

Lloyds Bank v Bank of America (1938), see above, 12.3.3.

22.7 Time of opening the credit

Garcia v Page & Co (1936)
A contract for sale stipulated that the buyer should immediately open a confirmed credit. However, the buyer took three months to do so.

Held the term was a condition precedent to the seller shipping the goods. The buyer's obligation to open a credit 'immediately' meant at once within such a time required for a person of reasonable diligence to establish the credit. The matter was referred back to the arbitrator to decide the law as stated.

Trans Trust SPRL v Danubian Trading Co (1952) CA
The plaintiffs contracted to sell 1,000 tons of steel to the defendants. The plaintiffs did not have the finances to obtain the steel from their suppliers, A Ltd, so an arrangement was made that the defendants would procure a credit to be opened in favour of the plaintiffs' suppliers, thus financing the transaction. However, the credit was never opened and the plaintiffs

claimed damages for breach of contract in respect of their loss of profit. The defendants claimed that the damages should be nominal because (i) the market price was rising and so the plaintiffs could resell the steel at a profit; and (ii) if they never obtained the steel from A Ltd, their loss of profit was caused by their own impecuniosity.

Held the plaintiffs were entitled to damages for breach of contract. Where the plaintiffs' impecuniosity was contemplated by the parties and it was foreseeable that the failure to open the credit would result in a loss of profit, damages would be awarded in respect of that loss of profit. *Per* Denning LJ, sometimes a stipulation to open a credit is a condition precedent to the formation of the contract. If no credit is provided, there is no contract. In other cases the stipulation for credit is an essential term (condition) of the contract. On the facts, that was the case here. The defendants were in breach of that term and so the plaintiffs were discharged from further obligations and were entitled to damages for breach of contract.

Pavia & Co SpA v Thurmann-Nielsen (1952) CA
Under a CIF (see above, 20.1) contract for the sale of groundnuts, it was agreed that the seller could ship the goods between 1 February and 30 April. Payment was to be by irrevocable letter of credit, but no date for opening the credit was stipulated. The buyers did not open the credit until 22 April. The seller claimed damages.

Held the credit should be open at the beginning of the shipping period. The seller was entitled to ship the goods on the first day of the shipping period; in that case he must be able to draw upon the credit. The sellers would succeed.

Sinason-Teicher Inter-American Grain v Oilcakes and Oilseeds Trading (1954) CA
Under a CIF (see above, 20.1) contract for the sale of barley it was agreed that the seller could ship the goods during October or November. The buyers agreed to give a bank guarantee, but no date was stipulated. However, when no guarantee was given by 10 September the sellers cancelled the contract.

Held the sellers were wrong to cancel as the buyers had not been at fault at that time. *Per* Denning LJ, unless otherwise agreed the buyers only need provide a letter of credit or bank guarantee within a reasonable time before the first date for shipment.

Ian Stach Ltd v Baker Bosley Ltd (1958)
Stach contracted to sell to Baker 500 tonnes of steel, shipment August or September, payment by confirmed irrevocable credit. Under this FOB (see above, 19.1) contract the buyers (Baker) were responsible for the shipping arrangements and for choosing the exact shipping date. Baker failed to open a credit before 1 August and when none was opened by 14 August the seller treated this as a repudiatory breach and later resold the goods at a lower price. Baker argued that since they, the buyers, were responsible

for the exact date of shipment, the credit only need be opened a reasonable time before the actual shipping date.

Held the seller was entitled to treat the buyer's failure to open the credit as a repudiatory breach. The *prima facie* rule is that the credit must be opened at the latest by the earliest shipping date.

22.8 Contract between buyer and issuing bank

Midland Bank Ltd v Seymour (1955)

Seymour, in England, contracted to buy ducks' feathers from sellers in Hong Kong C & F (see above, 20.1) Hamburg. Seymour instructed his bank to accept documents which described the goods as 'Hong Kong duck feathers – 85% clean; 12 bales each weighing about 190 lbs; 5 s per lb'. When the documents were presented to the bank for payment, the bill of lading described the goods merely as '12 bales; Hong Kong duck feathers'. However, all the documents (bills of lading, invoices, weight account and certificate of origin), when read together, fully described the goods in accordance with Seymour's instructions. The bank accepted the documents and then paid out against them. In the event, the seller shipped only rubbish and Seymour refused to reimburse the bank, claiming, *inter alia*, that the bank should not have accepted the documents because the bill of lading did not fully describe the goods in accordance with their instructions.

Held Seymour's claim was rejected because the instructions did not require each document to contain a full description of the goods. See, now, Art 41(c) of the UCP, applied in *Soprama SpA v Marine & Animal By-Products Corp* (1966) (above, 22.6). In any case it is up to the applicant to offer reasonably clear instructions: if Seymour desired that the bill of lading should fully describe the goods, he should have specified this to the bank.

22.9 Contract between issuing bank and advising or confirming bank

Bank Melli Iran v Barclays Bank DCO (1951)

For the facts, see above, 22.6.

Held unless otherwise agreed, the relationship between the issuing bank and the confirming bank (here, Barclays) was that of principal and agent. There was nothing in the facts of this case to suggest otherwise.

Bankers Trust Co v State Bank of India (1991) CA

Under a contract for steel plates costing over £10 million, payment was to be by confirmed irrevocable documentary credit, which was subject to the UCP. The plaintiffs (BT) were the issuing bank and the defendants (SBI) the confirming bank. SBI paid on the presentation of the documents and were immediately reimbursed by BT. BT then received the documents (comprising 967 sheets of paper) from SBI on Wednesday 21 September. BT finished checking the documents the following Monday and, having found some discrepancies, sent them to the buyer. On the Thursday (29 September), the buyer, having identified additional discrepancies, returned the documents to BT. The next day (Friday 30 September), BT informed SBI that they were rejecting the documents for non-compliance. Accordingly, BT claimed the return of money paid to SBI, who argued that the rejection of the documents came too late; under what was then Art 16(c) of the UCP (now amended as Art 13(b)) a bank had a reasonable time to examine the documents.

Held in favour of SBI, a major London bank, such as BT, should be able to check the documents in substantially less time than eight working days. Therefore, the rejection came too late. Also, the documents should not be sent to the buyer for the purpose of him searching for further discrepancies, although he may be consulted as to whether he would waive any discrepancies.

Notes

1   Article 13(b) of the 1993 revision of the UCP (UCP-500, in effect from 1 January 1994) provides that in any case a reasonable time shall not exceed seven banking days. Also note that Art 14(c) provides that the issuing bank may consult with the applicant on the question of waiver, but this does not extend the reasonable time for examination.

2   See, also, *Seaconsar Far East Ltd v Bank Markazi Jomhouri Islami Iran* (above, 22.6).

22.10 Contract between banks and seller

Banque de l'Indochine et de Suez SA v JH Rayner (Mincing Lane) (1983) CA
An irrevocable credit was opened by a Djbouti bank and confirmed by the plaintiff bank. The plaintiff bank considered the documents to be defective but, nonetheless, paid the sellers 'under reserve'. The issuing bank rejected the documents on grounds including some of those given by the plaintiff bank. And so the plaintiff bank, not being reimbursed, demanded repayment from the seller. The question arose whether 'payment under reserve' entitled the bank to recover from the seller:

(i)   where the issuing bank or the buyer rejects the documents; or
(ii) only if the documents are genuinely defective.

Held 'payment under reserve' means that the confirming bank can recover from the seller if the issuing bank or the buyer rejects the documents. In the present case the documents were genuinely defective and the grounds for rejection given by each bank coincided, thus the plaintiff bank could recover. *Obiter*, as a 'payment under reserve' is made against the background of the confirming bank's doubts over the documents, that bank should not be able to recover if the issuing bank or buyer reject the documents on other grounds.

Note ──────────────────────────────────────

Schmitthoff, *The Law and Practice of International Trade*, 9th edn, 1990, thinks that this view is 'doubtful', see p 439.

Also note that the expression 'under reserve' is not defined in the UCP.

22.11 Performance bonds and guarantees

Elian and Rabbath v Matsas and Matsas (1966) CA

Shipowners claimed a lien over goods based upon demurrage (delay by the party freighting the ship). The sender of the goods provided a banker's first demand guarantee to cover the demurrage. The shipowners then lifted the lien but immediately claimed a second lien in respect of another claim. The sender then sought an injunction restraining the shipowners from claiming on the guarantee.

Held the injunction was granted. The guarantee was provided on the understanding that the lien would be lifted and no further lien would be imposed. The shipowners were in breach of that understanding and so could not call on the guarantee.

Howe Richardson Scale Co v Polimex-Cekop (1978) CA

English manufacturers, Howe, contracted to sell equipment to buyers in Poland for £500,000. The buyers agreed to make an advance payment of £25,000 and part of the balance, £50,000, was to be paid by irrevocable letter of credit. The sellers agreed to provide a bank guarantee assuring the buyers of the repayment of their advance should they fail to deliver the goods by a certain date. Howe dispatched some of the goods but then refused to send the balance because the credit had not been opened. The buyers called upon repayment of the advance under the bank guarantee. Howe sought an injunction to restrain the buyers from claiming under the guarantee.

Held an injunction was refused. The bank was in a position not identical but very similar to a bank which had opened a confirmed irrevocable letter of credit. Thus the bank must perform that particular contract (the guarantee) and that obligation does not depend on the performance of the underlying supply contract.

Edward Owen Engineering v Barclays Bank International (1978) CA

Owens contracted with Libyan buyers to supply and erect glasshouses in Libya, payment to be made by an irrevocable confirmed credit. Owens agreed to furnish the buyers with a performance bond for 10% of the contract price. (A performance bond is held by a reputable third party, normally a bank, and gives the buyer security against default by the supplier.) Owens instructed Barclays to provide the bond and pay 'on first demand without proof or conditions'. Barclays instructed the Umma Bank in Libya to issue the bond. In the event, the buyers failed to open a credit and so Owens terminated the supply contract. The buyers then demanded payment under the performance bond from the Umma Bank who paid and demanded reimbursement from Barclays. Owens brought this action to prevent Barclays reimbursing the Umma Bank.

Held performance bonds and guarantees stand on a similar footing to documentary credits. A bank must honour them according to their terms, irrespective of the underlying contract and its performance. The only exception is where the bank has notice of clear fraud.

Northwood Development Company v Aegon Insurance (1994)

A building company contracted to erect some flats for the plaintiff. The contract provided that, should the building company go into liquidation, the contract would be terminated. The defendant gave a surety on a performance bond. Before the flats were completed, the building company went into liquidation. The plaintiff sought to enforce the bond. The defendant argued that the plaintiffs must show a breach of contract to call on the bond.

Held the bond was more than a guarantee. Its plain purpose was to cover non-performance. Thus the plaintiffs were entitled to damages from the bond without showing breach of contract.

Cargill International SA v Bangladesh Sugar and Food Industries Corporation (1997) CA

Cargill agreed to sell BSFI sugar. The contract provided that the sugar must be shipped in a vessel not more than 20 years old and that delivery would be before 15 September 1994. The contract contained a performance bond covering 10% of the total cost and freight. The contract provided that the buyer's (BSFI's) bond was liable to be forfeited by the seller (Cargill) if the seller (i) failed to perform in accordance with the contract; and, also, (ii) was responsible to the buyer for any loss or damage. The ship used was over 20 years old and it arrived late. BSFI rejected the shipment and called on the bond. Cargill sought to restrain this, arguing that as BSFI had suffered no loss they were not entitled to call on the bond.

Held in the absence of clear words to the contrary, it was implicit in the nature of a performance bond that the parties give account after the bond had been called upon, so that if, for instance, the amount of the bond exceeded the actual loss, the overpayment could be reclaimed. The term 'forfeit' used in the contract referred to the bond and not the money paid under it. Thus although BSFI could call upon the bond, they could only retain such money to account for their loss.

Index